MARKS OF TOIL

ALSO BY JUSTIN VICARI
AND FROM MCFARLAND

*Nicolas Winding Refn and the Violence of Art:
A Critical Study of the Films* (2014)

*The Gus Van Sant Touch: A Thematic Study—
Drugstore Cowboy, Milk and Beyond* (2012)

Mad Muses and the Early Surrealists (2012)

*Male Bisexuality in Current Cinema: Images of
Growth, Rebellion and Survival* (2011)

Marks of Toil

*Work and Disfigurement
in Literature, Film
and Philosophy*

Justin Vicari

McFarland & Company, Inc., Publishers
Jefferson, North Carolina

LIBRARY OF CONGRESS CATALOGUING-IN-PUBLICATION DATA

Vicari, Justin, 1968–
    Marks of toil : work and disfigurement in literature, film and philosophy / Justin Vicari.
       p.   cm.
    Includes bibliographical references and index.

    ISBN 978-0-7864-9588-7 (softcover : acid free paper)
    ISBN 978-1-4766-1704-6 (ebook)

    1. Manual work—Philosophy. 2. Mutilation—Philosophy. 3. Human capital—Philosophy. 4. Work in literature. 5. Literature and society. 6. Work in motion pictures. 7. Motion pictures—Social aspects. I. Title.
    HD4904.V545 2014
    306.3'6—dc23   2014032944

BRITISH LIBRARY CATALOGUING DATA ARE AVAILABLE

© 2014 Justin Vicari. All rights reserved

No part of this book may be reproduced or transmitted in any form or by any means, electronic or mechanical, including photocopying or recording, or by any information storage and retrieval system, without permission in writing from the publisher.

On the cover: Photograph by Lewis Hine, *Power house mechanic working on steam pump,* 1920 (National Archives and Records Administration)

Printed in the United States of America

McFarland & Company, Inc., Publishers
  Box 611, Jefferson, North Carolina 28640
  www.mcfarlandpub.com

Table of Contents

Preface — 1
Introduction: We Halcyonians — 7

1. Motifs of Physical Capital and Bodily Transformation — 17
2. Eternity and the Body — 43
3. Fictional Bodies of the Great Depression — 57
4. The Dean's Laughing Fit — 83
5. The Road to Kotka at Night — 97
6. The Aesthetics of Limbo — 107
7. Window Babies — 118
8. Surplus and Sacrifice — 129
9. This Animal Which Is Not One — 141
10. Dialectics at an Impasse — 167

(In)conclusion: On the Evanescent — 179
Chapter Notes — 191
Works Cited — 201
Index — 205

Preface

As a unit of being, in its ideal role as the nonmetaphorical container of our life force, the body is perhaps the only thing within consciousness that resists dialectical synthesis. What is its dialectical other? For the body—that most corporeal, immanent and utile of objects, whose boundaries are often virtually coextensive with the boundaries of selfhood and consciousness—has always and only had as its proposed other a pitifully incommensurable abstraction: eternity, the only conception in which the body has no role to play. (Eternity and death are two separate conceptions, not unrelated but not synonymous; in fact it is a foundational mistake to confuse eternity and death, for only the latter has a concrete significance for us and then only as an active transformation rather than a definable state.) This only serves to demonstrate the crucial meaning of the body, its utter incommensurability *avant la lettre*. It has no "other" that can define it; it stubbornly stands beyond dialectics, it marks the place where dialectical thought becomes irrelevant and where life nonetheless goes on without it, or does not, as the case may be.

Bodily transformations form a kind of shadow history of capitalism and other systemic orders. The alienated labor created by industrialization turned the body into a machine, a tool, and also into a special enemy within the system, an enemy whose natural powers had to be restrained and channeled into work. The work itself turned against the body who performed it, making the worker's body a kind of slate on which were inscribed literal exploitations and abuses in the form of physical damage and deteriorated health. These included maimings, disfigurements and deaths (farm and factory workers who lost limbs in machinery; the seamstresses who died in the Triangle Shirtwaist fire; the folk hero John Henry who dies with a hammer in his hand, trying to clear a tunnel through a mountain faster than a steam-drill); also mental, emotional and psychical derangements, which are somewhat extra-physical in nature but which affect the life of the body. Moreover, there was the more general sense of the body's essence being forced to change over a period of time, in order to adapt itself to capitalist regimes of utility and obedience. And Stalinist Communism and Maoism were no less harsh toward the human body.

The heartlessness of systemic orders is usually revealed to us piecemeal and haphazardly, through tragic "accidents" which seem to interrupt the regimentation of life. Actually, these are far from wholly accidental, not deliberate but also not random either, occasioned as they are by a lack of concern, a priori, for the safety and well-being of individuals within the systems themselves. We cannot even feel secure in saying that grisly, fatal industrial accidents are strictly a thing of the past. As I began to construct this preface to a book about bodies, and about death, eternity, dogma, and systemic orders, there was a heartbreaking news story in which a 62-year-old man, an employee of Bumble Bee Seafood, was found inside one of the giant ovens, roasted alive. His name was José Melena.

Somehow, Mr. Melena had been left alone to tend the oven, a job which normally required three men, not just for safety regulations but because the trays of tuna that are cooked en masse are so large and heavy that it takes three men to push them into the oven. (When we think of the Pharaoh's tombs in ancient Egypt, we shudder at the brutal system that required several slaves to push a single stone of a pyramid into place, slaves who gave their life energies for the glorification of their kings.) Could it be that Mr. Melena found himself forced to do the work of three men, and died somehow as a result of this?

Moreover, although only three years away from the standard retirement age of sixty-five, Mr. Melena had only begun working at the seafood processing plant five years prior, at the age of fifty-seven. The kind of cumulative benefits that once applied to working-class lives—seniority, a benefits plan, stability, a pension, retirement—no longer apply, and both blue and white collar employees are now forced to start over in entry level positions, even at an age when past generations were contentedly looking forward to their golden years.[1]

Preface

This might not be so terrible if job opportunities were plentiful and flexible, and if economic upward mobility, through home equity, modest stock investments, or readily affordable higher education, could be counted upon. It may be true that uncertainty, as well as the need to take risks, is a powerful impetus for growth, whereas routinization of life is damaging and moribund. However, alienated labor is already a routine which tends toward stagnation; for it to be physically hazardous or insultingly insecure on top of this is something which has already throughout history proven to be a pre-revolutionary condition. At any rate, it matters greatly whether the risks in question are undertaken with some degree of sovereign agency on the part of the individual, or whether one is simply buffeted about. People who have been "trained," as it were, to be the famous organization-men, the followers, cannot simply be abandoned by the system that they have served, and which has come to define their existence. It is equal to taking a domesticated pet and dropping it off in the wilderness.

In the U.S., the capitalist system is sovereign, but its masses of servants have not been encouraged to become so, even as the system turns more and more into wilderness on all sides. It is not government safety nets, head-start programs, and welfare that promote a lack of sovereign agency—indeed, such way-stations along the road of life are far less defining of an individual than his or her career, the job that becomes associated with a person's competence, fulfillment, livelihood and respectability, and which consumes the majority of his or her life. And the most helpless and over-weaned in such an inbred state of late-capitalist hothouse economics is invariably the ruling elite, which has had to mortgage its own credibility, its benign public face, in order to sustain itself through ever more savage encroachments on civil rights and the ability of citizens to simply live and get by. Neoconservatives accuse people of needing to be weaned from a "nanny state"; but the corporate tit is horrifying because it literally must suckle itself—or else siphon off the mother's milk of others in ghastly and disguised lactic amputations. Public monies now flow as a matter of course toward private coffers, which remain secure in the bosom of offshore accounts and hedge funds. Accruing, expanding or simply maintaining income today has never been less creative or individualistic; instead it amounts to the learned skill of sucking dry the remaining sources that are in place—all growth industries today are essentially interconnected industries of death: toxic food makes more sick patients for privately owned hospitals; the military-industrial complex ensures that we will need to be in permanent war.

Thus, we should not think of the tragic death of Mr. Melena as an isolated incident or even as an accident; capitalism is completely anti-life. Historically, it follows the same brutal course again and again: the luring of unskilled physical workers, often from a less developed nation or a minority-ethnicity; the sacrifice of these workers in arduous, dangerous labors; the casting-off and stigmatization of these workers after the result of the labors are privatized according to plan all along—from the pyramids to the railroads to the modern white-collar service industries. The difference, as this latter progression indicates, is that more and more of the working world, even those industries which used to sustain a thriving middle class, is now subjected to the same brutal conditions as once befell slave labor and indentured servitude.

Since much of the developing world is now undergoing its own industrial revolutions, we might expect that lessons would be learned from the corner-cutting, anti-human mistakes of the past. But this is not so. Nineteenth-century Western headlines are being made all over again, in the East now. In 2012 a fire broke out in a Bangladesh sweatshop, killing 112 garment workers. The factory workers were making clothing for U.S. outlets such as Wal-Mart, Sears and Disney, and were being paid on average the equivalent of $56 a month.

It is bad enough that some of the wealthiest corporations in the world have their merchandise stitched together in a nation so poor that people are eager to work for sub-minimum pay and in substandard safety conditions. I do not even begrudge those Bangladeshi workers for hoping that the plant would reopen quickly so that they could return to remunerated work, however paltry and hazardous. But it is extremely sad that in such a case where corporations have found ways to rake in a nearly 100 percent markup profit on consumer goods, due to the cheap labor and lack of safety regulations, the corporate owners will not undertake personally to see that no blood is shed for the sake of their bottom line.[2]

The carrot on the end of capitalism's stick has withered and shrunk to such an extent that soon (if not already) all that will be left is the stick. Because it is, again, hardly normative in any natural schema for humans to labor without profit or reward, transformations, mutations, warpings must and do occur. Merely possessing what we might call *physical capital* (by which I primarily mean the ability to labor, although this term encompasses all of a person's potentially marketable bodily attributes) is no longer enough, if it ever was in the post-industrial age. No amount of innate physical capital can endure working three jobs, seven-day weeks, 18-hour days, lack of medical benefits and care, having to work while going without food or a home, and so on. In real life, we have grown miserably accustomed to these systemic drainings of our physical capital, and their attendant health risks: the side effects of energy drinks, speed, alcohol and sleeping pills; ulcers; cancers; heart disease; isolation; chronic depression; and diminished life expectancy.

Within modern Western narrative traditions (from the nineteenth century to the present day), allegorical or magic-realist bodily transformations often serve a double purpose. On one hand, they speak to a resigned or hysterical acknowledgment of the bondage produced by alienated labor; the body is so profoundly acted-upon that it becomes unrecognizable to others and to itself. Yet this possibility of transformation can also suggest a fantasmatic of would-be escape and overcoming. In any event, transformations often represent the death of the body as a natural, pre-social entity and its subsequent rebirth as something often wholly defined by social conditioning and utilitarian value. The occasional sin of overstating this imposed value (without always allowing for "free will," for instance, or our nominal constitutional liberties) is proportionate to the stark fact that underlies narratives of bodily transformation: whether we gain or lose it, physical capital is mainly what we are within the socioeconomic realm and within systemic social orders.[3]

In this speculative discourse, I would like to trace several phenomena. First of all, I would like to describe ways in which Western narrative arts of story, novel and film have inscribed the presence of uncanny bodies—deformities, shape-shifters, Doppelgängers, etc.—as modes of resistance to a double social message, in which the immanent world becomes invested in the utilitarian, functional, exhaustive and finally fatal labors of the body, and then in which the metaphysical world (afterlife, eternity, and other abstract, non-empirical and unprovable concepts) is tendentiously codified as further endless punishment of the body, invisible in its heaven, relentlessly tortured in its hell. The uncanny body is only partly legible as a successful mode of resistance, since, by its own "freakishness," it ends up recapitulating normative standards of appearance or functionalism which make it easier to herd the proletariat in this world and in the fabulized "next world," world to come.

Second, I am interested in looking at the ways in which conservative and neoconservative thinkers have made free use of the tenets of dialectical theory, and even dialectical materialism, but pointedly against the interests of the proletariat. Dialectical theory has always been flexible, but since the 1970s if not earlier it has had real fault lines revealed in the way that it is made to glove the iron hand of fiscal power in the West. When relentlessly abstracted as cogs in a mental mechanism, "oppressors" and "victims" lose their corporeal integrity; imperial, capitalist power confronts periods of social change by claiming that it has now been subjugated to the ascendant rights of disenfranchised others. The "othering" movement of the dialectic, by which power is usurped through a thoroughgoing spectacle of one's own abasement, facilitates the poor-mouthing of upper-tier tax brackets, anti-union corporations, and deregulated investors. Money is the fictionalized weapon, and eternity the strange fabulized battleground, yoking together the locked-in yet dissembled terms of the dialectic—workers, bourgeoisie, owners—in a dance with no grace or resolution, and no definitive way of changing partners.

Introduction:
We Halcyonians

Even after thousands of years of civilized life, humankind is still struggling with the question of fulfillment. It is a kind of macro-problem; we can solve every other problem but cannot secure our ultimate fulfillment. It remains a forked, ambiguous responsibility, partly about the valorization of individual desire and partly about remaining close enough to the collective herd to feel safe and accepted. For in the Western imaginary, complete fulfillment has always been a scary prospect, endlessly mitigated and controlled by our own inventions of money, labor and religion. Just as man himself is fallen in the eyes of religion, so the worker is no less fallen in the eyes of capitalism. If we accept that alienated labor is a profoundly unnatural condition, "a negation of matter," as Fredric Jameson calls it,[1] then this negation has had the effect of deforming our view of laborers and their own view of themselves. The worker is easily demonized in the U.S. because this figure invariably must do *what he or she does not wish to do*. Subject to the control of external authority, the worker enacts the turgid and farcical play of punishment and painfully earned reward. Fulfillment, in this systemic order, must remain out of reach, deferred until later, always later, and finally until that later which can never be comprehended let alone answered: what we call "eternity."

The demands of dialectical thought would have our condition no other way: revolutionary praxis must be carved out from the grinding status quo of oppression. Once set in motion, neither of these terms—revolution and status quo—ever disappears from the equation. The best that can be done is to subsume more and more of the status quo under the aegis of revolution, while foolishly hoping that this process will dilute the status quo and not the revolution itself. But revolution can also turn into labor, and oppression; finally it must perpetuate some form of the old status quo or else it would no longer remain what it was; would no longer dwell beneath that sense of purpose to which everything pious and pedantic is hopelessly doomed.

Nietzsche has the lovely phrase, "we halcyonians," to describe those who wish to go on their own way to fulfillment, and to "banish the concept of guilt and punishment with all our might from the world." Halcyonians are on the side of fulfillment, of exalting humanity—in this, they are hard to define sociologically, they could be bosses or workers, it really doesn't matter. What is crucial, of course, is that halcyonians are a small threatened band whose "mortal enemies," Nietzsche asserts, are responsible for the fact that society "seems to have taken the contrary direction."[2] Filmmaker and theorist Rainer Werner Fassbinder meant something similar, I believe, when he referred to "us birds of Paradise" during the late 1970s when he frequently spoke about wanting to emigrate from West Germany, whose conformity to capitalist values he felt to be stifling and disturbing.[3]

For both Nietzsche and Fassbinder this exalted state of being (halcyonians, birds of Paradise) should not be a mere luxury, the entitlement of a privileged few. Yet we are accustomed to thinking of the apex, by definition, as an exclusive place, a tapered summit that has winnowed more and more excess as it climbs higher and higher. This elitism is part of what drags on the spirit, the collective spirit of humankind as a whole. And of course, this correlates with the consolidation of wealth and power; where the system allows or indeed requires such consolidation, the idea of equitable sharing becomes opinion rather than certainty, a quixotic hope or a battleground at best. Could all of us become truly free and fulfilled—not only the ones at or near the bottom, who are neither, but also the ones at the top—rather than falsely and expediently? All are socially oppressed, the oppressors as well—a truth that Marx told and which we would do well to recall. It would necessitate transforming the entirety of bourgeois capitalist structures, redefining society along non-materialist terms, since the wish for nobility, the wish to be more than "a mediocre, petty person,"[4] is incompatible with an alienated labor that demands constant mundane foreshortenings of selfhood, constant falsehood and obedience, at both the top and bottom of the hierarchy.

Halcyonians and birds of Paradise are utopian exceptions. Indeed, we might see both of these rhetorical conceits as synonyms for "artists," that special group which labors out of love and expends itself often without immediate economic reward; artists whose work is hard and time-consuming but individualized and self-motivated—a transversal of the demands of alienated labor, which have us work to another's satisfaction, another's timetable, another's idea of appropriate compensation.

When this sort of labor is imposed on the body and passed off as normative, the only means of escape is through a transversal by which one aggressively pursues all forms of non-normativity and non-utilitarianism in compensation. Under pressure, the body mutates, and here I am no longer speaking of something strictly utopian, which is to say, beneficial or ideal; the mutated, non-normative body is seemingly salvaged from labor but at the cost of making it available to other, specialized labors, or to unique punishments. Such exceptionalized bodily transformations often become indistinguishable from subsumption in their inevitable upholding of alienated labor as the rule, the prima facie of systemic power to control and dis-order the body itself, deflecting it at all turns from what it would naturally do or be. Yet the possibility of life exists today, as Derrida suggested, "only under the species of the nonspecies, in the formless, mute, infant, and terrifying form of the monstrosity."[5]

One's body never did belong properly to oneself, but to self-serving institutions that have designs on it. The neoconservative fear and hatred of a "welfare state" is predicated on this threat of the body which evades control, even though the "welfare body" is just trying to survive under harsh economic conditions and is likely to feel its diminished physical capital (in cases of disability, for example) as a loss or disadvantage. We are not permitted to redefine ourselves as something other than physical capital without trespassing on Western ideas of what is sacred. Stories of the loss of physical capital and the concomitant need for bodily transformation recall some of the West's most potent, primal martyrdoms—the trial of Socrates, the barring of Moses from the Promised Land, the crucifixion.

In the early decades of industrialization Arthur Rimbaud delivered this sarcastic epitaph for mankind's anarchistic yearnings:

> Nous t'affirmons, méthode! Nous n'oublions pas que tu as glorifié hier chacun de nos âges. Nous avons foi au poison. Nous savons donner notre vie tout entière tous les jours.
>
> [We affirm you, system! We are not forgetting how yesterday you glorified each of our ages. We have faith in the poison. We know how to give our whole life every day.][6]

To give our whole life every day. What kind of extreme mutations might be necessary in order to imbibe poison on a daily basis and not die? Or is there an even deeper issue here: the denial of death itself through legends in which people expend all of their physical capital, only to somehow magically regain it in a myth of immortality or indestructibility, a myth of the eternal. "Something" will sweep you up and carry you when even your last strength gives out, but the collapse must be total, the carrying (unlike a social safety net) a pacification to surviving others rather than a source of partial fulfillment to the one who has gone under.

This recalls Jameson's accusation of labor, or even systemic collectivization itself, as "negation of matter." During the high industrial age, there was still much superstition surrounding the nature of matter, where it came from, where it belonged. But we have not been able to prevaricate about matter for some time now; modern science has replaced God not with evolution as such but with something even more foundational: molecular theory. Being a development-narrative, evolution can still contain the career of spirituality; whereas molecular theory is the decimation of all narrative(s), the preemption of narrative's relationality (also the preemption of the uneasy embrace of dialectical thought—the irreducible molecule resists reduction into divided parts or internal synthesis). Jorge Luis Borges writes: "For us, the final, solid reality of things is matter—the spinning electrons that cross interstellar distances in their atomic solitude."[7]

That "solitude" is a perfect word, since by finally reducing the world to matter, we have made it more possible than ever to *lose* the world in all its forms. And so we end up coming full circle. This vertigo of lost world or worlds provides the stage setting for a resurgence of ancient dogma disguised in politicized rhetoric, the decisive problem of modern totalitarianism in all its crypto forms, as Hannah Arendt notes in her important essay, "History and Immortality" (1957):

> For mass society is nothing more than that kind of organized living which automatically establishes itself among human beings who are still related to each other, but have *lost the world* once common to all of them.[8]

Nonetheless, we solitary molecules try to cleave to the fissuring world and contrive our transcendent self-inventions. One thinks of ancient doctors who knew few remedies for treating internal ailments. Their pet leeches, which might nearly kill a patient by drawing off too much of the "toxic" blood within, are still with us, wherever physical capital is rapaciously amassed, foolishly risked, and grievously wasted. The wild hope for miraculous rebirth is everywhere in the culture of the U.S., a nation forged in stages, remapping its boundaries again and again, warring its way toward various plateaus of cohesion and identity, always chasing a supposed destiny, a predetermined idea of itself through Manifest Destiny or imperialism in general. Our reigning myth is the joyous coming-together after some disastrous setback; our anthem tells a story about waiting through a war-torn night and seeing our flag still flying in the morning. The idea of being born again, phoenix-like, from a disastrous crucible connects everything we are: the Fundamentalist becoming re-baptized, the celebrity making a splashy comeback, the addict getting clean, the immature becoming parents, the mature availing themselves of surgeries and drugs in order to be young again.

It is like the epileptically flashing reshuffle of one of Nietzsche's eternal returns. Meanwhile, we hammer ourselves into the ground with defeating, inflexible truisms, such as "closure is a myth," "addictions are incurable," and "no one ever changes." The folklore of our age practically demands continuous depression and substance abuse, just as the use of high fructose corn syrup in everything guarantees ever-rising rates of obesity and diabetes. Still, we wait through grim night praying for the best, hoping for the revelation of something, blessings to count, a beloved coming home. We do not question why the wait is always much longer than it should be, and the night much darker.

Again, these traits are, I believe, deeply coded in the American genes, going back to the first generations spawned by the European colonial imperialists. What sort of unknown, hybridized person would survive in the New World—or be produced by the need to adapt to it? "Democracy" did not mean that we individuals would create our own system (which we basically inherited wholesale from pre-revolutionary Europe, mainly Britain and Holland) but that over the centuries we would be forced or allowed or persuaded to imagine that we had, to view it as somehow natural and made to our own particular measure, arising from our organic needs and behaviors. We vaguely inspired the French and later the Russian revolutions, but in fact we were the enshrinement of all of the traditions that Europe was in the throes of divesting itself of; the *ancien régime* in arrested development, particularly the wish to safeguard money at the expense of human life itself. We met the old ideas of Europe more than halfway, and we managed, with the help of certain *mental leeches,* to bleed both ourselves and those ideas enough that we could make our new national conscience blurry and amnesiac around things like feudalism, colonialism, imperialism, exploitation, militarism, and religious dogma. New beings had indeed mutated into existence, but not out of thin air; we were in the image of what we once could have permanently resisted and dispelled.

We find this tension between the individual and society, and this counterfeit of "new," transformed beings, in Nietzsche's philosophy: "Everything that a man does in the service of the State is against his own nature. Similarly, everything he learns in view of future service of the State."[9] The use of capital-s "State" indicates that Nietzsche is addressing Hegelianism, specifically the dialectic whereby we could, in Hegel, recognize some form of the individual before his or her absorption into state, society, institutional law. Nietzsche's post–Hegelian "division of labour" is seemingly meant to imply little difference between those who rule and those who serve: "The legislator—and he who fulfills the law. The teacher of discipline—and those who have grown hard and severe under discipline."[10] These are the "countless generations" forced to "sacrifice themselves to [the] cause"[11] of maintaining an abstract ideal of power that belongs properly to no one. For we understand that the legislator is as much a product of the law as he who fulfills it, and that the teacher was himself made hard and severe under the same discipline which he now imparts.

If we substitute "the ruling class" for the word "State," we find a tenet of Marxist theory—especially as espoused by Theodor W. Adorno and the Frankfurt School—in which postindustrial capitalism takes on the character of a totalitarian system where everything is made to conform through a certain twisting or mutation of natural life. One could be born, live and die in some city exactly like a serf on an aristocrat's land, and not even realize this because, if one is lucky, one superficially chooses the work one does or the products one consumes. One remains generally baffled, fallow, increasingly apathetic, and most significantly *unfulfilled*. (This is similar to what Nietzsche calls "the problem of those who are waiting."[12])

Indeed, "mutations" of all kinds are subsumed as frightening imagoes of brutal, enduring exploitation, the natural body's last card played, the canard revealed and passively swallowed as if it were truth. From the same *fin-de-siècle* as Rimbaud, there are Melville's shape-shifting Confidence Man and the rejuvenated vampire in Henry James's *The Sacred Fount,* characters who seem to aggressively revise the rules of physical capital against a panicked backdrop of radically shifting societal needs, desires and expressions. One transforms in some way, first as a *relief* from the thought that one is merely another average laborer defined solely by his or her labor; but in the end one is brought inescapably around to a second "relief," delirious and harrowing, precisely that one has been *nothing* but another average laborer all along, and that everything in social life, even the most intimate of personal relations, has been distorted and deformed by the artificial structure of alienated labor. This is a lowest common denominator of capitalist experience, by no means universal but starkly revealed as fact in cases of industrial maimings and deaths, sweatshop fires, slavery and "coolie"

INTRODUCTION

labor, the suicides of jobless men and women, and the plight of disenfranchised migrants.

What more can possibly be said (or experienced, for that matter) about the actual condition of alienated labor as we have seen it in operation from the Industrial Revolution to the current bedraggled temp- and-fast-food state of things? Not much; anyway, we have learned from the ideological failures of communism that it is best not to generalize about the experience of workers. It would be sheer hubris for me to think that I could address actual labor through any form of discourse. Moreover, although workers are often oppressed as a general class, and should be liberated as a general class, this liberation probably cannot be administered wholesale and entirely non-circumstantially. But this does not mean that we should not try to administer it.

In the West, a certain ideal of individualism has acted to disguise the workings of systemic collectivization, and also to hamper the practice of communal, one-size-fits-all solutions. We have yet to name and delineate the precise ideology that corresponds to the mixed-feature economies of the West, partly laissez-faire, partly centrally planned. A communism that embraces individualist strivings? A capitalism that understands managed patterns of social needs and growths? Both of those sound too optimistic. The "embracing" and "understanding" on either side are still far from genuine, or perhaps it is the individualism and the needs and growths that are vague and misty for us. In pragmatic terms China's economy leads the way when it comes to being able to step outside of categorical distinctions; but China remains far more centrally controlled by the government than the major Western nations are or want to be. Of course, the U.S. economy is entirely centrally *controlled*—by Wall Street. Long-range development and cross-class outreach are put off in favor of shortfall schemes and guaranteed protections for those already at the top. And China, on its side, is far from perfect: they have no transparency, nor do they have labor unions—a serious omission for an ostensibly Communist nation. The workers, in China as in the U.S., need more power in their own workplaces and over their own production and its material rewards. This is indisputable. But China's economy as well as the U.S. economy (when it has functioned well) are proof that we need to stop lying to ourselves in the U.S. about totally "free," laissez-faire markets: the fact is that only mixed-feature economies (as opposed to all-out laissez-faire capitalism or all-out Communism) have the balance and stability to endure and thrive.

At any rate, we are not concerned here with formulating policy, and only obliquely concerned with the *effects of policies* as such. We are concerned with issues of representation, specifically how the condition of alienated labor has been expressed in the narrative arts of literature and film through the tropes of physical capital and bodily transformation.[13] Fiction renews life, through the exaggeration which makes the unsayable take shape, and through the thematics, which allow us to extrapolate from particulars to panoramas. We will examine a variety of narratives in which bodily non-normativity and bodily transformation—defined rather broadly as any forced, willed or helpless changing of the human body's natural shape, properties, functions or boundaries—become connected to socioeconomic status and appear as a kind of adaptation in something like social–Darwinian evolution. The transformed body, then, bears a special relation to the rigorous demands of labor and production under capitalism; but not exclusively there. Any *system* can produce mutations of the kind I will be describing, in which an individual radically morphs under the strain of the pronounced effort to belong, to survive, to accumulate the necessary physical capital in order to function.

This is doubtlessly because collectivized systems are always incommensurable with the human. For Étienne Balibar, class structure "is a dissociation" which can be said to breed mutations, since "the opposing terms are seen not as entities external to one another, to which individuals have to belong unambiguously, but as incompatible modes of existence which can, in very large measure, affect the same individuals or enjoin them to choose against themselves."[14] The terms of dialectical thought itself would have it no other way: just as the parts break down and destabilize the whole, so the whole enforces its assimilationist logic on the parts. For either side to win within dialectical thought is tantamount only to creating new ranks of the

INTRODUCTION

oppressed. So the wealthy and the neocons today can argue their need for unfettered markets, no taxes, no unions, etc., with the exact same terms that Marxism uses to defend the rights of workers and the disenfranchised: in a society that responds largely to phony sensitizations and phony solutions, the perception of favoritism or bias is all that is needed to turn the discourse of human rights into a sidewalk shell game (or an investment banking Ponzi scheme).

Fassbinder once said: "In our society there's no one who isn't mentally ill."[15] Likewise, within collectivized systems, there is no such thing as a non-mutated individual; everyone is compelled to adapt. How would the individual appear who can step outside the chain of transformations, and could it ever be more than quixotic to imagine such a person? Many of the sharpest, most invigorating thinkers of the last century—Adorno, Bataille, Borges, Fassbinder, among others considered here—devoted themselves to conjuring such an apparition, unreal and utopian, able, in his or her absolute will to freedom, to contemplate even mortality serenely. In *Minima Moralia,* Adorno wrote: "What would happiness be that is not measured by the immeasurable grief at what is? For the world is deeply ailing. He who cautiously adapts to it by this very act shares in its madness, while the eccentric alone would stand his ground and bid it rave no more."[16] The spirit of this lone eccentric will be evoked throughout the book as an extreme, even a mystical, refusal to change—refusal to passively adapt to the madness of the ailing world.

1

Motifs of Physical Capital and Bodily Transformation

Georges Bataille acknowledges the possibility of a kind of love between the feudal masters and their serfs, since the relation between them was human and face-to-face, characterized, as Bataille puts it, by "generosity and nobility."[1] Feudalism had hardly been good for the serfs, but their labor entailed a relation to the land that was purposeful, honorable, intimate. They were not entirely left in peace, and the land was not their own, but given their realistic expectations, we can imagine that the serfs were able to simulate independent families and communities under the circumstances. This possibility of love was entirely absent, however, from the relation between workers and bourgeois capitalists, unseen factory owners and absentee landlords, since the bourgeoisie were "incapable of concealing a sordid face, a face so rapacious and lacking in nobility, so frighteningly small, that all human life, upon seeing it, seems degraded."[2]

A pitiless, miserly restraint marked the capitalists of the bourgeois era and their new conception of an industrial labor which took place outside of home and family, finally outside of self. It was the bourgeois capitalists' supposed disconnection from their own bodily lives, from the free play of pleasures, that made their presiding over other people's labor so terrible. Here were people seemingly *without bodies*, demanding the systematic usage and draining of the bodies, the physical capital, of workers. "A fundamental grievance of the bourgeois," Bataille writes, "was the prodigality of feudal society and, after coming to power, they believed that, because of their habits of accumulation, they were capable of acceptably dominating the poorer classes."[3]

We can thus denote the founding principle of post-industrial bourgeois capitalism as a true horror, an empire based on total suffering and abnegation, a dialectic of lack:

> *From each according to his inability to escape a life of labor; to each according to his lack of need.*

Or, as Calvin once preached and as current evangelical Christians believe, God loves the wealthy and despises the poor; obnoxiously, the sign of financial blessing (whether earned, inherited or in some cases stolen and defrauded) is already the mark of "grace," whereas the poor deserve only the fallen marks of toil, certainly no special help or safety net.

Indeed, the bourgeois era marked the first time in history (not counting wars of conquest) when large numbers of people had to acquiesce passively to watching their bodies being used on a daily basis for alien purposes, conducted solely at the behest of others. Michael Watts writes: "Marx and Engels commented quite specifically on these revolutionary capacities of capitalism, the 'uninterrupted disturbances of all social relations,' the 'everlasting uncertainty and agitation' … that distinguished the bourgeois epoch."[4] What is euphemistically called modernity's "broad mesh of sensibilities" is, in fact, "a maelstrom of perpetual disintegration and renewal"[5]: troubled traces of psychological, spiritual, and physical mutations. As Steven Shaviro notes, this is "what Marx calls the *formal subsumption* of labor under capital: one of the 'processes whereby capital incorporates under its own relations of production laboring practices that originated outside its domain.'"[6]

Life and capitalist labor were no longer joined together; life was now over here, labor over there, the human split down the middle, as it were—hence, the urgent appeal of the Doppelgänger, one of the more obvious representations of bodily transformation which arose in the wake of the early industrial revolution. Although supernatural in origin, the Doppelgänger is part of a material fantasmatic of plenitude meant to dissemble an originary lack. It is a sign of the body under pressure from the demands of being physical capital, of amassing material goods. A double is an imitation-self, produced by the original person, who in turn becomes the double's cheap imitation, since what is

1. Motifs of Physical Capital and Bodily Transformation

produced in capitalist societies is always valued more highly than the individual who produces it.

The Doppelgänger is rooted in the need for a "back-up" body, one more liberated and independent. Of course, things tend to end badly with one's Doppelgänger, when the original discovers that he wants his unique self back. The fact that mass-production makes one view the unique self as a paradise lost, and the fact that this paradise cannot be regained (or its loss survived), indicate the urgent ways in which the Doppelgänger attempts to fill a gaping need created by the regimens of alienated labor. This is not I at work in this factory or office for ten hours every day; it is my double. Or, I wish I had a double whom I could send to the factory or the office in my place while I (the real I) am free to do as I please. But there is a grammatical-linguistic problem right off the bat, for no language has ever accommodated such a subject as "the real I." One cannot say, "The real I am going...." Subjectivity resists adjectival qualifications, even at the level of basic grammar, because there had never been an ontological need for grasping a wholly objective subject. The Real I, in this sense, is already a disjunctive, objective thing, to be referred to in third person: the Real I *is* free to do as *he or she pleases*. "JE est un autre," as Rimbaud said,[7] and can we have any doubt which I he was referring to?

For another, perhaps harsher turn of the societal screw was coming: even as alienated labor became the dominant mode of Western life, leisure and personal expression (still held up as ideals of the "life well-lived") were already being neutralized through commodification and consumption, or else placed untouchably on reserve for the elite class as a way of justifying the ascendancy of the wealthy few via the wage-slavery of millions. By this point, of course, we are heading into the twentieth century and post-industrialism; machines are making labor easier for some, and more cost-effective, thus the basic principle of class structure, of alienated labor, had to be organized and justified all over again. Scholars Richard Wightman Fox and T. J. Jackson Lears write:

> Perhaps the key development was the rapid expansion of the professional-managerial stratum, which included (among others) both the technicians who staffed the new corporate bureaucracies and the

corps of reformers who consciously undertook to "harmonize" the relations between labor and capital. Accredited experts set out to manage not only the economic arena, but the rest of the social order as well. For the masses of employees who in a corporate economy could no longer aspire to become their own bosses, new authorities in personal adjustment promised not power through work but, in the phrase of the popular therapist Annie Payson Call, "power through repose." For these ordinary Americans the prophets of adjustment, of therapeutic consumption, provided the promise of health and worldly contentment. But for a still powerful group—the northeastern, Protestant upper bourgeoisie—the new experts in social and psychological harmony provided more than the hope of health: [t]hey offered a new legitimation.[8]

In Orwellian fashion, which is to say, counter to their stated linguistic meanings, the *empowering repose* became more fleeting, expensive and illusory, and the *disempowering work* more burdensome and time-consuming. Leisure itself became an extension of work, a new series of tests to pass, of standards to measure up to. This was the caste system of feudalism mated with the disequilibrium of labor outside of home, family, and self, a veritable corkscrew of alienation largely unknown to the serfs, or even to the peasants and workers from, say, Jonathan Swift's time.[9] Put otherwise: no working class prior to post-industrialization ever had to deal with fashion models, or the advertising industry, or the movies at their most meretricious—or any of the concerted efforts to turn people into imitations and types in order to exploit them more thoroughly and surreptitiously.

There was also a sense that what one could be at home perhaps (relaxed, benevolent, caring) was not an option within the workplace; the projection of a public self that was more repressed and controlled than the family self was a way of preserving the sanctity of family within the potentially hostile outside world of work. One represented one's family best in front of others by denying the comforts and liberties which the family haven otherwise allowed, and so the family, once integrated with labor (as it still is in rural agricultural communities), began to bear its own burden of overcompensatory meanings. It could never be authentically loving enough to make up for the elaborate fiction that it spun around itself like a cocoon; like butterflies regressing

1. Motifs of Physical Capital and Bodily Transformation

into moths, the anxieties set aside at work in order to protect the family at home returned to the family itself, where the reality could never match the overdetermined ideal, and the promise of being allowed to "be oneself" became so hystericized that it was no longer possible without psychosis.

The Doppelgänger selves were quickly multiplying as the capitalist system bred new, unprecedented prototypes. The go-getter and the self-made millionaire are among the first of capitalism's useful monsters, hatched under a sign of exceptionalism which valorizes the selfishness of capitalism even as it seems to mitigate against the stark necessity which reigns in the fact that, for some to be rich, many others always have to be poor. So the poor man is forced to imagine a double of himself out there somewhere, leading the life of luxury, and one day he and this double will meet and fuse together: this is the kind of everyday schizophrenia which capitalism requires. One becomes the double of one's own double, and at the same time even this double grows weary and disgusted, and gives rise to yet another double, who cannot possibly be us, since no one can find true self-expression, dignity or purpose in a sweatshop, an assembly line, a lick-spittle department store. But who is "us"? Who is "no one"? Life is always elsewhere; the Real I is another.

These problems of the body as physical capital, locked within its inescapable destiny of being never anything more than physical capital, and also the attendant problems of bodily transformation, are uniquely relevant to Edgar Allan Poe's story, "William Wilson" (1839), itself a version of the Doppelgänger myth. In this tale, the narrator's body is a mutational entity which seems to split off into an exact double on those occasions when the narrator is plying his avocation of robbery. In the end he is the one who is robbed—of himself, disquietingly to say the least. "I would not here embody, if indeed I could, the record of my later years of unspeakable misery and unpardonable crime,"[10] Poe writes as the story begins, and his verb "embody" feels particularly resonant. At that time, and since the mid-eighteenth century, according to the O.E.D., the word had carried the meaning of fully representing an abstraction or idea in speech or on paper, a kind of irrefutable textual evidence. However, in this usage, it was typically spelled "imbody" until at least 1859.[11] Poe is creating something of a neologism by mating the physical connotation of "embody" with the abstract, representational connotation of "imbody." The result is a word which sounds modern to our ears, and which carries a strong sense of the lineaments of the human body and its physical capital.

In fact, the usage of this unique verb sets the tone for Poe's story, in which language and bodies (of various kinds, not only human but architectural and spatial) will become dangerously enmeshed. Poe's prose is always rich with word-clots that accrue around intangible things; sometimes this takes the form of a reiteration that seems almost too blunt, until one realizes that we are seeing the same thing from slightly different angles, as in a film montage, and that this sort of extended stammer or stagger of description is replicating a progressive process of mutation. So, the boarding school where Wilson first encounters his double is "irregular" and "overshadowed."[12] And then it is "[i]rregular in form, having many capacious recesses," and then again, with "no end to its windings, its incomprehensible subdivisions."[13] This could be a first cancer cell metastasizing, some new bloom inside the organs of the blood. Everything within the endlessly metamorphic building anticipates what will happen to the narrator's body; it will soon subdivide, its recesses will turn inside out, it will wind and wind like a crazy top, and finally, it will become overshadowed. The somewhat overemphatic descriptive language, inviting us to look and then look again at seemingly the same entity, guides us between the two objective correlatives of the school building and the narrator's body. Similarly, the building's different "stories" (and here we find another meta-pun, similar to "embody") relentlessly morph into each other, as if unable to maintain their own identities and functions ("the wings were innumerable, inconceivable, and so turned in upon themselves"[14]). The benches and desks, in particular, have been worn down into things that are unrecognizable. "[They] have entirely lost what little of original form might have been their portion in days long departed."[15] Mass-reproduction of forms has undermined the idea that things can be traced back to singular "original forms" or that these

1. Motifs of Physical Capital and Bodily Transformation

forms (artisanal, conceptual) might retain any cachet as ideals. Physical capital is close to bankrupt: here is a spawning ground of Doppelgängers *par excellence.*

The degraded physical capital of the overused desks and benches is one of Poe's few hints, in "William Wilson," about any kind of societal macroeconomics: other than this, the whole of the story's critique goes into exposing the decadence of the narrator, as a spoiled rich kid who never attempts to earn a living in any other way except through chicanery and fraud. But even these crimes—shortcuts through the systemic demands of labor, of production—give rise to mutation. Just as the massive inert school building is acted upon by processes of transformation over time, both in rebellion from or conformity to its own endless labor of providing shelter, so alienated labor can fit in any social schema with those larger processes of restriction, routine and implicit threat which have been stamped upon the brow of social man, as it were. (The mark of Cain: one of the West's early images of bodily transformation in the service of systemic order.)

There is much futility in the school's "vast number of gigantic and gnarled trees"—the two adjectives suggesting that to grow at all is to grow twisted and diseased—as well as "the fretted Gothic steeple [which] lay imbedded and asleep"—again, as if to rise at all already contained the seeds of a concomitant flattening.[16] In Chapter 5, we will investigate a Don DeLillo novel, *The Body Artist,* that has a church in it with no steeple at all, thereby suggesting not only this same flattening but a complete loss of even symbolic function, which is also possible to read as *liberation* from symbolic function via physical transformation.[17] The deeper we go into (postmodern) fiction, the more we will see that transformations of all kinds become par for the course, a ubiquitous, none-too-special language that eventually links with concepts such as virtuality and cyberspace to fashion, out of what would once have fallen into the domain of magic realism or even supernaturalism, a new (social) realism that is nonetheless wholly dependent on the precise articulation of illusion, deceptiveness, mutability.

Meanwhile, back in the nineteenth century boarding school of "William Wilson," the idea of physical transformation is still relatively new and implicative enough for its incommensurable, Escher-like architectures to make us suitably uneasy. The boarding school is, in fact, a place where space attempts to mimic time, creating the sense of a vast eternity lurking behind obstacles and weird dimensional illusions. This is similar to the way Steven Shaviro will describe the Internet: "No panoramic view is possible, for the space is always folding, dividing, expanding, and contracting."[18] There is a kind of definitive loss of phenomenological innocence when time and space no longer help us but instead take turns distracting us. Normally, when we become lost in time, daydreaming or even dozing on a bus, say, we look to the physical world to bring us back—did we miss our stop, how far have we gone? "William Wilson's" physical world, however, is in conspiracy with the most malign and bewildering aspects of time: déjà vu, memory loss, repetition, mortality.

Scariest of all in Poe's recurring nightmare is the school's main gate, "riveted and studded with iron bolts and surmounted with jagged iron spikes. What impressions of deep awe did it inspire!"[19] If this spiked gate suggests a prison more than a school,[20] then it is hardly surprising that the students pass this gate only at the regular intervals (three times a week) when they are allowed outside.[21] The regimentation of time, as well as the threatening barriers of confinement, reproduce themselves in all these various settings, school, prison, church (for the gate suggests an enormous crucifix too) and finally, by extrapolation, factory, thereby linking them all as metonymic segments of the same general system. From childhood to adulthood and death it is the same imprisoning force, the same enclosure repeated again and again. Through poetic metaphor, lines of political force are made to connect and intersect.

Poe's intuition, in "William Wilson," is that we are somehow born into toil, no matter what our ostensible situation; any status that we might possess is always only temporary. The narrator is to the manor born. His first coup, while still a child, is to gain control over his parents so as to have full access to the family finances. This is, we are told, "the despotism of a mastermind in boyhood,"[22] and rather than there being anything ludicrous in this phrase, it is depicted as a serious, albeit not legitimate, enterprise. "William Wilson" is about the shadowy side of free enterprise, its kinship with robbery, assault and other

1. Motifs of Physical Capital and Bodily Transformation

crimes and betrayals; it's free enterprise for sociopaths. Often Wilson refers to his double as attempting to thwart "the ambition which urged me, and ... the passionate energy of mind which enabled me to excel."[23]

"William Wilson," only obliquely concerned with labor as such and reconfiguring the world of enterprise as a criminal world, is nonetheless a story of physical capital in a state of downward mobility, a series of demotions (in life) whereby the original Wilson loses more and more status and authority. Wilson's double is a creature of contained energy, of radical humility, marked by his strange whisper, the one trait in which he strikes Wilson as not resembling him at all; to Wilson, this whisper is a "weakness" because it seems to curtail his power[24] (the strong voice is part of one's physical capital), but this seeming weakness is already growing like a vine around the tree (gnarled, perhaps) of Wilson's own strength: so we are startled to read "in his singular whisper grew the very echo of my voice,"[25] as if speaking were suddenly to be defined only by muteness, by what is unable to speak—a potentially revolutionary dialectic. Always the double triumphs by doing and showing very little: Wilson schemes, the double sleeps; Wilson plots and machinates, the double merely arrives at the last minute and makes insinuations. The double finally triumphs completely by allowing Wilson to stab him to death, a seeming sacrifice which is quickly revealed as the shattering of the illusion: Wilson has committed suicide.

It seems too easy to read the double as an externalized conscience; although it is, among other things, a kind of petri dish in which cells of aggravated human conscience are cloned into sentient existence much against Wilson's will. In the mysterious room where Wilson finally confronts and kills his double, the descriptions reveal how far the story has gone beyond the merely human. Being is in chaotic, grandiose flux. "I was frantic with wild excitement," the narrator says, "and felt superhuman energy and power with my single arm."[26] Akin to the rooms of the old boarding school, this showdown room is a shape-shifter, with its ominous mirror (another objective correlative) appearing out of nowhere. And language, the conduit, is exposed as a final inability to meet the demands of death, just as it had been inadequate to meet the demands of mutational life, to "embody" the bodies that would not stay put. "But what *human* language can adequately portray that astonishment, that horror which possessed me at the spectacle then presented to view?"²⁷ The final gasp reifies the first one, earlier in the story, when Wilson gazed upon his sleeping double and asked himself in wonder, "Were these the lineaments of William Wilson?"²⁸ The double, here, is the impossible, poignant person that one might have been allowed to be in a world that did not demand toil for money and prestige, and financial independence that comes (if it does) only in the squelching of every other kind.

The next example of physical transformation that I would like to consider draws more explicitly on the background concepts of capitalism, commerce, and even imperialism. It posits transformation as a process in which an object in the production-consumption nexus—a trading ship—divests itself of its own physical capital as part of a systematic journey to the end of its own purposefulness, its own utilitarianism. I refer to Rimbaud's "Le Bateau ivre" (1871) or "The Drunken Boat," surely one of the greatest lyric poems ever written, and one which has also been claimed as a political text. In *The Emergence of Social Space: Rimbaud and the Paris Commune,* Kristin Ross traces a line of Marxist thought about this poem, beginning with a remark which Bertolt Brecht made in conversation with Walter Benjamin. Benjamin was certainly the right person to whom to impart the remark, since he always yearned to establish legitimate left-wing credentials for great writers whom he already loved but whose work did not overtly exemplify Marxist theory (Kafka, Baudelaire, Proust, etc.):

> [Brecht] thinks that Marx and Engels, had they read "Le Bateau ivre," would have sensed in it the great historical movement of which it is the expression. They would have clearly recognized that what it describes is not an eccentric poet going for a walk, but the flight, the escape of a man who cannot live any longer inside the barriers of a class which—with the Crimean War, with the Mexican adventure—was then beginning to open up even the most exotic lands to mercantile interests.²⁹

This is why Rimbaud punctuates the dreamlike odyssey of the drunken boat with headline-specific reminders that the goods it freights are

1. Motifs of Physical Capital and Bodily Transformation

Dutch and British, and that at one point it passes through "d'incroyables Florides" [unbelievable Floridas][30] and even rubs sterns with the U.S. Civil War battleship, the *Monitor*.[31] Like so much of Rimbaud's prescient writing, "The Drunken Boat" is an early assessment, visionary yet shrewd, of a world already transformed and interlinked by what we now call global capitalism.

Specifically, as Ross writes, the drunken boat becomes an emblem of defiance against "the expropriation of the body by the institution of wage labor: the economic obligation of people who cannot otherwise survive to sell the only commodity they possess, their labor power."[32] Freed from its duties, its burden of cargo and crew, the boat finds itself like a dropped-out hippie, examining its former life of labor from the inside-out. It resigns itself to no longer being a tool in the service of commerce, and gradually this resignation, without entirely losing the poignancy of a resignation, becomes something more like a vow, never to go back, and instead to embrace its own disintegration through a series of ecstatic, narcotic visions.

Or rather, in actuality, the boat leaves behind ordinary human narcosis for something that resembles narcosis but is much rarer and more transcendent. Alcohol and drugs are quantifiable and therefore controllable; plus, their effects are only fleeting. The boat is "drunken" finally on nature and liberty themselves:

> Plus douce qu'aux enfants la chair des pommes sures,
> L'eau verte pénétra ma coque de sapin
> Et des taches de vins bleus et des vomissures
> Me lava, dispersant gouvernail et grappin.
>
> [Sweeter than flesh of green apples to children,
> The green water penetrated my pine hull
> And cleansed me of those stains of blue wine
> And vomit, dissolving steerage and grappling.][33]

The nature-identified color "green" supplants "blue," traditionally used to designate human misery, wastedness, and tawdry eroticism. The linking of "wine/And vomit" seals the dismissal of intoxication as a finite cycle of liberation, thus false and lesser than the boat's ultimate journey of self-uncovering and transcendent annihilation. The boat's drunkenness has an essentially different character, for example, from what is said of the poet Baal in Bertolt Brecht's early play, partly inspired by the aura of Rimbaud: "Drinking brings out the bad in him and then he feels good. He's too strong."[34] *Baal* is one of Brecht's pre-Marxist plays, influenced by French decadence and pulp fiction, but there is something about the word "strong" which connotes physical capital. Baal, who is not a laborer but an artist, must combat his own surplus of physical capital by numbing his heart with alcohol. For all of his grandiose sovereignty, however, Baal is a hobo, a bisexual and a killer, definitively outside of society, and as such, fairly easily destroyed by the end of the play. His physical capital running out, he dies in a shack among strangers who spit on him and shrug off his death as meaningless:

> Sometimes a guy bites the dust who might still get a lot of fun out of life, a millionaire. But you—you haven't even identification papers. Don't be afraid: round as a ball, the world will roll on. Tomorrow morning the wind will be whistling. Try to be more detached. Say to yourself: "A rat is dying. So what?" Just take it easy. You haven't any teeth left.[35]

Disease and infirmity catch up to Baal only at the end, and then quite suddenly. From organic accouterments (teeth) to inorganic ones (I.D. papers), he is bereft of physical capital. Even in a context where there is no alienated labor per se, physical capital defines, again as in "William Wilson," the lineaments of a life.

The drunken boat, on the other hand, is apotheosized by its cumulative loss of physical capital as an entity of spiritual and societal liberation. Yet there almost seems to be an innate tendency on the boat's part to want this slipping, this freedom that is found in headlong submission to uselessness and self-destruction. Much more than Baal, it finds its meaning in its decay, a state which it seems to recognize, cosmically, without having necessarily experienced it before. Thus, the boat is not disoriented, but re-oriented; it finds out who it is. Indeed, it cannot be said to ever have been particularly strong in terms of physical capital. Rather, its physical capital has mainly been invested in it by the people who used it. This has caused the boat to suffer the ignominy and trauma which Baudelaire described as the demeaned lot of modern men, "esclave de l'esclave" [slave of a slave].[36] It bears

1. Motifs of Physical Capital and Bodily Transformation

trace memories of being under the command of seamen who, in turn, felt themselves to be uniquely powerless and weak; in turn, they abused the ship. But again, as we see, their generic stains (of wine-vomit) are not indicative of Baal's lofty, decadent sovereignty of getting drunk and doing "wicked" things,[37] but instead a passive, proletarian numbness that explicitly resembles, a priori, symptoms of disease and infirmity.

In Rimbaud's poem, drunkenness is a faulty human remedy for the miseries of alienated labor, and a trap if one thirsts after true, permanent independence. Thus, it is like some heavenly kingdom awarded to the boat when it finds it can become drunk on water alone, a beautiful image of needs being freely fulfilled and of real empowerment, and perhaps a passing allegory of the working class (the boat) seizing for itself the "means of production" (the water which the boat sails). This allows us to understand Rimbaud's complex pun:

> Moi dont les Monitors et les voilliers des Hanses
> N'auraient pas repêché la carcasse ivre d'eau…
> [I whose carcass, drunk on water,
> No Monitors and Hanseatic sailboats will have rescued….][38]

The subjunctive tense, as well as the way the "*dont*" attaches "*carcasse*" back to the singular pronoun "*Moi*," suggest the secondary meaning of "*avoir repêcher*," which in the context of pedagogy means: to have passed a test. The lines are therefore delivering not a fatalistic verdict on the boat's downward-and-out mobility, but the news that it has achieved something beyond all other ships. It has broken through:

> I whose carcass, drunk on water,
> No Monitors or Hanseatic sailboats *will have surpassed…*

Like Bodhisattva, the drunken boat has become the Enlightened One. By the end of reading Rimbaud's poem, in true revolutionary fashion, we no longer wonder why this ship is speaking to us; we wonder instead why all ships are not.

It can be argued that Rimbaud's utter modernity caused him to see everything as mutation—life, the body, thought and discourse themselves, all of human existence a series of alienated adaptations, dislocated, indeterminate, anti-utilitarian. As Hans-Jost Frey writes:

"Self-awareness [for Rimbaud] is the awareness of being an other, of being isolated from oneself; it is an awareness of the other in me."[39] The Real I, the Other I. Far from being "univocal," writes Étienne Balibar, identity "is always in transit between several symbolic references.... It always has to express itself successively through different commitments."[40] In Rimbaud's work, this is often the case with inanimate objects or architectural structures as much as with beings: we are reminded of those cityscapes in *The Illuminations* where endless terraces are stacked on top of each other, and where the turning-off of a simple street takes us into a wholly different geography and climate.[41] One is tempted to say that anything *structural* for Rimbaud required deranging, a counter-derangement to the individual's bewildered lack of free coordinates. It is the same spatial derangement that coincides with, or gives rise to, blurry, wrenched selfhood in Poe's "William Wilson." Someone else is always leading this dance of where one finds oneself and what one does there.

Moreover, there is no such thing as space, either external or internal, that can be definitively demarcated as private and intact. Rimbaud, in a letter: "C'est faux de dire: Je pense. On devrait dire: On me pense [It's wrong to say: I think. We should say: someone thinks me]."[42] Rimbaud's "*on,*" the pronoun in "*on me pense,*" could be translated as "someone" or "they," at any rate one or more others, the societal "they" whose creature we become even when engaged in something as traditionally self-defined and private as "thinking." This matter-of-fact statement—someone thinks me—is a startling reversal of the entire Western philosophical *monologue* tradition that begins famously with René Descartes' *cogito ergo sum*, instead choosing to pick up much farther back in pre–Christian antiquity where Socratic doubt and symbiotic *dialogue* left off.[43]

The hybridized nature of the philosophical dialogue would have made for a better model in terms of Western art and culture. Rimbaud was a great seeker of new forms, new ways of using language and writing to reveal societal fissures and fractures. "There is, in short, a homology between [Rimbaud's] prose poems and the fashioning of the barricades."[44] In terms of literary expression, any hybrid form can be a sophisticated mutation in the direction of greater liberty. Thus, in

1. Motifs of Physical Capital and Bodily Transformation

the end, the central movement of transformation in "The Drunken Boat" is not that the ship gains human consciousness, but that this human consciousness is *raised,* in the political sense of becoming more aware of the flaws of the mercantile and imperial system whose slave it had been. The ship is more human, possessed of an expanding universal consciousness, and uniquely open to recalling those aspects of the self which defy the social order through deterritorialization, lawlessness, rebellion. The opening stanza, in which screaming redskins nail the white crewmen to poles to use them as living targets,[45] is a jarring return of repressed materials, which precipitates the whole drifting departure from Europe and from white identity in the final stanzas. It is those screaming redskins whom the boat, rising more and more into declamation, finally comes to join:

> Si je désire une eau d'Europe, c'est la flache
> Noire et froide où vers le crépuscule embaumé
> Un enfant accroupi plein de tristesses, lâche
> Un bateau frêle comme un papillon de mai.
>
> Je ne puis plus, baigné de vos langueurs, ô lames,
> Enlever leur sillage aux porteurs de cotons,
> Ni traverser l'orgueil des drapeaux et des flammes,
> Ni nager sous les yeux horribles des pontons.
>
> [If I crave any water of Europe, it's the icy
> Black pond where, toward the embalmed twilight,
> An unhappy child crouches and sets adrift
> A boat as frail as a butterfly in May.
>
> Bathed in your idleness, oh waves, I will never again
> Foam a wake for the cotton exporters,
> Nor plow through storms of flags and flames,
> Nor swim below the bridges' fearsome eyes.][46]

The ship as an inveterate tool of capitalist trade has been remade in the playful and non-utile image of the child's paper boat and literally reborn as a butterfly; the last stanza's litany of what the boat is now incapable of doing forevermore needs to be read not as an elegy but as a kind of declaration of freedom. The boat may capsize and drown, but it rises anew in the sudden bird's-eye view that it takes of the European waters to which it will never return even if it could. It is like a workers' strike or, beyond that, complete transfiguration of the world of alienated labor into a world of harmony and peace, that idyllic laziness which Ross describes as "revolutionary praxis."[47] And we recognize a classic Rimbaudian mutation in the "If I crave any water of Europe…," which is to say, the invocation of a special adaptation to survive without food and water, or to learn how to eat the inedible (e.g., the poem "Faim"[48]; the "merde" letter to Verlaine: "Quand vous me verrez manger positivement de la merde, alors seulement vous ne trouverez plus que je coûte trop cher à nourrir! [When you see me eat shit with a smile on my face, only then will you realize how cheaply you can keep me!]"[49]). The most opportune transformation is one that allows you to replenish your physical capital for free, even in the midst of a world where everything has a price—a transformation that evades the "great sale of human labor that makes merchandise of people and an immense boutique of society."[50]

Suddenly one day, a man becomes a bridge, or a bridge becomes a man:

> I was stiff and cold, I was a bridge, I lay over a ravine. My toes on one side, my fingers clutching the other, I had clamped myself fast into the crumbling clay. The tails of my coat fluttered at my sides. Far below brawled the icy trout stream. No tourist strayed to this impassable height, the bridge was not yet traced on any map. So I lay and waited; I could only wait. Without falling, no bridge, once spanned, can cease to be a bridge.
> It was towards evening one day—was it the first? was it the thousandth? I cannot tell—my thoughts were always in confusion and perpetually moving in a circle. It was towards evening in summer, the roar of the stream had grown deeper, when I heard the sound of a human step! To me, to me. Straighten yourself, bridge, make ready, railless beams, to hold up the passenger entrusted to you. If his steps are uncertain steady them unobtrusively, but if he stumbles show what you are made of and like a mountain god hurl him across to land.[51]

This is the halfway point in this short-short story—a pedestrian has come to this light-headed height, not yet traced on any map, this impassable mountain gorge where we were certain that no tourist had ever strayed. How is this possible? The enigma of the story, thus far,

1. Motifs of Physical Capital and Bodily Transformation

is not the anomalous mutation of the bridge-man, but rather the unassuming human presence, which, in enunciating itself as a token of order, brings the true chaos. We can only assume that, while the bridge-man lay stretched above the ravine, waiting for his destiny of passive service to be fulfilled, society quietly expanded, claiming yet another swathe of unheard-of, even imaginary, space for its own colonial enterprise. The pedestrian is an advance guard from imperial powers that be.[52] (He could even be an implacable insurance adjuster trying to track down the drunken boat and reclaim whatever is left of its cargo.) At the same time, he is also just a blasé stroller, wearing (it turns out) a frock coat exactly like the bridge-man. In some ways, he is a Doppelgänger vaguely like the one in "William Wilson," in that he may have been summoned forth precisely by the bridge-man's futile waiting, in order to *do something about it*—to fulfill or thwart the long-held, long-unproductive ambition. The arrival of the pedestrian quickly reveals to us, for example, that the bridge-man, though he may be many things, is hardly "a mountain god," for his dimensions are essentially those of an average man stretched isometrically across a narrow, deep ravine. At the same time, the pedestrian is nothing like a conventional Doppelgänger, for the bridge-man does not recognize him as such, does not view him as an uncanny threat but instead as a kind of mechanical counterpart, whose function of strolling is needed to test the bridge-man's function of providing passage from one side of the gorge to the other.

The story continues:

> He came, he tapped me with the iron point of his stick, then he lifted my coattails with it and put them in order upon me. He plunged the point of his stick into my bushy hair and let it lie there for a long time, forgetting me no doubt while he wildly gazed around him. But then—I was just following him in thought over mountain and valley—he jumped with both feet on the middle of my body. I shuddered with wild pain, not knowing what was happening. Who was it? A child? A dream? A wayfarer? A suicide? A tempter? A destroyer? And I turned around so as to see him. A bridge to turn around! I had not yet turned quite around when I already began to fall, I fell and in a moment I was torn and transpierced by the sharp rocks which had always gazed up at me so peacefully from the rushing water.[53]

That is the entirety of the vignette, titled (with emphatic and delusional certainty) "The Bridge" (written between 1914 and 1917). Of course, it is Kafka—who else could it be, especially after the arrival of the second man who ruins everything by revealing the dysfunction at the heart of the bridge-man's straining effort, the literal lack of support or structure ("railless beams"); in short, the bridge-man's paucity of physical capital even in the face of his desperate and perhaps hubristic denial of this lack.

Thus, the bridge-man is not similar to the drunken boat at all; the bridge-man's seeming escape to geographical remoteness and to the status of an ostensibly non-sentient object (neither remote nor non-sentient enough, as it happens) has not succeeded in bringing about a real transformation even within the bridge-man himself. Nor is this an emblem of freedom's lazy drift, this straining, stretching attempt to defy gravity, to meld with the rock on either side, to solidify where the body remains soft. The boat could cease to be a boat per se, and find triumphant meaning in that; the man cannot succeed in becoming that endless, static worker known as "a bridge," permitted no break times or days off, no vacations or sick days, and no malfunctions.

Moreover, the transformation is not gradual, dynamic or progressive; we are given to understand neither its origins nor its objective purpose. The story's narrator simply "was a bridge," in the ongoing past tense, the way some obituary might state "he was a machinist" or "he was an office worker." In fact, it wasn't something he *became* one day, although in introducing the text I could not help but try to give it some riddling chicken-and-the-egg logic, since this plunging-in is by far the most disturbing part of the entire text—the purpose of that first phrase is to acclimate us all at once to Kafka's *realism*, for this text is meant neither to be dream or metaphor.[54]

The emphasis given to treating non-logical circumstances as if they were fact and thus possessed of a certain inherent logic is a fiat which suggests tyrannical thinking, irrational whim codified as unlivable law. Likewise, what the tyranny decrees is upheld only by a paralytic passivity, on the part of the worker, that is close to death or a death wish. We could be in the world of current *Saw*-like thrillers,

1. Motifs of Physical Capital and Bodily Transformation

where drugged and kidnapped people awake to find themselves tied up in remote locations where they must perform certain tests or be immediately killed. One way or another, anyone in the bridge-man's situation would need lots of physical capital, inordinate, even surplus and superhuman amounts. But now there is a stick, a simple prop for short walks, for measuring the physical world, far less mechanically advanced than the most provisional sort of working bridge, but in this case unerringly reliable: for as the second man pokes his stick among the bridge's coattails and then into the bridge's head of hair, we see that the bridge's span can only be the average body length of a man, whose head is close enough to his feet to be reachable from either side. It is at this point that we understand the bridge-man's impossible drive to undertake a greater share of labor, even an unnecessary share, in this case a job that cannot even be performed by a human. The only alternative to succumbing to the tyrannical decree that has made the man a bridge would have been a kind of revolutionary action; yet, somehow, this is beyond the man's capacity, even though he stretches himself to the breaking point and finally dies in the attempt to oblige the tyrannical decree. Thus, there is no teleology here, any potential for development is brutally arrested from the start.

Jorge Luis Borges has astutely recognized Zeno as a precursor of Kafka, particularly in the theoretical "paradox against motion":

> A moving body at point *A* (Aristotle states) will not be able to reach point *B*, because it must cover half of the distance between the two, and before that, half of the half, and before that, half of the half of the half, and so on to infinity; the form of this famous problem is precisely that of *The Castle,* and the moving body and the arrow and Achilles are the first Kafkaesque characters in literature.[55]

Physical being itself contains something of the impossible, of the necessary overcoming of severe limitations, and the only intermittent or theoretical success of this overcoming. Like sleepwalkers who cannot be awakened, Kafka's characters set out on their impossible journeys, build up a little more of their Great Walls and burrows ... or stretch themselves out across ravines and pretend to be bridges. What does such mutation represent? Is it the work ethic run amok? Learning to stop worrying and love the alienated labor? Nothing so blunt. Kafka's use of the trope of bodily mutation, or what Gilles Deleuze and Félix Guattari term "absolute molecular deterritorialization,"[56] is a kind of shaming mockery of the order as such, but only through an absurd extremity that leaves the reader with neither the false consolation of the ridiculed order nor a coherent program of recuperation. "It is by the power of his noncritique," Deleuze and Guattari suggest, "that Kafka is so dangerous."[57]

Deleuze and Guattari use the word "*assemblage*" for any spatial or psychological cathexis at which oppressors and oppressed unite in their shared desire to be part of the same machine. The machine is made of desire, although it might appear to be made of something more like power: "There isn't a desire for power; it is power itself that is desire. Not a desire-lack, but desire as a plenitude, exercise, and functioning, even in the most subaltern of workers."[58] There is no way to misplace power in the concept of fulfillment. It may be benevolent, benign, passive, understated, unabused, but where there is fulfillment there is power. The bridge-man would be happy (thus empowered) if the pedestrian could walk across him—as in masochism, there is power achieved through the overcoming of thresholds of submission, of nominal powerlessness. Alienated labor is submission without accomplishment, enforced masochism without fulfillment. It is that resigned bourgeois scourging of need and desire which places any possibility of true freedom for anyone beyond reach, under lock and key. The whimsicality of actions in "The Bridge" define it as a scrounging search for liberty in a world that is not free: the bridge-man ecstatically surrenders to his doomed function, just as the pedestrian energetically destroys the bridge-man. Together they form a desire-machine that is fulfilled in the shared exercise and display of power, the power to enact and fulfill the desire (however odd) on both sides.

According to Nietzsche, the "desire for freedom" is only one of the disguised forms of will to power.[59] There is a strain in Nietzschean thought, rarely pursued and one which we will investigate in this work, that suggests that what Marxism really meant to redistribute to the masses was not material wealth but the value of a power that encompasses total human energy—mental, spiritual, emotional, psychosexual. This is a bit like the folkloric wisdom that states, if you give a man

1. Motifs of Physical Capital and Bodily Transformation

a fish he will eat for a day, whereas if you teach him how to fish he will eat for a lifetime. It is true that Nietzsche moves decisively against the herd at every moment; yet it is also abundantly clear that his vision of individual sovereignty depends upon everyone possessing this sovereignty. Here is a statement which makes sense only when we read it inside-out, or "transvaluate" it: "The time of kings has gone by, because people are no longer worthy of them."[60] Put otherwise: in order to have kings, every person must be kingly. Is this not a semantic cousin to Marx's dictatorship of the proletariat? And here is another statement: "Are we to suppose that there are any pains which 'the species' feel, and which the individual does not?"[61] Refinement of feeling, and the ability to redress wrongs, are only comprehensible at the level of individuals, or what Nietzsche (in anticipation of Deleuze and Guattari's machinic assemblages) calls "units."[62]

Of course, this does not mean that free individuals will live in peace; in fact, they will most likely attack one another. Nietzsche writes: "Even the body [group] within which individuals treat each other as equals ... has to do to other bodies [groups] what the individuals within it refrain from doing to each other...."[63] This is one of the pessimistic limits of Nietzsche's thought, which strains against limits and, in doing so, always reveals them. We might call this a problem of post-revolutionary societies, what Marx, too, noted as an ongoing struggle. The units must become equal without sickening from equality itself, without needing to exert a lesser form of will-to-power which is not true freedom but only the fleeting satisfaction of an urge. Sovereignty, again, is learning to fish, not simply gobbling up whatever fish is at hand.

Where Nietzsche implies a refutation of Hegelian dialectic is precisely in this thought, again somewhat recessive in his work but unmistakably present, that the way to rid society of oppression was not to abolish power, which is an impossible canard, but to make everyone equally powerful. Both Marx and Nietzsche were ardent pursuers of *value* (in German, *Wert*), which turns out to have affinities in both its material (Marxist) definition and its human-energy (Nietzschean) one. The key to physical capital beyond the bondage of alienated labor lies partly in these half-buried affinities. Marx's debt to Hegel has been critiqued before; this book is not a comprehensive or final severing of ties with Hegelianism (were this even possible or entirely desirable), but one of its aims is to ask if we have not in many ways outlived the usefulness and sense of the dialectic.

The dialectic has ironically hampered Hegel's own originary vision of history "as one uninterrupted development of the Spirit"[64] by providing it with a structured means of interruption: a binding of unfettered thought at intervals where we sense an endgame or goal in sight. Hence, there is no way of resolving forever the problem of fulfillment, since the seeking of fulfillment drives the process of development. Calvinist capitalism childishly attempts to resolve fulfillment by restricting it to the realm of death and afterlife, thereby cheapening the immanent world with rituals of guilt and abnegation. Fulfillment is, therefore, not an end in itself, after which we have nothing left to do, but a means of bringing our humanity more and more into focus by discovering the true purpose of our physical capital, our life energy. Without naming him directly, Hannah Arendt brought Nietzsche squarely into play against the Hegelian problem of Marxist thought, whose "danger is … the transformation of meanings into ends, which is what happens in Marx's philosophy when he takes the Hegelian meaning of all history—the progressive development and realization of the idea of Freedom—to be an end of human action."[65] It was Nietzsche who explicitly asserted that all life, power, and freedom were different names for the same energy, and that this energy was always only a means in an ongoing series of Becomings, not an end, not a fixed state of Being.[66] Any final resolution, no matter how liberatory (or indeed, at the farthest extreme of liberation), is equivalent to the death of the organism; the cessation of chronic Becoming is not Being but death. Or, as Fassbinder has his heroine Geesche say in the play, *Bremen Freedom:* "Peace means death, father, and I want to live. I can't see myself longing for peace."[67] However, Marx, "in accordance with [dialectical] tradition, views this [Freedom] as the end-product of a manufacturing process, just as the table is clearly the end-product of the carpenter's activity."[68]

Thus, we note that transformation can sometimes be defined by its determined incompletion, its lack, indeed "a certain ambiguity that leads to [its] insufficiency and condemns [it] to defeat"[69]; the transpar-

1. Motifs of Physical Capital and Bodily Transformation

ent way in which the form-to-be-escaped (man) remains visible within the mutated and capitulating form (bridge).[70] Brought to standstill, sick with dialectical ambivalence, one waits to be chosen as it were, while knowing that when one is chosen, one's inevitable unworthiness will be exposed. But if there is nowhere to run, the organism can adapt by forgetting the instinct to run in the first place, or forgetting how. "There is only a single man in [Kafka's] work," Borges writes, "*homo domesticus* … desirous of a place, no matter how humble, in some Order."[71] For this man, willing to cripple or smother himself as the need arises, bodily transformation "is presented as a simple imitation."[72] Given the bridge-man's capitulation, and his ultimate fulfillment in the co-enactment of desire with the pedestrian, we understand that the bridge-man's oppression exists at the level of consciousness itself, in his limited options. As a worker, the bridge must be only that one thing which he purports to be. Although already a hybrid of bridge and man, he cannot afford to squander any precious physical capital on the kind of changeling freedom disturbingly ascribed to the pedestrian, to be any number of possible identities, none of them employable or productive: *child, dream, wayfarer, suicide, tempter, destroyer*. These are the faces of non-work, of excess physical capital and its expenditure, of those who cannot take responsibility, or those who toss it away, anyway those who go on their way without caring and who *might not even truly exist*: the ultimate luxury. At any rate, only "in thought" can the worker let himself follow where this oblivious pedestrian might actually go, and we know from Rimbaud that thought is no refuge, no line of escape: *someone thinks me*. Instead of a progression, the bridge-man's thoughts move "in a circle," like clockwork or a vicious cycle of undifferentiated repetition. Still, he exposes the faults of the system from within, by exposing his own inability to measure up to the tyrannical demands. This is revolt through attrition, or the revolutionary corollary of Zeno's paradox of movement: as Étienne Balibar writes, "*The capitalist structure of society cannot but change*, by virtue of its own constraints."[73]

A devotee of Kafka, Paul Goodman offers a narrative of ruined physical capital in his short story, "Terry Fleming—Or, Are You Planning a Universe?" (1947). Goodman describes intense and complete transformations wrought in a father and his son through their resistance to repressive social institutions: Dick Fleming is a prison lifer, while Terry attends a tough, unsympathetic high school. The father rises from the dead, so to speak; Terry's mother, in an attempt to spare her son's feelings (and Dick's dignity perhaps) has lied to Terry all his life that his father is dead. When the young man finds the newspaper clipping it is as if antimatter has become matter: "His father was not dead but alive, not nothing but a person, not nowhere but in a place called jail."[74] Goodman's reiterated use of double negatives tortures the syntax in a way that incipiently suggests the colloquial speech patterns of the story's uneducated, un-bookish males. At another point, Terry crows, "He's not nowhere."[75] Of course, grammatically, these constructions are correct, if we view "not" (the way Terry does) as the negation of an affirmed lack: nothing is the thing that the father is *not*, nowhere is the place where the father is *not*. The double negatives *sound* wrong to most ears, though, and this is because, in their vernacular second meaning, they could easily denote a real, existent lack. "He's not nowhere," meaning the father is gone, the painful truth of Terry's boyhood existence whether he acknowledges it or not. Negating a lack is finally not the same as fostering a benefit or plenitude.

Indeed, lack begins to win in the story's psychological warfares. Terry proceeds to isolate himself from his mother by concocting the myth that she is a Gypsy who raised him after he was stolen as a baby. As the maternal side of his origins dwindles away, the paternal side (also fictive) blobs out of proportion: "'My father is a king,' thought Terry. 'Enemies have locked him in jail. They have cruel guards and use heavy stone and iron to keep him unknown. But his dignity shines.'"[76] Empathy with a convict necessitates the removal of guilt through a fantasy of persecution. Here we see a more forwardly and outspokenly revolutionary twist on the bridge man's vigil in Kafka's story. The false mythos transforms justice into injustice, punishment into oppression, and contains within it the rationale for symbolic and literal insurgency. The laws are unfair, the reigning social order is a murderous coup d'état.

From this point, Terry slides behaviorally: he has already gotten

1. Motifs of Physical Capital and Bodily Transformation

in trouble at school by insulting a teacher and picking a fight with a group of boys; under the aegis of his own false mythos he is not effecting revolutionary change but instead becoming surly and antisocial, a criminal type like his father Dick. Terry becomes psychopathic, furiously masturbating to thoughts of a long-lost sister who could help him to rescue their father the king.[77] Meanwhile, Dick has also become incipiently pathologized by his long imprisonment in a dehumanizing penal system. "Inured" is the word Goodman uses to describe the caged man, and we see that this is yet another kind of socially conditioned and enforced mutation. Dick has learned to digest every kind of rage into stark scientific law, isolated, bereft and pure:

> But when he slept, he dreamed of dark fire. We others dream of fire with its forms and colors and licking its objects: houses burning, explosions and bolts of electricity. But the fire that Dick dreamed of was more like the dark fire of physics, an invisible mass not even hot because it touches no objects—the fire itself, filling a space where nothing else can be, except that occasionally there is a white flash and annihilation because of some flaw in the perfect vacuum.[78]

It is "just the purpose" of prison "to create such an inward-turning relation" of a man to himself,[79] Goodman tells us; when a human is broken to the point where he is only fit for aloneness, then he is finally left alone—the sour reward earned by his torment. Given the nature of the social order to reward mindless production over contemplation, it is much more difficult to become an agent of truly revolutionary change than it is to lapse into incipiently revolutionary but ultimately self-defeating stalemates: to become psychopaths, in a word, addicts, sybarites, gamblers, debtors, the impulse-control-challenged; the sad monsters of the human zoo. Put otherwise, the "fellow mammalians" addressed at the end of Philip Roth's novella *The Breast* (which we shall consider in depth in Chapter 4): "Morons and madmen, tough guys and skeptics, friends, students, relatives, colleagues"—for everyone is a monster, everyone is in this zoo—"and all you distracted strangers, with your billion different fingerprints and faces."[80] Are these still men?

Among other transformational dramas which Goodman's hybrid text embodies (its final section takes us outside the story to deliver a wry utopian program for planning the perfect universe), there is the poignant and radical implication that this is literature for the functionally illiterate, the lumpen prole, the gum-chewing kid. Yet, of course, it remains more truly *about* them than *for* them. Can literature evade, repurpose, or shed its own physical capital to become a more direct instrument of revolution? It is an uncanny trick of Goodman's to match the abused and lost physical capital of his heroes by creating a piece of writing that lacks physical capital of its own. It is not perfectly written; its various "plots" never connect; its title, at once difficult and perfunctory, must work harder than most titles at bridging the text's gaps. Like that faulty, "disinterested" humanity which it invokes, the story has its own unique fingerprints, its own weird DNA. It feels guilty about something. Yet it demands to be set free.

2

Eternity and the Body

Many Ur-narratives tell a similar story: that of an individual sacrifice made for the sake of the collective. Persephone is given to Hades for half of each year so that we may enjoy spring and summer in the other half; Moses the law-giver was not permitted to accompany his people into the Promised Land; Christ was put to death to redeem the sins of the world. The hero typically gives up the right to his or her *family*, and it is because the hero mutates first away from family that we can remain within our own families and love them. We can say that we are always given to cherish something through the representation of its sacrificial loss (family, identity, life, status, work) and this thing is nearly always something which holds the collective together. As Bataille spent much of his life pointing out in various ways, Western societies never construct myths around the cherishing of things that would be destructive of collective bonds: sexual freedom, for example, or wanton destruction of property. In his essay, "The Sorcerer's Apprentice," he wrote:

> The greatest part of activity is subordinated to the production of useful goods, no decisive change seeming possible, and man is all too inclined to make his enslavement by work an insuperable limit…. He can tolerate his existence only on the condition that he forgets what it really is.[1]

Forgetting one's existence: through narcotic stupors and blackouts, through acts of violence and sex, through madness, through religious frenzy. The individual who forgets who he is might be seen as mad or impaired in some way, even though Bataille makes it clear that in a bourgeois capitalist society this self-forgetting (or self-denying) has to be the norm. This is why true individual freedom is isolating in Western cultures; it is seen as the mark of attempting to destroy the collective by setting an example of freedom which, if it spread, would lead to a thorough overturning of hierarchies.

What is specifically taboo in the West is to be casual or carefree regarding death. I am not talking about someone readily taking the lives of others, nor about someone laughing in mockery at an actual corpse. I am talking about the acceptance of mortality and the placement of it within a perspective that can allow one to fully live. Fassbinder expressed this when he stated: "Life doesn't become manageable and accessible until the moment when death is accepted as the true aspect of existence. As long as death is treated as a taboo, life remains uninteresting. *A society based on the exploitation of human beings has to treat death as a taboo.*"[2]

I have italicized that last sentence because it has always struck me like a bolt of lightning. The internalization of the idea of death, minus the placebo of being certain of an afterlife in heaven, is the beginning of all true freedom for the individual, since it places stress on the moment of living as free and conscious choice. Only then can one *value* oneself as truly living, truly alive. Whereas, if one is reduced to nothing but exploited physical capital, then one might feel a rebellious urge, even a duty, to hurl away that physical capital in acts of self-destruction.

I am more interested in Fassbinder as a philosopher than as a filmmaker, here, although this theme certainly runs throughout his films as well as his writings and interviews. As a philosopher Fassbinder is very close to Bataille, who also explored this tension of learning to live through the acceptance and even welcoming of "death"—both literal and what could be categorized as extreme, transformative experience. Fassbinder saw life coming down to a central choice, "the decision in favor of a short but fulfilled life or a long but unaware or on the whole alienated existence."[3] This was not a choice that a work of art could make for someone, but instead should be "left entirely up to the audience."[4] Each spectator must be like the poet Rilke before the ancient torso of Apollo in the famous sonnet, hearing the fragmented sculpture's command to "change your life" within a kind of internal or spiritual ear. There is, of course, great melancholy in Fassbinder's perception that one cannot, somehow, have both a long life *and* fulfillment; yet there are many ways in which life, when carried on outside of social and institutional regimentation, becomes exceedingly fragile. And of course, Fassbinder wanted to provoke a response and even revolutionary action (both individual and collective) on the part of his audiences, as did Bataille.

We are reminded of another of Bataille's essays, "The Practice of Joy Before Death," in which he describes the power that comes from ridding oneself of the tyranny of "eternity," which holds all of empirical life hostage, as it were, to an oppressive imaginary: "He alone is happy who, having experienced vertigo to the point of trembling in his bones, to the point of being incapable of measuring the extent of his fall, finds the unhoped-for strength to turn his agony into a joy capable of freezing and transfiguring those who meet it."[5] Rock legend Jimi Hendrix breaks things down even more explicitly in the song "If 6 Was 9" on the album *Axis: Bold as Love*: in a spoken aside he muses that each of us must die when it is our time, so we have the right to live as we wish, for ourselves first and foremost, rather than for the approval of others.

Eternity has been, since its origins in theological thought, an enemy to empirical freedom. The seemingly unchanging concept of eternity is challenged by Nietzsche's doctrine of Becoming, for him the highest principle and aspiration, the ultimate mark of being alive.[6] Nietzsche viewed the eternal as part of a kind of conspiracy against Becoming, in the sense of making "everything temporal and limited subordinate to eternal rights!"[7] Eternity would have things rigidly fixed and ossified; whereas Becoming derives from a recognition that there is no such thing as a final state; instead, we should aspire to an absolute temporality that is non-successive, individualistic and unstable.[8] Becoming gains its prime importance as a value because, Nietzsche writes, values "may all be reduced to that scale of numbers and measures representing energy."[9] Energy is synonymous with Becoming, and with life.

Nietzsche denounced the falsity of an ego supposedly "liberated from Becoming and declared to belong to the sphere of Being."[10] Becoming will not let us go free from it; it is a taskmaster, precisely as burdening and oppressive as life itself can be. It is like the opposite of the cruel image of eternity depicted in Michel Gondry's *Human Nature* (2001), a white room with two doors on either side, and when the room-dweller tries to leave through one door he ends up coming right back in through the other one. With Becoming, as with life, you never (need) enter the same room twice. Whether you find this proposition exhilarating or terrifying is perhaps the basic measure of who you are as a person; whereas the doctrine of eternity presupposes that we are all essentially the same in the end (in a position of being irrevocably judged for a kind of characterological essence) and that we can do nothing to obfuscate this.

There has been very little written about eternity in recent times. Carlos Eire's *A Very Brief History of Eternity* places a high premium on the idea of an endless span of time: "there is no concept more central to the definition of transcendent reality" or what Eire calls "lived religion."[11] Eire depicts it as "an odd sort of comfort" that humanity has "imagined something beyond material existence ... beyond constant flux and evanescence."[12] However, not everything that can be imagined is helpful or even necessary; rather than interrogate the assumptions of the eternity-imaginary, Eire takes those assumptions fully at face value, which leads to some intellectual denial on his part. He very movingly relates the abuses of the Castro regime in his native Cuba, acknowledging the pain of "having lost some of my family to its dungeons and firing squads simply because they dared to challenge dialectical materialism in public."[13] However, a few pages later, he invokes Saint Augustine as the last (theological) word on those who might be tempted to question eternity and an eternal God: "the best I can do is to quote St. Augustine.... Before God created heaven and earth, he was busy designing hell for people who ask such questions."[14] When asserting any kind of institutional doctrine, it apparently helps, no matter what side you are on, to have a few dungeons handy.

For the ancients, eternity was a kind of superstructure which predated human time. A great connoisseur of theories of time and eternity, Borges writes that, for Plato, "time is a moving image of eternity," while for modern man, "eternity is a game or a spent hope."[15] Considering the concept of Hell, Borges calls it "a wearisome speculation,"[16] because, among other things, "to eternalize punishment is to eternalize Evil."[17]

2. Eternity and the Body

Eternity begins as a value judgment in the guise of universal law. Nothing is eternal *as an exception* to anything else. The fallacy that some things have a special, higher claim on eternity is partly the object of Nietzsche's argument that a series of strawmen have been placed in the path of man's Becoming, interrogating his origins and character the way the sphinx interrogated Oedipus; eternity being one of these "desiderata" which act as obstacles and stumbling blocks. And we also see that with eternity it is actually the opposite of what Plato believed; it is time which predates the concept of eternity, which Borges calls "an image wrought in the substance of time"[18] and nothing more. If time is the designer original, then eternity—"still, monstrous, and classified"[19]—is the knockoff.

According to Hannah Arendt, Augustine was the first thinker to mark the death and resurrection of Christ as the single turning point of world history, and also its obliteration, since this became "the supreme event of human history, when eternity, as it were, broke into the course of earthly mortality," inaugurating a nontemporal time outside of the secular. Arendt regards this as a flaw, tendentiously based in Augustine's effort to minimize the importance of the fall of Rome as "a decisive event." It was a matter of sheer coincidence, then—Rome falling during Augustine's lifetime—that caused eternity to become so central to the already ahistorical cast of Christian thought. "The simple fact that the problem of history arose in Christian thought only with Augustine should make us doubt its Christian origin, and this all the more as it arose, in terms of Augustine's own philosophy and theology, because of an accident."[20]

Because of this denial of temporal change, there can be no such thing as teleological development. "Secular history repeats itself," Arendt explains, "and the only story in which unique and unrepeatable events take place ends with the birth and death of Christ."[21] It is not difficult to see how the twentieth century in general refuted the stark faith in this conception with its plethora of unprecedented inventions and events, although religious thought has attempted a counter-refutation by placing recent history in the context of a march toward apocalypse, the "last days." This is nothing but an attempt to reassert, in the face of widespread doubt, disbelief and disproval, Augustine's beloved eternity, that exceptional nontemporal time which supposedly bookends the meaningless stasis of human temporality.

Eternity, therefore, remains a stultifying barrier to man's growth, sealing off in a metaphysical imaginary what the ancient Greeks, for example, recognized as the responsibility of the earthly, secular polis, namely the preservation of humanity into an ever improving and immortalized future. In its ideal responsiveness to social needs and moments, democracy is a pragmatic, optimistic, daily undoing of the tyranny of eternity over the immanent world. Arendt writes:

> Did not Pericles think as Thucydides (II 41) tells us, that the highest praise he could bestow upon Athens was to claim that it no longer needed "a Homer or others of his craft," but that thanks to the *polis* Athenians everywhere would leave "imperishable monuments" behind them? What Homer had done was to immortalize human deeds, and the polis could dispense with the service of "others of his craft" because it offered each of its citizens that public-political space that it assumed would confer immortality upon his acts.[22]

The privilege of God—to make the world in his own image—is given not to the state but directly to the people themselves, the ones who live in and for and by the world.

This democratic assumption was reversed in Christian thought, in which "only individual men were immortal, but nothing else of this world, neither mankind as a whole nor the earth itself, least of all the human artifice."[23] Arendt writes: "Nothing could be more alien to Christian thought than this concept of an earthly immortality of mankind."[24] This "earthly immortality" is not to be confused with nationalistic fervors or despotic empires, although both of those are specious attempts to establish "imperishable monuments." The comparison to Homer's poetry is precise and apt, since poetry is an exaltation of humanity; the mindset is, in any event, something deeply foreign to us today, but it comes from and speaks to an extreme and a priori lack of cynicism regarding sociopolitical ideals. A perfected society stands as a monument to its citizens who have striven for that perfection. As we say of the greatest art throughout history, earthly mankind, in order to earn immortalization, would have to have that indispensable touch of the secular-divine. Each person would aspire to be the equivalent (whether artistic or not) of a Homer, a Dickinson, a Hendrix.

Needless to say, a highly poisonous cynicism enters into life with the Christian refusal to see collectivization as anything but the means to control beings who are merely "passing through" on their way to the intended eternity that is their true environment. No society based on the belief in religious eternity has a truly vested interest in trying to overcome problems which can always be sloughed off as examples of creation's ineffable mystery. The goal of culture in a nutshell is to rediscover the ancient hope in "the potential immortality of mankind,"[25] which is so inimical to Christianity. For Borges, it comes down to "the ridiculousness of the Logos dying on the cross like an acrobat in an interminable sequence of performances."[26] There is no dignity in this or in eternity. There can be some dignity in life but only if we accept that it will at some point end. There is sobriety in this thought, and the epiphany of liberation.

Bodily transformation, for me, also takes on the sense of "epiphany," especially one experienced epiphenomenologically. One sees oneself clearly, sees through the disguise, so to speak. Mortality, as a positive awareness which confers supreme value upon life, is another epiphany. Specifically related to what we are addressing here, Fassbinder went on to describe the precise moment when he awakened to his individual mortality and thus his individual freedom: "In my life there came an important moment when my body suddenly realized it was mortal. Since then life's been much more fun for me."[27] Now, both Fassbinder and Hendrix died far too young, and actual death is not the ideal that we (or they) were pursuing in their statements or their lives. The ideal is probably closer to Buddhism, in which the death of self is not literal but a stage in individual growth or evolution (expansion of consciousness, gaining of experience or chakras). One grows through and beyond the acceptance of death. For Fassbinder, this is what makes the body "terrifying," its "repulsive feature that it can refuse to meet the needs of my spirit."[28] This is not because the body is grubby where the spirit is supposedly pure, but because there are limits to the body; for many the body is not yet a thing of transcendence, hence not yet a thing at all, since true selfhood is when body and spirit are both equally immortal and equally vulnerable. The goal is the enlargement of self and the *reversal* of the process by which one only forms what Adorno called "an aborted, unformed self, withdrawing from the process of experience and asserting [itself] as the ultimate That's-the-way-I-am."[29]

For our purposes, then, mutation will not always be a negative, the "regression" imposed by "social form"[30]; as an adaptation, it can be a benefit, even a necessity. When the self is free, perhaps in flux, then death is the moment that defines the character of that self in whatever form it took—not as an alien and dogmatic judgment over humanity that has failed or succeeded to obey certain given injunctions, but as the spontaneous revelation of a living, organic dynamism of the self engaged with other selves in active improvement and fulfillment. This is what Borges beautifully describes about the death of Socrates in the *Phaedo,* the true form of the philosopher's life revealed by his impending death:

> How wonderful it is that, in that moment, on the last day of his life, he doesn't say that he is going to die, but rather he reflects on the fact that pleasure and pain are inseparable. It shows us a valiant man, a man who is going to die and doesn't speak of his immediate death.[31]

Death is inevitable and finally natural. Even the most unjust homicide is a more natural act than forcing someone to spend a lifetime in slavery or servitude. Few of us are presented with this choice in stark, definite terms, but that does not make it strictly theoretical. It is familiar on some conscious or unconscious level to all of us, what Étienne Balibar has eloquently called the "subjection of individuals to the rule of a spiritual authority which is sufficiently ferocious and incomprehensible to demand 'more than death.'"[32] That "more than death" is the cumulative exhaustion of physical capital through alienated labor over the course of a lifetime, to be followed by the reified exhaustion of "eternity."

For the ancients, the dead were never gone, they were always physically there, always on the verge of coming back. Death was how the concept of eternity began to form, doubtlessly not very concretely at first, since no one could conceive of a transformation that was lim-

2. Eternity and the Body

itless and in that sense truly final, the transformation of all transformations. In fact, eternity begins as the aghast primitive horror that the dead would never reawaken, which grew into the hope that—since we ourselves forgot them, kept living, and let them decay—there might never be some reversal of death, some corridor whereby the dead could return to the living to accuse us of discarding them. The need to account for the dead as staying put *somewhere* arose to ameliorate the terror of having to confront or combat the dead on guilty and unequal footing. Eventually, we accepted that death belonged to an ahistorical eternity, and this sense of eternity—non-empirical, metaphysical by nature—began to take in more than death; that "more than death" which Balibar identifies as the greatest torment of capitalism, essentially a life of servitude and suffering, of bodily denial and unfulfillment.

Indeed, sometimes the purpose of mutation, as a trope, is to suggest that there may be things far worse than death. David Kepesh, the mutant hero of Philip Roth's *The Breast*, feels himself at one point strangely "reborn" into a primeval era before the before, before the beginning, before all the disfigurements of measured and measurable time: "I have returned, I tell the doctor, to the dawn of my life, to my first thousand hours after the eons of hours of nothing—back to when all is oneself and oneself is all."[33] In a kind of state of irreversible living death, Kepesh attempts to find the beginning of eternity, convinced that his own particular eternity and eternity in general are the same. Although impossible to grasp, we carve out flashes of eternity through the available emotions of love and loss—what we hope will last forever, or what saddens us with the despair that it will go on without us. That frightening death which we are terrified both of surviving and of not surviving, and which is held as identical to the wait for birth in non-temporal time: "But where else to begin but there? Only there there is nothing. It is all *too* far back, back where I am."[34]

Eternity becomes a bizarre form of science unto itself. Even if the universe is not preordained, it is, according to physics, one long chain reaction in which everything has a prior cause leading back to the Big Bang. Put otherwise: the molecules scattered with no rhyme or reason, but once they had scattered, there was no way of undoing the processes which they began. They would not be re-scattered from scratch, only tweaked in a series of transformations and developments. This is not to say that nothing can be spontaneous in the moment; rather, things can only be spontaneous *in moments*. Any attempt to comprehend existence as a totality will always lead back to the interconnectedness of things, and to the fact that there is a kind of history behind everything: genetics, philology, geography, anatomy, and all other kinds of knowledge are predicated on the certainty that there are traceable developments, interdependent on other developments and on circumstances that were random only in the sense that they were unforeseeable, but which ceased to be random once they had done their work of pushing consciousness further along.

Eternity, as a concept of religious faith, displaces the empiricism of momentary time by substituting an incomprehensible and ineffable abstraction for something that would otherwise be too painfully concrete. One of the names that Bataille calls this abstraction is "beatitude." He writes: "The mystical existence of the one whose 'joy before death' has attained inner violence can never enjoy the satisfying beatitude of the Christian who gives himself a foretaste of eternity." This sentence employs Nietzschean irony; while seeming to valorize eternity, it actually forces us to view it inescapably as the enemy. Bataille comes to bury eternity, not to praise it, for the next sentence immediately enters into combat with the prior one: "The mystic of 'joy before death' can never be seen as cornered, for he is able to laugh complacently at every human endeavor and to know every accessible enthusiasm: but the totality of life—ecstatic contemplation and lucid knowledge *accomplished in a single action* that cannot fail to become risk—is, however, just as inexorably his lot as death is that of the condemned man."[35]

Can one subject totality to a rupture of the chain of circumstantial developments? Can one say, in effect, yes, the continents drifted apart, these mountains formed, my ancestors remained on one side, I grew from their specialized skill sets and experiences and superstitions, their self-regarding gene pool—but what of it? I am here now, a man without past if I so choose, without accountabilities. To ask the question differently—because of course one can always choose to disregard the past or even cross the mountains if one has the will—would the weight of the past even be an issue if it weren't for the uncertainty of

2. Eternity and the Body

the future? What if—eternity? But it is eternity that Bataille's mystic no longer believes in. The man who brushes away the past and lives out an anarchy of risk does not live nonexistently; rather, he makes death *feel* nonexistent, Bataille writes, "as soon as he stops behaving like a cripple, glorifying necessary work and letting himself be emasculated by the fear of tomorrow."[36]

The individual's risk, which leads to fulfillment and the loss of fear of death and of eternity, comes at the detriment of the collective. It leads away from the false fulfillment of alienated labor, what Bataille calls "sacred drunkenness" (much like the false narcosis which the drunken boat transcends in Rimbaud's poem) toward the "happy *loss of self.*"[37] So, according to the numbing certainties of the collective, the lineaments of selfhood must never be trespassed, one must never go so far as to lose oneself; even the dead must never be wholly lost, and for all of this we need eternity, as threat and promise. Also, the dead must go on working somehow, give a responsible account of themselves, and be reabsorbed into our sense of routine, so as to remain calm and inert through their incomprehensible and angry forever. Civilization is largely the story of how eternity and labor-based existence grew enmeshed as systemic imaginaries and symbiotic processes: temporal routine offsets an eternal imaginary as bondage offsets perpetually deferred freedom.

Although many primitive cultures certainly tried to oblate their dead as much as possible to keep them contented and at bay, they seem generally less inclined to make their dead go on "working" for them in various psychical capacities. The death itself was perhaps enough, freeing up, as it did, precious communal resources. Indeed, one has the sense of an active, expulsive death, emphasizing courage more than sorrow, or even something like Bataillean orgiastic ecstasy. For example, in *Crowds and Power* Elias Canetti writes about a Central Australian aboriginal tribe, the Warramunga, who savagely pummel the bodies of the dying:

> The whole thing begins with the news that death is near.... The pack breaks out; it has been waiting for its opportunity and will not allow its victim to escape. The tremendous violence with which it falls on its object seals its fate. It is scarcely conceivable that a dangerously sick

man should ever recover from such treatment. In the rabid howling of his people he is almost smothered; it is probable that he is sometimes actually stifled. In any event, his death is accelerated.[38]

Can this strange ritual be anything other than the need to be an active rather than passive participant in the person's death, so as to feel in control of it, thereby making absolutely certain that the body in question would really never move or rise again? Embroidering on our surmises here, natural death, in prescientific times, must have been an unfathomable riddle: a supernatural escape into a sleep-like limbo where who knows what would happen. But with the taking of life by one's peers, there is a sense that the death can be explained or accounted for. In taking active responsibility for the death, the tribesmen earned the right to mourn, to incorporate the strength and virtue of the dead person while also giving themselves a reason to propitiate the dead spirit. It represents the assignment of meaning to what would otherwise be uncontrollable and impossible to know. Indeed, the frenzy which the pack displays is nothing else but its excessive tribute of mourning, of paying respects and registering trauma, though nothing like our modern rites of death and burial. Canetti: "The feeling, so natural to us, that a man should be allowed to die in peace, would be utterly incomprehensible to [the Warramunga], intent as they are on their own excitement."[39]

Canetti distinguishes the Warramunga in this behavior as a certain type of pack-crowd, the Lamenting Pack, and ascribes their behavior to a kind of mass hysteria. However, nothing suggests that the Warramunga acted completely beyond a certain reason or logic, even at their most violently extreme. For days afterwards, the mourners would injure themselves, bleeding profusely, but even this seems to suggest a means of distinguishing between the fatal and the non-fatal, that which will end life far into the foreseeable future (death) and that which will eventually heal over and allow life to continue. By literalizing this process with every death, the aborigines were displaying a version of prescientific scientific method, repeating a formula again and again to ascertain the desired results: the dead remained dead, the living survived. And survival was precisely the point: "It is like a war, but it is they who inflict on themselves what an enemy might. A man

2. Eternity and the Body

who carried on his body the scars of twenty-three such wounds regarded them as badges of honor, as though he had received them in war."[40]

Again, it is not the moment of dying that occasions horror (indeed, this moment is hastened) but rather the prospect that an unimaginably long period, nameless and unstoppable, will follow upon this moment. Before it was identified, eternity was sensed as being synonymous with the horrible unknown power of the dead, to remain gone or to come back. The living had to move decisively against the dead. "Equally essential, however," Canetti notes, "is the way [the tribe] rejects [the dying man] after he is really dead":

> Every trace of his existence is destroyed, his tools, his hut and everything belonging to him; even the camp where he lived with the rest is destroyed and burnt.... He has become dangerous because he has left them. Because he is dead, he may become jealous of the living and take his revenge on them.[41]

Whether bodies were burned in an act of total cleansing and severance from the world, or simply left exposed to decay over time as a watchable process, the living took steps to contain the long slow waiting to see if death would, in fact, mutate into something else, return or reversal. There had to be nothing left to entice the dead: instead, the dead were *shamed* into politely staying away, shamed by a kind of potlatch (the burning of the whole village, even the neighbors' huts; the scarifications of the living, etc.), coming as close as possible to total destruction in order to prove oneself somehow indestructible.

Humanity's dawning consciousness that a corpse would remain a corpse "eternally" was reassuring in one sense—they now could stop fearing the dead so much—and melancholy in another way—they now had something conceptually new to deal with: the oppressive idea of eternity. But does eternity really exist, or is it a kind of logical deduction that we accept more or less on faith, with no way of proving it empirically? Eternity is where physics and sentiment collide in a heart-stopping shriek. What does Rimbaud say? "Cela commença par quelques dégoûts et cela finit,—ne pouvant nous saisir sur-le-champ de cette éternité,—cela finit par une débandade de parfums. [This began with a few revulsions and this ends,—we being unable to grasp this eternity all at once,—this ends with a riot of perfumes]."[42] Senses, fleeting traces stand in for the ungraspable eternity, helping obscure its larger outlines from conscious perception. In the *Diaries,* Kafka writes (not completely unlike a self-help guru) about finally learning to live in the moment: "Yes, in the moment, the terrible moment. It is not terrible. Only your fear of the future makes it so."[43] This is also like Bataille's castigation of "the fear of tomorrow" as a source of self-oppression.[44]

Eternity was conceived as an unknown quantity; the only way of defining it was that it was not-life, decidedly not-body. Whatever was of the body could not be translated into eternity, and vice versa. Because it was so thoroughly disembodied, eternity became the natural correlative of all sorts of extreme and imponderable religious feeling. However mystical, though, it also became oddly domesticated, in the sense that the Judeo-Christian religion placed a kind of "end" on eternity, in which the dead would rise again to be judged, and then a whole new "authentic" eternity would begin, one in which time as we know it will have ceased to exist altogether. With this even greater horror, a special job was given to the living, to prepare for final judgment, and a special job was also given to the dead: to wait.

3

Fictional Bodies of the Great Depression

Pain and the Law

Systemic law is directly enforced through human pain, not love. "For on love," Nietzsche wrote, "no institution can be founded."[1] What herds humans together into collectives is seldom the positive good that could stem from patterns of collectivization, but rather the specter of pain that is held out as the inevitable alternative. From tribalism and the earliest civilizations down to our current global interconnectedness, the message has always been: "Join, or go backwards, or worse." To join is merely to have access to a definable identity, a less bewildering set of options, some focused, stage-managed information about events: a lucky fetish, as it were, of supposed security and well-being. Put otherwise, it is to cede the terrors of freedom for the certainty of being part of a successful enterprise, a juggernaut. Its fulfillment can be distantly read and claimed as one's own.

Like a throughline, the allegory of Hegel's all-powerful state crushing the individual has haunted dialectical thinking even in its progressive and post–Marxist incarnations. Society claims to venerate the tokens of individual freedom (increasingly abstract and intangible notions of life, liberty and the pursuit of happiness, etc.) while managing to make those tokens worthless through ongoing systemic abuses. To go backwards, after all, is to be excluded from modernity itself, from progress, and to dwell in cardboard huts and eat exotic prey and have no currency, written language, or technology more advanced than a spear and a spit. One thing about those free spirits who do light out for some kind of wilderness is that they often leave no records behind; what they do is never "for" a posterity that has arisen naturally from the same social enterprises as the past. Just as we have far more historic records of devastation—plagues, wars, massacres, economic depressions—than we do of relatively cheerful and prosperous times. (Would we even read the cheerful, prosperous historic records if we possessed them?)

The more advanced the systemic order is, the more ubiquitous and well-enforced becomes the pain of exclusion. It no longer comes all at once, as a fatal blow, but in increments, Céline's "death on the installment plan." There are warning signs, threats, gradual removals and divestments, demotions of every kind. The pain itself changes, neither better nor worse in the advanced systems but more murky and attenuated, more like chronic depression. Indeed, once enmeshed with advanced systems, the human comes to apprehend pain itself very differently, or rather on a different scale or by a different series of coordinates. For many who attain some moderate standard of living (what we have traditionally called "the middle classes") the fear of pain becomes something like slipping down from one's current status, losing any of the amenities that make one comfortable.

When a job holds no meaning or satisfaction in itself, but only serves as access to the amenities of consumption, then there can be virtually nothing which does not take place beneath the aegis of strictly collective agendas. Individual fulfillment ceases to matter except insofar as it serves the collective through labor and consumption. In current U.S. capitalism, for instance, we are an oil-based society and an economy that has become increasingly driven not by industrial production but by financial speculation; it is hardly possible for anyone to function outside of this oil-based and speculation driven structure. Just as there is no way to be "a little bit pregnant," activists in our time must make peace with the potential redundancy and hypocrisy of having no place to critique the system except within the system itself. At one time, the grid was not so tight; one could feel purified simply by refusing to own a television set; gas-powered cars were not an issue, nor were electric, electronic and computerized systems that are also oil- and investment-bank-powered.

Marshall MacLuhan was right in ways he never dreamed of: the

3. Fictional Bodies of the Great Depression

medium is the message, since one's cultural tastes signify more or less that one has the money to purchase the latest electronic gadgetry. The quality of the film does not matter, only that it is Blu-ray high definition, so our noses can be rubbed more definitively in the fact that we are given mostly insubstantial trash to view; today, we do not *watch* films, we *look at* gradients of picture quality. Every endeavor is covered by the passive cast of having had to buy one's way in, so to speak. The environmental organizer, who draws a very clear and crucial *ideological* line between himself and "oilmen," nonetheless functions within the same paradigm of fossil-fuel power (computers, lights, the many everyday items made from petroleum, transportation, etc.). One can only minimize these dependencies, not eradicate them. Likewise, the most ideologically radical college professor works within an institution that not only functions through those fossil fuels but is likely to be owned outright by an investment bank.

This does not thoroughly nullify the hope of protest; it is true that in different hands what can be used as a weapon can sometimes also be used as a tool of progress. It makes a difference whether one is actively exploiting, through greed, or passively exploiting, through survival. The one thing we can be certain of, in the U.S. today, is that there has never been a greater basis for the solidarity of all workers: blue- and white-collar, manual and intellectual, entry level and seniority. There is no one who works today who does not in some sense work for corporate and banking interests; much of the income tax on the poor and the middle class is now funneled to big business instead of being reinvested in infrastructure.[2] All revolutions—like workers' strikes but on a larger scale—have been produced by exactly this expanded vulnerability across disparate classes and professions, this relentless and forced movement *downwards*.

When a society loses *all* sense of revolt there is always a steep price to pay for not being (willingly or unwillingly) part of collective experience. The ones who evade collectivization the most—societal drop-outs, homeless, criminals, and the mentally ill—experience the savage pain of facing the wilderness alone, which we associate, again, with primitive tribal groups. Collectivization, which sometimes gives the merely ideological position of despising relativisms as morally injurious (a common shibboleth among U.S. neoconservative capitalists when addressing their Fundamentalist Christian base), inevitably thrive on relativisms of the most neurotic and disgusting kind, such as: the complaint of someone who must go from driving a BMW to a Hyundai, versus the usually unheard pain of someone whose baby dies from malnutrition; the complaint of a consumer who did not get enough foam in his cappuccino versus the begging placard of someone who camps beneath a bridge.

Because, even in the most advanced and bureaucratically organized collectives (capitalist and communist both), there are always elements of "First World" and "Third World" extremities living uneasily side by side. This is a commonplace, of course, although it bears scrutiny. Too often, in representing this idea in art, the extremities are seen as divergent rather than contiguous, meeting only at a point of severe rupture and even then remaining antitypical, mutually othered. In fact, the connecting points between privileged and disenfranchised members of a collective are everywhere and take the form of various mutational oddities or hybrids: servants who come to love their masters; masters addicted to slumming; a popular culture so irrefutably bland that it nets the high and the low together in the same numb apathy, which keeps the gears of injustice grinding. The way in which both sides concoct and build up one another, becoming composites of each other, exposing the fiction of equality and justice while maintaining lip service to it—this is best expressed in art by exaggerating the cracks in the system as "real" physical defects and deformities, forced mutations to an inhuman way of collectivized existence.

In this chapter we shall begin by examining a quintessential Depression-era horror film, Erle C. Kenton's *Island of Lost Souls* (1933), as an allegory of the capitalist socioeconomic crises then occurring. The Great Depression remains a complex phenomenon. If we look at documented numbers, we see that unemployment during the peak Depression years of 1929 to 1933 fell by less than a quarter, 24 percent, and total factor productivity (the amount of goods produced by the amount of labor in force) fell by less than that, 14 percent. So, more than three quarters of the population were working, and working rather hard, it seems. However, the numbers on the consumption side

3. Fictional Bodies of the Great Depression

of the production-consumption nexus paint a grimmer portrait: "U.S. per capita GNP fell 38 percent below its long-run trend path (of 2 percent per annum growth) from 1929 to 1933. Real capita nondurables consumption fell nearly 30 percent, durables consumption fell over 55 percent, and business investment fell nearly 80 percent." There was also a shrinking per capita monetary base and far fewer loans granted.[3]

These numbers strongly suggest that average households were working harder but for less benefit, clearly less pay, and also that the general infrastructure of society was losing ground. The obvious human pain behind these numbers is what we need to focus on. There is data showing that throughout the depression the wealthy abstained from paying back their fair share into a broken economy whose collapse was largely due to reckless speculation by the wealthy themselves: shopkeepers often display signs that read, "You break it, you buy it," cautioning browsers not to damage the merchandise, but in the case of the depression-era economy, the wealthy broke it, but they would not buy it. Meanwhile, the wealthy were putting their resources into being able to continuously abstain from funding recovery efforts, by fighting President Roosevelt tooth and nail on automatic salary increases for workers, say.[4] The law of collectivization, unstated or otherwise, is that the wealthy take first, as much as they need, more than they will ever need; whatever is leftover (if anything) gets scattered like breadcrumbs to everyone else. Pain is what enforces this law, or more specifically, the threat of even greater pain outside of the collective than the pain that comes to the exploited ones within it. This law of collectivization, which Hegel identified in dialecticism with some optimism and which Marx identified in dialectic materialism with great righteous anger, persists today because neither Hegel nor Marx was able to transcend the essential dialectic itself—that human energy and power require some ghost of powerlessness in order to validate and define them. How to imagine human energy as boundless and free, not confined within quasi-sadomasochistic desire-machines, and not invested in the dualistic seesaw that always keeps someone or something abased even as it uplifts someone or something else?

The close symbiosis between pain and the law is directly embodied in *Island of Lost Souls,* which concerns, in the broadest sense, a dictatorship within a geographically isolated tropical community. The dictator is Dr. Moreau (Charles Laughton), the epitome of a ritzy gent in his neatly trimmed goatee and spotless white-on-white suit; he often reminds his swarthy, hirsute, brutish subjects, and by extension us the audience, about "the Law." "What is the Law?" he asks, always with a tinny gong and a cracking whip, and later (when it is too late) an ineffectual pop-gun. Time and again he stands above his ragtag subjects on a little hill and asks, angrily, smugly, "What is the Law?" Laughton mouths this question in as many different permutations as is performatively possible, emphasizing a different word in the sentence, or seething the whole thing in an undertone of supercilious menace. His subjects shuffle below him, gesticulating, hunching their shoulders and raising themselves erect; they begin to groan and grunt in unison, the Law always being enunciated collectively:

> *Dr. Moreau:* What is the *Law?*
> *Subjects:* Not to run on all fours, that is the Law. Are we not men?
> *Dr. Moreau: What* is the Law?
> *Subjects:* Not to eat meat, that is the Law. Are we not men?
> *Dr. Moreau:* What *is* the Law?
> *Subjects:* Not to spill blood, that is the Law. Are we not men?

It is this complex enunciation which Moreau possesses as a special item of physical capital, above and beyond the slurred, guttural accents of his subjects. The sadism of the recitation scenes lies in the way that Moreau makes his slaves instruct him in how to oppress them; by forcing them to reiterate the laws that keep them down, he is shifting responsibility for the oppression to the oppressed themselves. Moreau's tyranny is brainwashing, and it would be too much to say that he bears a humanity which his zombie-like subjects lack. Moreau's humanity is stunted; but then again, in collectivized systems, "humanity" has never been an element of any kind of human capital except in revolutionary times, when the human (humanist) element becomes ascendant.

On Moreau's island, this human capital is about to be discovered by his subjects, whose repeated question—"Are we not men?"—is a leading one in another sense, since they are not exactly men, but mutant beings whom Moreau has created in his laboratory. This lab is the one space on the jungle-covered island where modernity reigns absolutely, through bright tube-lighting and antiseptic metallic surfaces. His creations were animals, whom, through various surgeries, Moreau has dragged up the evolutionary scale, if not to a complete, perfected humanity then to its passable semblance: they walk upright, they have opposable thumbs, they can even speak. The film is as vague about the science of these surgeries as is the original source novel by H. G. Wells, although we would probably assume it is a radical form of gene-splicing; the intention seems to be more cosmetic than anything else, since human appearance is overvalued by Moreau, given the fact that he considers his crowning achievement to be Lota the Panther Woman (Kathleen Burke) because she is beautiful enough to pass for an actual female human. True science aside, the horror of these experiments is that they are conducted on the mutants while fully conscious and sentient—they are vivisections. As forward-thinking as Moreau is in terms of engineering new life forms, he takes pleasure in reversing a century of modern medicine's humanitarian concerns.

Thus, we see that Moreau is a creature of mutation himself; he is brilliant and idiotic, idealistic and unprincipled, brave and cowardly, charismatic and effete, glamorous and ungainly. He hides the weak or problem areas of his own physical capital with unnatural power: this is what has led him to want to make more abased mutants over whom to rule. And this is a systemic mutation as well, since it concerns social institutions: medicine, here infected by sadism; science, here infected by messianic egotism; government, here infected by self-glorying authoritarianism. It is, of course, axiomatic of the mad-scientist genre that Moreau is not allowed to practice medicine anymore "in society," which is to say, the world of collective systems. Moreau's mission is to replicate a systemic collective in his own mutated image.

To be sure, this mutated image is not far from the systemic class society whose hierarchies obsess Moreau. In his protected isolation he can afford to be more blatant about the antisocialness at the heart of the social collective itself. Aside from whatever pride he takes in the mutants' tribute to his scientific prowess, Moreau essentially treats them as a servant or slave caste. A mutated dog is, in fact, the houseboy at the doctor's mansion. This dog-man is also sent on the expeditions to bring back fresh animals for Moreau; in the beginning of the film, before we see the island or meet Moreau, we encounter the dog-man aboard the freighter, attempting to slop the beasts in their cages and receiving a beating from the drunken ship's captain. We see all this through the eyes of Edward Parker (Richard Arlen), a man who is first incensed by the captain's violence, then horrified by the fur and pointed ears which he discovers on the abused servant. Neither end of the class spectrum is appealing, both the upper and lower are deformed by their participation in collectivized power.

Through a series of unlucky circumstances, Parker soon ends up stranded on Moreau's island. Although Moreau behaves charmingly to his unexpected guest, it becomes clear that he does not view Parker as a person but as a subject for laboratory study. Now, in addition to his animals and mutants, he has an actual genetic human being to experiment on. The experiment he has in mind, which forms much of the plot in this kinky pre–Code movie, and which Wells angrily viewed as a tawdry bowdlerization when he saw the finished film, is to encourage Parker to mate with Lota the Panther Woman, thereby producing—what exactly, we are never sure. Vaguely, the thought of a natural mutant offspring, although "natural mutant" would be an oxymoron in any realm but the preternaturally deformed one of collectivized systemic power. Thus, contra Wells, the smuttiness of Moreau's vision is crucial and compelling; nothing concrete can come of the mating act except the act itself, it is a barren, perverse and would-be sovereign expenditure which reveals Moreau's privilege to exact his own fulfillment at the expense of the others, the lower orders. The authoritarian anthropomorphic laws which he imposes on his mutant subjects are not meant to apply to him, who is profligate with his own beast-like tendencies.

The mating scene, extraordinarily composed and lit, is a mini-masterpiece of creepiness. Voyeuristically, Moreau hovers in the shadows spying on Lota's mostly unsuccessful attempts to seduce her flattered but distinctly disconcerted beau. An iron grate casts bar-like shadows on Moreau as if he himself were the prisoner of his own

3. Fictional Bodies of the Great Depression

power, again an insight into the ubiquitous deformities of systemic orders. This also helps us to see Moreau's control as a projection. As a later scene makes clear, in which Moreau dotes on the appearance of Lota's hands as if he were not a surgeon but a kind of hell-bent Nazi manicurist ("This time I'll burn out *all* the animal in her!"), Moreau triangulates the seduction scene with his own lust, a transexualism enacted through Lota. It is held as shameful and potentially destabilizing for a master to live sexually through a slave's fulfillment—this is one of the main reasons why fulfillment is abrogated to the collective in a systemic order, and thereby placed out of anyone's reach.

Moreau has reached a tipping point whereby his god-like authority has begun to slip and its days are plainly numbered. The mutant subjects begin to resist enunciating the Law on command, or they seem to confuse its terms, although they remain abjectly terrified of the "House of Pain," the name which even Moreau himself has given to his lab. Like the thought of expulsion from any collective system, the conjured pain of the vivisections is so great that the mutants are cowed into obeying at the very reminder of it; but of course, at some point, the pain will outweigh the fear. This is where nature, neither purely human nor animal but allied with both, asserts itself in the unnatural mutants, the revolutionary moment when they stumble on the realization that the spectrum is different from what they have been led to believe: they are not "men" serving an omnipotent God (Moreau), but instead beleaguered lab-rats at the whims of an impotent man.

In the all-important relation between pain and the law, Moreau's "Law" is transparently worded in such a way as to forbid the reverting to animal instincts which remain predominant in the mutant animal-men. These animal instincts are seen, in an anthropomorphic context, as being not only no longer natural but unproductive, destructive rather than generative. Whereas the mutants' successful adaptation is measured by how obediently they follow rules and do menial work. There is nothing pedagogical about the Law, or about Moreau's methods. The Law is not written anywhere, it is not read by the mutants but recited rotely from memory and then only when there is the threat of being whipped, shot or otherwise tortured. It is not an evolutionary teleology of improvement which Moreau wishes to impose but what Adorno calls "permanent regression." "The mindless tasks imposed by authoritarian culture on the subject classes," Adorno writes, "can be performed only at the cost of permanent regression. Their formlessness is, precisely, the product of social form."[5]

In this sense, the animal-men's labor goes beyond menial jobs to a more all-consuming labor that we might rightly say is concomitant with their existence itself. They are born proletarians for whom to live is to constantly work at the difficulties of living. We have seen how Moreau attempts to turn the Panther Woman's sex drive into alienated or exploited labor; but her sex drive would be a form of alienated or exploited labor even if Moreau did not go to the extent of baiting her with an actual mate, or trying to watch. This is because it *cannot be fulfilled.* The definition of the mutant in *Island of Lost Souls* is nearly identical with the definition of the prole in capitalism or the peasant in communism: someone born to suffer under a set of innate needs which cannot be fulfilled, or which can be fulfilled only at great pain and hardship—indeed, more or less illegally, in defiance of the Law.

To defy the Law is to go the House of Pain, which could be anything and anywhere. It is borderless. It takes shape in the reality of going hungry, going without medicine, being homeless, or having children whom one cannot care for. It is being profiled by street cops and store security guards. It is getting a substandard education or no education at all. For those living at and below the poverty line, the entire social world becomes a House of Pain.

There is an allegorical element in the faces of the animal-men themselves, in close-up in their heavy special make-up, as they come rushing forward one by one, thrusting their scarred snouts, puffy lips, oddly spaced eyes, and hirsuteness at the camera. What reflection of ourselves and our own deformities are we being asked to see in this series of close-ups? It is much like the way the camera's lingering attention allows us to warm to the misfits in Tod Browning's *Freaks* (1932), another Depression-era shocker in which it is possible to see the circus oddities as alienated labor being preyed on and kept down by despotic, heartless exploiters. (Of course, in *Freaks,* we are not confronted with merely *fictional* bodies but actual human oddities.) These films were hardly comforting to an audience that saw their fellow men if not themselves becoming more and more scruffy and ragged, visibly marked by outsider status, and with an enormous and widening gap between them and what we call "the beautiful people." Indeed, both of these films remain uncomfortable and chilling to this day because of the stark societal lines they draw.

The parade of pathetic faces in *Island of Lost Souls* is finally reminiscent of another work from the Great Depression, Nathanael West's novel, *Miss Lonelyhearts,* above all the sequence of agony letters in its first chapter. The male reporter who writes a newspaper advice column under the pen name, "Miss Lonelyhearts" (his real male name is never given; he is only referred to as either "he" or "Miss Lonelyhearts," a meta-mutation within the text) is poring depressively over a sample of advice-seeking letters as the novel opens. Like him, the supplicants lack full names and are identified by their pen names. There is Sick-of-It-All whose kidneys are failing from being forced by her religious husband to abstain from birth control and thus to bear too many children; Desperate, born without a nose; Harold S., whose deaf-mute, retarded baby sister has been gang-raped and impregnated. These letters form italicized blocks of text stretching down the page, with spelling errors, run-on sentences, bad grammar, all the gritty, anti-literary rhythms of actual uneducated speech. What we also hear in these relentless confessions is the droning of liturgical speech—the reiterative and rote occur again and again throughout the short novel, always bearing some relation (mocking or harrowingly sincere) to the guilt that pursues Miss Lonelyhearts everywhere he goes; church rituals hang like choking smoke over all the worldly, sleazy places which the hero pilgrims through, unable to add real comfort or redemption but only casting a deeper pall of regret and despair. Indeed, the hero's need for Christ haunts the novel like a junkie's fix. During his episodes of religious hysteria, Miss Lonelyhearts chants the name of Christ over and over again.[6] But the liturgical is more often obliquely evoked in formal uses of repetition, such as all of the chapter titles beginning "Miss Lonelyhearts…," or in the idea of sacred or protected language existing within language itself: the novel's complex meta-language of newspaper and advertising catchphrases; urban slang; and parodies of prayers scrawled on cardboard placards. Nearly as esoteric as Latin and comprehensible only within an insider coterie, such meta-language has something in common with the chanted Law in *Island of Lost Souls;* it is self-sufficient in its ritualistic meaning yet a symptom of dependency and groupthink. Like the idea of the reporter's career, which ends up going sour when he finds himself stuck in the advice department, there is a token consolation of being part of something seemingly greater and more respectable than oneself, but ultimately defeatist and draining. Still other Westian reiterations are social interactions in which sexual experience is rendered uniquely ghastly: the sickening accounts of endless gang-rapes in one of the novel's bar scenes,[7] or the set-piece in which a wife's tragic story of her dying mother is intoned again and again during adulterous sex in order to throw off her husband, who might be listening in the next room.[8]

Truly authentic spiritual feeling, however, does not arise through these token and sarcastic ritual utterances. The only pages in the book that do not clack and clatter with glum or jazzed-up or hectic chatter, or secondhand cultural references, are found in the idyllic "Miss Lonelyhearts in the Country" chapter, in which the hero spends time away from the city with his girlfriend Betty: in fact, West banishes all dialogue from this chapter, and writes each sentence with as "straight" a syntax as possible, short and direct, and natural-sounding. There are no wasted words; it is as if all meanings were being rediscovered, reborn as far outside of the symbolic as possible. This brief reprieve, although it does not "cure" him, offers Miss Lonelyhearts the banal yet sincere experience of heterosexual romance untroubled by neurosis (West hardly even calls him "Miss Lonelyhearts" in this chapter; just the generic or archetypal gender-pronoun, "he").[9]

Everything else in the novel, however, becomes the sign of a rote collective experience, even the way Dostoevsky is evoked several times as a talismanic name, part of a group code among the book's boozy, cynical "intellectuals." Again, one could say that West indicts such collective ritual codes as playing an active role in keeping the disempowered in line, numbing social outcasts and victims with the temporary release of being able to put a name or face to their painfully unfulfilled needs, just like the letters from the tragic seekers who present themselves so desperately for Miss Lonelyhearts' ministration, all of them "stamped from the dough of suffering with a heart-shaped cookie knife."[10] (Their misery is even exploited to sell newspapers within the production-consumption nexus.)

Litanic utterance is also a trope of Browning's *Freaks*, for that matter, there emerging as a defiant attempt on the part of the title characters to howl down their own outcast status, pounding on a banquet table and hollering, "Gobba, gobba, we accept you, we accept you, one of us!" (later adopted as a quintessential punk cri de coeur by the Ramones). However, this attempt is brought to crashing silence by the "normal" woman's expression of revulsion. She will later be attacked and maimed by the freaks for that revulsion, offending all of them in her attempt to poison the sideshow's star midget, who worships her. Likewise, the mutants in *Island of Lost Souls* get to kill their oppressor Moreau in the end (they vivisect *him*), but never get to become something other than mutants. In adopting Moreau's own scientific, man-made weapons against him, they reveal an inability to fully return to their natural origins and an equal inability to grasp that tiny measure of conceptual rationalization which at least provided the doctor's sadism with flimsy disguise. The force of mutation wins out, consuming all it touches. These particular mutants may be headed inexorably toward extinction, but like mechanical reproductions, or like the lumpenproletariat used to absorb a society's dirty work, they will be kept going as long as a need for them exists.

Dead and Still Working

Does even death offer reprieve for the worker, or is it merely an extension of his or her imperative to labor? Étienne Balibar has noted that the harshness of capitalist systems can be defined by the fact that they demand "more than death" from their individual members.[11] Balibar is referring generally to the violent nature of subjection and exploitation in class-based societies; although we can infer that this is also a clear reference to what he terms the "spiritual authority"[12] of the church, which has demonized life and threatened an eternity of torment for those who do not accept enslavement with resigned obedience. Even without this metaphysical dimension, which has weakened greatly in its hold over the past one hundred years, there are ways in which capitalism now literalizes that "more than death": for example, the dead peasants' life-insurance policies whereby corporations can profit financially from the untimely deaths of their employees.[13] In keeping with our focus on fictional bodies of the Great Depression, we will now investigate two other horror films of that era, Michael Curtiz's *The Mystery of the Wax Museum* (1933) and Edgar G. Ulmer's *The Black Cat* (1934). Both films suggest that for the working class and members of social collectives, death is hardly the end but only an endless reification of alienated labor.

In *The Mystery of the Wax Museum,* a London sculptor named Ivan Igor (Lionel Atwill) is acclaimed for his lifelike waxworks figures of historical personages, among them Marie Antoinette whom he regards as his masterpiece. However, artistic acclaim does not equal commercial profits, and one night Ivan's unscrupulous business partner (Edwin Maxwell) burns down the museum to collect the insurance money, destroying the sculptor's work and leaving him disfigured. More than a decade later, in 1933, the sculptor has relocated to New York City, where he is preparing to open a new version of the former museum with his masterpieces fully "restored." Ivan's hands were damaged in the fire; the loss of his prime physical capital has forced him into the instruction of apprentice sculptors in this restoration process. The results seem perfect, but an enterprising reporter, Florence Dempsey (Glenda Farrell), stumbles onto the fact that the sculptor is using dead bodies for the new wax statues. Some of these bodies are stolen from the morgue, others are murdered directly. Florence enlists the aid of friends and police to break up the ghoulish ring in time to save her pretty roommate Charlotte (Fay Wray) from becoming the reincarnation of Marie Antoinette.

Behind this deceptively simple premise is a parable of warring physical capital set against a background of widespread unemployment and misery. The corpse used for the Joan of Arc statue is a woman who committed suicide because her millionaire playboy lover abandoned her. The sculptor, covering his scarred face under a wax mask, steals the physical capital (corpses) of others and exploits it as a kind of free and eternal labor. The corpse makes the ideal worker, uncomplaining, untiring, and completely divested of the need for wages. This exorbitant standard seeps upward to constrain the living laborers who still have bodily needs: the reporter, constantly threatened with "the breadlines" by her hardnosed editor Jim (Frank McHugh), is literally fighting for her livelihood and deploying every ounce of her own physical capital to get her exposé on the wax museum—"I'll make news," she vows, "even if I have to bite a dog!" In much of this, we see the brisk effort to overcome the harsh economy through sheer force of will.

In economically deprived times, the individualism that is associated with fulfillment (for example, doing "the work you love") becomes even more of a luxury, and those who can attain this fulfillment are already reproaches to those who are not so fortunate. This is Adorno's "permanent regression" of capitalism: the ease with which failing markets (already exploitative of labor and penury in their periods of prosperity) scramble and cow their victims even more by making a garbled dirty name of fulfillment itself. Therefore, as crucial as it is, physical capital in *The Mystery of the Wax Museum* (a deeply subversive film in many ways) is depicted not only as an asset but a kind of curse, a mark that makes one a target. The sculptor's victims are selected because of their chance likenesses to the original statues that had been destroyed in the fire; "Ramsay was murdered because he looked like Voltaire!" a horrified witness squeals under police interrogation. Even as society shades into groupings of endlessly reified "types," the saintly expression that we imagine Joan of Arc to have had, or the beak-like nose that we want to exaggerate on the shrewd Voltaire, has become something exploitable. Long before there was a concept of "retro," or a pop culture sustained largely by cinematic remakes and new stars who look or sound or behave like stars of the past, *The Mystery of the Wax Museum* points toward this vanishing point of noncreative reification.

Moreover, there is no art left in the sculptor's artistry, merely technological gimcracks that cut labor and cost while mass-producing "the human" in inhuman fashion. Why labor to sculpt statues when one can embalm and wax-coat dead bodies? Walter Benjamin's sorrow at the loss of the aura in artisanal, handmade works is brutally avenged (in a way that would have horrified but fascinated Benjamin) in the outright theft of human auras. In one stroke, art is reduced to mere overhead in the running of a profitable business; we are meant to see how this hard lesson was tortured into the once-idealistic sculptor by the violent treachery of his business partner. What is most subversive about *The Mystery of the Wax Museum* is the offhanded, semi-vulgar touch with which the film celebrates the dynamics of exploitation. By the last fifteen minutes of the film, director Michael Curtiz is having great fun with the trope of living bodies and inert statues trading places: the eyes of a masked head open and leer; also, one of the sculptor's assistants, crouching behind a work table, appears as one more head in a row of decapitated heads, until his sudden movement causes Charlotte to scream. On a formal level, Curtiz's exquisite, painterly use of Technicolor blithely technologizes the Fine Arts, making the technique of individual artists something that is, again, mechanically reproduceable.

The sculptor's derangement, then, is akin to the derangement of all art in the wake of mechanical reproduction, its protracted loss of human *essence*. "It is a cruel irony," the sculptor says, "that you people without souls should have hands." This derangement leads to a mean-spirited baiting of people, art's savage pain at the hands of corrupt business making it now unable to scrounge up that quotient of love which it once harbored for its human subject. Dr. Moreau's "House of Pain" has become the sculptor's quintessentially passive-aggressive (and pain-denying) House of Wax. Art moves from its former glory of being able to mock or imitate imprecise notions of eternity, into a realm where it is closer to disposability, a link in a chain of imitations.

"Don't you think that they know that those figures'd be recognized?" the skeptical Jim says to Florence when she is outlining her conspiracy theory; he misses the brazen Dadaist nature of the sculptor's new work of repurposing the dead. The actual human body is now expendable, particularly where it can be given a claim on immortalism. This is a diabolical perversion of the ancient Greek concept of a polis so excellent in every way that each member would leave behind "imperishable monuments." Here, the attempt to achieve this is delusional, a hoax. "I am going to give you immortality," the sculptor "reassures" the horrified Charlotte as he bears down on her. "In a thousand years you will be as lovely as you are now.... Your beauty will be preserved forever." Ironically, preserved forever as Marie Antoinette, an irresponsible tyrant who lost her head in the revolution of her own downtrodden people.

The benevolent concept of "forever" was once a touching, tentative gift bestowed by the aura: the artisanship of crafted art works, lasting down the centuries; the awe-inspiring sense of the artist's stroke, what we can still see, for instance, when we look at a Van Gogh: those thick scallops of paint, not so much coloration as a kind of building up of three-dimensional texture on the canvas. Van Gogh's stroke at its thickest was close to an attempt to make actual flesh; yet the violence of this creation harmed no one, instead exalting the creative prowess of humans everywhere. Jackson Pollock is another great painter whose creativity loses all of its meaningful physical capital unless one sees the work in the flesh, as it were, rather than reproduced in a book, where the famous splatters often look like mess; only in person can one note the thicker globules where the spatters begin, the thinner tails where they trail away, in short a trajectory, a physical record of direct intention, and nearly a metonymy for the human spermatozoa in its far-flung expenditure through the act of fecundation.

If human fulfillment cannot be found naturally because of Draconian imperatives to suffer, then it will be found unnaturally, outside of law and order. *The Mystery of the Wax Museum* includes a number of moments which seem to question the point of staving off human fulfillment in the name of working to cement one's place in the collective. Charlotte asks Florence, "What about lunch?" and Florence, pursuing a hot lead and determined to stay on her news beat, quips, "I'll have it for supper!" It is tossed off as a joke but it is the testimony of the working poor and hungry. Also, long before it is required by the plot, we become aware that a number of the waxwork figures are not sculptures (which would have been costly to create en masse) but movie extras, dressed up elaborately and made to hold frozen poses for what would have probably been scale. Everywhere in the film we see labor presented in the open, as it were, undisguised, as when Curtiz employs a hallmark of '30s cinema, the transitional montage showing labor processes at work: switchboards, phones ringing in a newsroom, typewriters clacking away. Such montages assert that the mechanics of newspaper offices and police stations are still, on a quotidian level, human processes.

Could Curtiz have been nursing inchoate sympathies for a kind of anarchy that would push a superficial "disrespect" for death far enough to eventually provoke renewed respect for the living? In a 1980 essay, Fassbinder advanced his belief that Curtiz was an anarchist at heart, allowed to reveal himself only furtively within the commercial system of Hollywood. There is a danger that such untidiness can become counter-revolutionary, if one ends up frightening people and thereby unintentionally reinforcing patterns of repressive conformism by having one's anarchy misread as mere self-centeredness or dysfunction. "Anarchy is not so easy to deal with," Fassbinder wrote:

> First, people who haven't learned anything but to conform to society are thrown off and repelled by the wishes and actions of this [anarchic] individual, if, indeed, they don't decide that he's mentally ill. Second, their system, within which they're useful and know how to behave, is confirmed in their eyes as right and true, and they're filled with fear of their real wishes. They'll be terrified by their true urges. Their imagination will be stifled, they'll identify dreams of the freedom of beautiful madness with power, and in this way consolidate their pathetic helplessness, till finally they'll be ashamed of their dreams.[14]

Fassbinder does not pretend that it is easy to make inroads into a fulfillment that has been so thoroughly proofed against its own realization. The stakes are high, and the risks are great. And again we find Fassbinder situated very close to Bataille, whose ideal individual, having first liberated himself from the toxic idea of eternity, "clashes only with those who pretend to attain fulfillment in their lives, who act out a risk-free charade in order to be recognized as having attained fulfillment, while in fact they [merely] speak of fulfillment."[15]

3. Fictional Bodies of the Great Depression

The trope of the dead being made to go on working, performing functions for the living, attains a deranged and erotic purity in Edgar G. Ulmer's *The Black Cat* (1934). Dr. Vitus Werdegast (Bela Lugosi) has tracked down his arch-nemesis, Dr. Hjalmar Poelzig (Boris Karloff), who betrayed him to the Russians when both men were officers in the Austrian army. Werdegast spent fifteen years in a Siberian prison camp, a place, he says, "where the soul is killed slowly." Werdegast is someone from beyond the grave, here on a mission; he demands to know what Poelzig has done with his wife and daughter. Although he expects the worst, knowing Poelzig's cruelty, Werdegast is astonished when his enemy takes him to a dungeon deep below his Art Deco mansion and shows him a bizarre gallery of women, dead and perfectly preserved, upright in glass sarcophagus-like cases. The women could be stillborn porcelain flowers rising from unmarked graves. They wear prim, virginal white dresses. Their hair is upswept as if they were plunging into water; their eyes are closed.

For Poelzig, their dead state does not diminish their physical capital; rather, it enhances it. Preserved behind glass, they are controllable, a private harem for his pleasure and power. "Is she not beautiful?" Poelzig asks the tearful Werdegast in front of the case that contains Werdegast's dead wife. For Werdegast, this is clearly a desecration, an unnatural abuse. Poelzig reminds his guest that they themselves are both the "living dead"—as much "victims of the war as those whose bodies were torn asunder." This is identical to the way the sculptor in *The Mystery of the Wax Museum* describes himself as a "living dead man," destroyed long ago along with his life's work.

The living and dead can be made to trade places in an attempt to forestall life from taking on its own fulfillment outside of the realm of death and eternity. Poelzig regards others as so much physical capital for him to steal and squander, like his realistic chess pieces, small carved likenesses which he holds in his hand and whose faces he likes to rub with his thumb. Like Moreau, Poelzig suffers from his own inner mutation which causes him to want to produce other, lesser mutants for himself to rule. Death is not the end for anyone in *The Black Cat*. Werdegast's burly servant is shot but regains a zombie-like energy to help his master subdue the struggling Poelzig; Werdegast ties up

Poelzig and flays him alive; Werdegast is also shot but survives to dynamite the mansion. Even the feckless hero (David Manners) gets vilified by a reviewer later when the novel he goes on to write about Werdegast and Poelzig is dismissed as being too outlandish to believe.

Historical precedent is a kind of red herring. There is virtually no human problem that has not existed throughout recorded time. We know of no epoch that has not repeated the atrocities of the past, or refined them. In order to change, we would have to cease to make history a fetish, and instead internalize it as a true command to change, what Rilke hears echoing from the ancient torso of Apollo. Without change, historicization is not a force that keeps us on the right track but the enabler of our faults, our viciousness. It would probably be in our best interests to forget the past entirely, because whatever response we need to make to avoid future catastrophes is hardly one that history can give us: it will have to be conceived as something completely new.

Useful Monsters

In *Freaks* we encounter the unique paradox of the little person Hans (Harry Earles), a midget who is rich, from an old aristocratic family, but who nonetheless works as a circus sideshow attraction, allowing himself to be exploited. This paradox touches upon what Nietzsche called "pity *versus* pity." Nietzsche believed that there are two kinds of pity. First, there is the "higher and more farsighted" pity of the strong, who experience any pity directed toward them as a goad to immediately test themselves, to oppose themselves against the misfortune in question; this is a proactive awareness of pity which above all preserves the autonomy and pride of the one being pitied. Then there is the pity that is "the worst of all pamperings and weaknesses," Nietzsche asserts—actually not even valid pity but a sort of hypocritical ankle-biting by means of which "*you* make him smaller," you being the one who pities and "him" being the pitied one. For there is no ultimate panacea; life will always involve some suffering and struggle, and it does no good to defang someone through excessive, patronizing pity, thereby weakening him. Rather, there must be a way of inuring the

3. Fictional Bodies of the Great Depression

vulnerable person to greater and greater amounts of suffering and struggle, of hardening him. Anything else, as Nietzsche knew, would be the most destructive of little white lies: "You want, if possible—and there is no more insane 'if possible'—*to abolish suffering*. And we? It really seems that we would rather have it higher and worse than ever." This is not only, it turns out for Nietzsche, because suffering is unavoidable but also because there is value in his estimation to cultivating it to a certain extent. Life without suffering "soon makes man ridiculous and contemptible … [and] makes his destruction *desirable*."[16]

Of course, the goal of life is not wallowing in suffering; nonetheless, suffering entails an active relation to the self. The man who risks and engages suffering becomes the hammer that forges his own better self.[17] Thus we do not find pessimism here, but resolve. This is similar to the circus sideshow becoming an emblem of the life that is too impossible to bear whole, and so gets paid off in the small coins of admission tolls; the incommensurable rendered moot with a cheap price tag. The problem with "pampering" pity is that it deceptively tricks out passivity as (false) strength, defined as the successful garnering of the pampering but nothing more; on top of this it conceals the will to power hidden in the act of pitying itself, since the need for a constant supply of pity leads one to greater abjection in a vicious cycle.

There should be nothing wrong with pity in its best incarnation (although Nietzsche, to be sure, never credits good intention when he disapproves of the results so strongly). Nietzsche's argument has been bastardized by neoconservatives who refuse to help the poor; the synecdoche of this self-righteous Darwinism is the refusal to give to panhandlers, or to fund social programs, since, it is argued, this only keeps people in a state of dependent begging. It is dubious, though, whether the conservatives who do not want to help have ever really seen and identified the poor *as people*, let alone worried after their future dependency on a source of help which they wish to extinguish anyway. Nietzsche is hardly so reductive. The reason why we should not mistake neoconservatism with Nietzscheanism is this: neoconservatives refuse to acknowledge that there is real suffering in the lives of oppressed minorities, workers, the indigent, whereas for Nietzsche everything is predicated on the fact that suffering is real and crushing. Moreover, for Nietzsche this suffering is actively chosen: being helped or not does not change the fact that suffering is a necessary obstacle on the path to an ultimate fulfillment which we cannot recognize because we have never felt it before. This fulfillment, which is more than material, is neither difficult nor easy, neither hard-won nor freely given; it is something whose consistency does not yet exist among our human options.

In this sense, Hans exiles himself from the world of privilege in a Nietzschean attempt at superior fulfillment—he yearns to experience a world that need make no allowances for him. However, his bid ends disastrously; the protections and good graces of the world are shown to be endlessly necessary. Against the backdrop of the Depression, in which the working class was kept down, Hans's wish for self-sufficiency reveals only the fearsomeness of those social controls which block his way to fulfillment. In extreme times, and frequently even in normative ones, systemic orders equate fulfillment with bad risk and death. To want whatever is "more" than the systemic order has allowed is to be on a collision course with reality, to be literally in the wrong place at the wrong time.

In the end, defeated, Hans returns to his lavish mansion while totally withdrawing from the world. His shamed pride will not allow him to accept anything now, for nothing can be on his terms. In what might appear on the surface as a contradiction to his preaching against pity, Nietzsche also warned against those rigidly probative moralists who cannot forgive either themselves or their witnessing friends after they have been caught doing something stupid.[18] There are limits to the embracing of suffering, where it no longer reveals the brutality of the systemic order but instead only the obstinacy of the individual. Nietzsche would have us understand that even the best food can be burned in the cooking, that principles must be flexible enough to adapt themselves to the exigencies of life. Here is where a certain amount of proactive pity—pity that forgives everything, perhaps even the need for pity itself—would be helpful. Indeed, it is only with great, teeth-gritting resistance that Hans finally agrees to see his midget fiancée

3. Fictional Bodies of the Great Depression

Frieda and weep in her consoling embrace. In an illustration of proactive pity in filmic-visual terms, Browning films them with the camera tilted slightly upward (with the warm glow from the hearth behind them, they look almost like Jeannette MacDonald and Nelson Eddy in one of their glamorous musicals), training his perspective to their stature rather than the other way around.

    Freaks did not go over well. Audiences already demoralized by the Depression refused to support the idea of a wealthy man too strong and noble for his own good, even if that man was represented by a non-normative body. Hans's choice of drudgery and risk was a sort of *pacification signal* to a likely restive working-class public: this brave little person would literally die to be in your worn-out work shoes— do not bother to envy and despise the rich, they long to do their honest day's work. In fact, the feelings of proud, suffering, ruined men are a nearly constant leitmotif of Depression-era movies, not only thrillers and horror films but musical comedies. However, it is always from the viewpoint of the worker, and the cinematic image exalts him in less fraught and subtle ways than Browning's slightly upturned camera at the end of *Freaks*. Lloyd Bacon's *42nd Street* (1933) ended with a pugent tribute to unemployed veterans of World War I, "Remember My Forgotten Man." The humanist chord of the overlooked or forgotten man will always resonate throughout our capitalist society, and today *Freaks* plays best as a parable of capitalist-systemic mutation. Long after the oddity of the freaks has been mooted by our humane concerns (it is rather taboo, when discussing *Freaks* in current film circles, to express discomfort at the appearance of any of the title characters), what stands out most resonantly in the film is Hans, his pale blond hair burning on his head, his face twisted into a determined grimace of self-righteous anger. And perhaps what twists the mind so much when one watches Hans is the way his non-normative physical status is bound up with his chameleonic class status: his failure at being both rich man (potential exploiter) and worker (exploited) seems to mock any and every striving.

    As pacification signal, the character of Hans operates through a certain cognitive dissonance: one identifies with him, yet one clearly does not want to be him; this tiny, humbled millionaire is meant to forestall too much identification between real workers and "freaks," with their abused, exploited, stunted bodies. Little people, when employed symbolically, have sometimes seemed to awaken extremist political anger, perhaps because they so overwhelmingly imply the futile personal needs that often underlie every grandiose project to change the world. Of course, there would be something revolting about blatantly using human oddities as negative objects of political rhetoric; yet it is undeniable that the visceral fantasmatic of political extremism is energized by the idea of dwarfism or of gigantism, which is to say, the dialectical idea of one side expanding at the necessary shrinkage of its opposition. At the same time, the idealism of revolutionaries forces them to deny such pettiness, or indeed, to project it *only* onto the opposition. The problem of Western intersubjectivity is still (and likely always will be) the problem of freedom(s) as impinging, mutually exclusive states. When conflicting ideological freedoms become too incompatible—the freedom to make money by whatever means versus the freedom to get by without doing damage to human or natural ecologies—every stance becomes viewed as potentially reactionary.

When Werner Herzog made *Even Dwarves Started Small* (1969), he stumbled into a hornet's nest of political factions in then-divided Germany. His film is essentially a dark Kleistian poem about extremity and fate, depicting a futile and nightmarish "revolution" of midgets and dwarves within an institution where everyone is a little person; even the institution's director, who gets tied to a chair and tortured, is a midget. What begins as a plausible attempt to redress actual grievances descends into absolute chaos: for example, a pair of blind midgets beat each other with sticks in their feckless attempt to defend their hoard of supplies from the sighted dwarves. It is existential redress that seems to be sought by the little people, who are starkly revealed as profoundly damaged, in their incessant crazy laughter and in the desperate pettiness with which they abuse a litter of suckling piglets. Herzog reports that when the film wrapped, he hurled himself into a cactus patch in atonement.[19] Yet further problems would arise in terms of the hostile public response to his unique masterpiece.

3. Fictional Bodies of the Great Depression

Unlike *Freaks,* there is no pacification signal lurking at the heart of *Even Dwarves Started Small,* which takes little note of class or other political distinctions. More precisely, Herzog addresses Political Man in the same breath as Creative Man, Romanticist Man, and Religious Man—reducing all attempts at higher meaning to a kind of savage playtime. However, when the film premiered in West Germany, theaters received bomb threats from both leftwing and rightwing factions, each convinced that Herzog was mocking *them* by comparing them to dwarves; dubious reasons were found to ban the film completely. *Even Dwarves Started Small,* Herzog says, was "misunderstood as a statement against ... revolution, so either side tried to occupy this film for themselves." Instead, Herzog was, again, aiming at something far more universal than any political dogma: referring to a point in the film where chickens begin to cannibalize one another, he says, "There is something ultimately wrong in creation itself."[20]

Yet even Herzog cannot refrain from acknowledging the terrified root of the West German radicals' anxiety, because there is "something midget-like inside of us" and "we cannot put it aside."[21] It is not inaction or passivity which defines this "midget-like" soul, but instead exactly the opposite: the sword and the soapbox, the war whoop, the sovereign stance, particularly when these things depend (as they frequently do) on the blood and sacrifice of nameless followers. We are far from the off-kilter transcendentalism of *Freaks,* which only wanted to assert that the "freaks" were vaguely Rousseauian children of Nature. "Nature" could never be wrong, and in a society torn apart by class warfare waged by the rich against the poor, there was something consoling about this idea. It suggested that we might yet find a way of coming together, beyond all our socially constructed differences, as a human family.

In 1932, the same year as M-G-M's *Freaks,* Paramount released *If I Had a Million,* an omnibus film in which a millionaire decides to give away his fortune to random needy people. Not one of these beneficiaries is a "freak," and not one of them is too proud to take the money and save themselves from economic misery (for some, the gift literally saves their lives). The more desperate the problem, the simpler the solution needs to be—as if poverty could be erased by turning the poor into instant millionaires. The fact that this can only happen in a movie fantasy world is its own bewildered self-indictment. *If I Had a Million* dramatizes the birth of what neoconservatives would come to demonize as the "welfare state," and reveals how much the idea of charity is bound up with the perpetuation of the status quo, as a guilt-shedding token of how nothing macro ever changes; pity remains double-edged, a narcotic that maintains us in chronic discontent. Whether one bows to the collective order or not, one must consent to want what everyone else wants for the sake of that order, serving in the ranks of capitalism's useful monsters, happy to be made rich, as it were, by money alone.

4

The Dean's Laughing Fit

There is a scene toward the middle of Philip Roth's magic-realist and satiric novella, *The Breast*, where Arthur Schonbrunn, the staid Dean of Arts and Sciences at Stony Brook college, comes to visit his former colleague, Professor David Kepesh, in the hospital. The two men go back a long way, Kepesh describing Schonbrunn as an ambitious and successful academic who had helped Kepesh up the ladder of success.[1] Schonbrunn is still the same gracious, charming, socially adept person that he was. Kepesh, on the other hand, is now an enormous female breast. These men of letters find themselves in a situation that seems to belong to the world of literature rather than life. Roth peppers the entire narrative, told from David's viewpoint, with moments where the breast likens its transformation to something from classic literature. But now, encountering each other again for the first time since Kepesh's change, the two colleagues cannot find, so to speak, equal standing. In fact, what collapses between them is precisely that distance of phallic projection by which the literary-homosocial is accomplished. They cannot pretend anymore that they share a common meta-phallus named "literature," because Kepesh, as a breast, is so thoroughly de-phallicized. He has gone over, as it were, to the other side; he has blabbed the secret softness inside the male armature of thick door-stop books and syntactic impenetrability.

However, rather than becoming stern and lecturing, aggressive, angry, Schonbrunn drops his own phallic armor and becomes "soft," as it were, overcome by a prolonged fit of giggling that prevents him from speaking and soon necessitates his departure from Kepesh's hospital room.[2] Like a Lacanian answer of the Real, the Dean's giggling fit demands to be addressed by Kepesh. First, it drives him into an extended period of depressed denial in which he believes that he has gone mad. What he yearns for is his normal life back: "There was to be no magical awaking, no getting up out of bed, brushing my teeth, and going off to teach as though nothing more than a nightmare had interrupted my ordinary and peaceful life."[3] Ultimately, Schonbrunn's reaction becomes a kind of new re-certification of the academic as what he will be for the remainder of his conscious existence: the ambivalent, taboo, silly symbol of succor made flesh. The male symbol of old-fashioned professor (this is still the early '70s) becomes the female symbol of Breast—a dialectical opposition which Schonbrunn's laughter upholds. Not only is this "not a pipe"; it isn't (more damningly) literature anymore. Great literature cannot be a breast.

But why is this?, Roth's novella asks. Isn't succor part of the experience of art? Why must we conceal our dependency on art in order to feel that we have mastered it (or, in psychoanalytic terms, our dependency on the mother in order to feel that we have mastered human relationships)? Kepesh is now something of an unrequited lover, victim of the dean's (and Literature's) rejection. To be sure, he himself has not abandoned that great literature which seems to have abandoned him, and once again he attempts to explain his condition as a case of hero worship run amok, his unfulfilled "literary longings" leading him to internalize too fully the magic realism of Kafka, Gogol and Swift.[4] Of course, the fulfillment of his transformation is also his undoing, his failure to measure up, as it were, to the tyranny of the cult of the Great (Male) Artist. (All of the famous authors referenced in the book are male.) Certainly, the choice of belonging to this cult (but can one ever *choose* it—isn't it beyond our choice, and isn't that precisely the point of Kepesh's transformation?) is deeply inflected by self-pity, the yearning to be unique, and other, frankly petty ego needs: "Why David Kepesh?" David Kepesh laments. "Why me, of all people, endowed with such powers? ... Great art happens to people like anything else. And this is my great work of art!"[5]

Kepesh's self-sabotaging devotion to the cult of great art, as well as his ultimate revelation that great art "happens" to every kind of person, not just to supposedly Great Men, coincides with his dropping out of any kind of literary and academic establishment; indeed, dropping, or mutating, out of society and nearly humanity as a whole. Is

4. The Dean's Laughing Fit

this Roth's comment on the societal work of creating art as alienated labor (perhaps especially for female artists, a condition that cannot really be felt unless one is somehow "in their skin")? Or is it a sardonic comment on teaching as midwifery—those who cannot do, so to speak, become nurturing teats? And this, too, is alienated labor by default, a kind of mass-produced or institutional nurturance.

From the beginning, Kepesh's mutation seems to have everything to do with his position as a college professor, although this position is perhaps only revealed as alienated labor in retrospect. But Roth makes sure to weave in references to Kepesh's work life throughout the early pages, so that we cannot help associating his physical problems with his work-related problems of physical capital, so to speak, getting through the daily grind. Kepesh first notes his early symptoms while at work, in "the men's room adjacent to my office in the humanities building"[6] (even in neutral office spaces, there is blatant gender coding, a fact which may be inevitable in some respects but which also reifies other, less blatant forms of gender coding) and then "through the hectic day of teaching and conferences and commuting and dining out."[7] The workaday world shades into the social one, making "dining out" seem like one lengthy extension of Kepesh's job. And the sense of drudgery does not end there. Even sex with his girlfriend Claire has turned into a more or less onerous chore.[8] Meanwhile, the demands of work itself addle David and make him unable to look out for his own best interests. "Exhausted from a hard day's work," Kepesh puts off going to the hospital when his penis begins its grotesque change into an enlarged nipple.[9]

But once the transformation is complete, gone is any sense of labor; of course, Kepesh has mutated himself out of the workforce. However, there is a deeper level of relief, although Kepesh spends most of the novella fighting against the truth of this: his "professorial dignity" can finally get "a little rest...."[10] The breast does not have to do anything; it lays there; it experiences "purely tactile delight"[11] when caressed, a natural reflex, having nothing to do with will or consciousness or even desire. The controlling head is literally gone, the upright and erect completely leveled. And following its regular massage session, the breast enjoys "the sleep of the sated."[12]

Is this a chance for Kepesh to experience life from a different viewpoint, and does that still make it Kepesh's own? Again, as Kepesh himself notes, the model for this goes back to the creative world, to art and literature, where, since the early '70s especially, the performing of various roles, identities and shadow-selves has been an intrinsic part of the artist's (and teacher's) mission and of our collective experience of art. In literalizing performative transformation, thereby overdetermining something that is already sufficiently overdetermined (identity), the breast pushes through a new didacticism, bringing together the aims of art and teaching rather than leaving them at cross purposes. Not even the artist fully knows the message of truth which he bears, for in art, the only thing that cannot be planned out in advance is the essence of the truth that motivates and underlines everything. This truth is the elusive subject for which all artistic mutations go searching. I is another. "Autobiography in its fundamental sense," feminist artist Eleanor Antin has said, "is the self getting a grip on itself [and] can be considered a particular type of transformation in which the subject chooses a specific, as yet unarticulated image and proceeds to progressively define [herself].... The usual aids to self-definition—sex, age, talent, time, and space—are merely tyrannical limitations upon my freedom of choice."[13]

Lucy R. Lippard explains this openness of women's art as being reflective of the fact that women have had to be mutable, shifting, in society: "We play so many roles in our lives, while most men play only one or two."[14] Again, this may be changing for men, but the male's limited biological role in reproduction (crucial though it is to the entire process) still makes the statement *feel* true. In spite of Kepesh's seeming initiation—getting laughed at by Dean Schonbrunn—into the conflicted position of belittled women in the often male-dominated art world, it has no way of transforming this lesson into something proactive and creative. Indeed, although the mutated breast seems to have discovered an extra role beyond the traditional ones allotted to, or chosen by, males, it is an unfulfilled and unpromising one. It pointedly lacks solidarity with "the female," its true oddness not that it is a breast but that it is a lone breast, only one of an item that always naturally comes in pairs (or at least even rather than odd numbers), a forlorn refugee from the amputated, shadow side of life where nothing functions quite as intended, and where meaning is no longer assured.

It would be overly reductive to say that *The Breast* is merely "about" the huge cresting wave of the women's movement that cascaded upon Western culture in the early 1970s, changing it completely. (*The Breast* was written in 1972.) Clearly, on some levels, Roth employs Kepesh's mutation as a way of excavating the bewildered male pain and inadequacy at now having to make room for female consciousness. Put otherwise: being a man was no longer an automatic refuge, a safety zone, but a place that could draw ideological fire, simply, it seemed, for pursuing what came naturally. This is because the early feminists were dealing with a patriarchal desire that was still virtually of whole cloth and "supremacist" in its thinking. It had no reason not to be, since it had never really been thoroughly contested on an institutional level. *The Breast,* to the extent that it is a vaguely sci-fi allegory, can be read as the fear of a male venturing outside of patriarchal securities: who will he be now?

The breast ends up as an anomaly, or rather a mutation in progress, a lingering male, even sexist consciousness speaking from inside a body that is no longer precisely gendered but which has become an obvious synecdoche for everything that "woman" represented in patriarchal culture: the yielding, the passive, the consoling, the maternal. The breast, belying the male consciousness that still fights, kicking and screaming, deep within its adipose folds, speaks the language of this passivity right from the start of the narrative (and while still describing, significantly, its prior incarnation as Kepesh): "Still, I would submit to you, in all humility...."[15] When the breast describes what its forebear always wanted, the words resound with the idealized cultural meanings of receiving and providing succor: "calm," "placid," "content," "dependable," "warmth and security."[16] Likewise, the obliging breast behaves, bites its metaphorical tongue: "I restrain my rage and I restrain my misery...."[17]

This is the only sexism that I see in Roth's novella, and it's likely he thought that he was reaching out to women when he constructed it this way: the breast is only angry as long as the male Kepesh remains within it, holding on to faded masculine prerogatives and mindsets; once it fully embraces its new role as a female breast, it is not angry, and seemingly cannot be made angry. It is instead a self-administering panacea, not that any real breast ever thought of itself as such. But this closes in on the idea that the novella may really be about bad teaching, since the former teacher of poetry has become a poem, but only in that anodyne sense in which a poem cannot prickle or fang. (This might also amount to an inveterate prose writer's idea of what a poem is.) How audacious it would have been to make the breast grow less placid and more enraged as it fully assumes its femaleness. As it stands, it is as if the idea of female anger were precisely what Roth most wishes to forestall, by offering up a male as sacrifice to femaleness. In *The Breast,* gender remains a kind of prison: one speaks from within it; one never speaks one's way through it.

Lawrence Kramer has argued that for devotees of gender polarity (particularly, sexist males) terror is awakened by extremities of being and sensation: listening to emotional music, for example, or even the self-blurring throes of sex, which "continually subverts the sexual difference it is supposed to confirm."[18] Who possesses whom in coitus? That ultra-masculine premium placed on containment becomes violated in seductive, even addictive ways. And yet, as Kramer writes, "even the most 'feminine' traits can be tolerated within a sufficiently dissimulated claim to hold the absolutely masculine position...."[19] This is exactly like Kepesh, whose sexual demands on his girlfriend Claire grow ever more insistent and selfish for a period of time after his initial transformation: the masculine voice within is goaded to protest, to reassert its patriarchal identity.

As if thinking of Kepesh, Kramer refers rather startlingly to a different literary figure in his analysis, one who straddles the polarities of ultra-masculine and ultra-feminine: "the old farmer of Whitman's 'I Sing the Body Electric' is basically a breast, but he is none the less a man's man of a patriarch."[20] In fact, for Whitman himself and (as the poet conveys) for the farmer's extended clan, there is no conflict or dissimulation in the mixed-gender attributes. So, in the "basically a

4. The Dean's Laughing Fit

breast" category, we have the full roundness of his head with its extremely light wisps of hair, his eye (described as singular) suggesting a nipple, even the web of capillaries showing through his cheeks. But "all who saw him loved him ... with personal love ... as the most beautiful and vigorous of the gang." (We are told that he has spawned "five sons and many god-sons.")[21]

Perhaps there is no contradiction there at all, even on the surface, since a breast could and should be loveable to any mammal who has ever suckled. Obviously we would not always like to literally become what we love (or make love to), but one of the more uncanny themes teased out in *The Breast* is how Kepesh loathes his new form, and cannot imagine how anyone could fail to see him as utterly ridiculous—hence, the crucial breaking-point reached with the Dean's laughing fit. A straight male is forced to admit *just how much* he loathes the shape of the thing from which he has derived life and pleasure. What the male finds fine and natural on the female form is a bad mark on his own, too much brainless flesh, too much softness—it is as if Roth is addressing the burden of expectation placed on women through the ages: to have always been there at the ready for patriarchal needs and desires, to have had no "lives of their own," so to speak, and on top of all that, to have been relegated to a corner of kid-like silliness in human consciousness. Look, Ma, boobies!

Ultimately, this has as much to do with masculinist self-esteem as it does with sexism and the oppression of women. For males are similarly hard and condescending toward other things that please them; not to be able to resist the lure of pleasure is to be feminized, engulfed. This is Lawrence Kramer's point. But it is a self-esteem issue because it is the pleasure of the self that is singularly distrusted. To want anything is to want too much; to need is to be doomed to neediness. A tiny, fragile space set aside for love can only be maintained by the male ego (at its most immature) if it has been carefully carved out of a powerful and enormous space of inflexible disdain. We might think of fanboys' Top Ten lists, for example, at their most recondite: love for obscure, unseen and unseeable films, or for recording artists who barely recorded, has something of the exclusive taste for the virginal, the female whom no other has possessed.

This grudging nature of masculinist surrender can sometimes express itself inappropriately, as a lashing out. I suppose that female guilt can do this as well, but it seems that much of men's defensiveness around what turns them on, what makes them feel good, has to do with the underlying anxiety of having made the wrong choice, having put oneself too far out there, as it were, and become vulnerable. Desire threatens and terrifies that hard-won self-sufficiency which the male often aspires to. In this sense, we might be reminded of Norman Mailer's *The Prisoner of Sex*, written in the year before *The Breast*, 1971. *The Prisoner of Sex* is one of Mailer's most disconcerting books, but also one of his most honest (it also includes a lovely, light-handed *précis* of D. H. Lawrence[22] that is one of my favorite models of intuitive, intimate literary criticism). *The Breast* and *The Prisoner of Sex* are hair-raising in similar ways: the latter because Mailer in some ways refuses responsibility for the heterosexual desire which women awakened in him (he's the prisoner in the title) and the former because the male is forced to change but the change doesn't quite take, or essentially solves little. It is the extinction of male power with the male still brutally trapped within his now-amputated patriarchal thinking. For the breast is the emblem of a castrated sexism, a disempowered patriarchy. It is now the feminized quarry which it once pursued and still attempts to pursue. After it realizes that its nipple is a highly sensitized and semi-phallic sex organ (capable of erection), it wants to penetrate female nurses as well as Claire, addressing them, in some cases, through demeaning language and offering to pay them to prostitute themselves to "him."[23] Along with this, however, Kepesh also feels uniquely vulnerable, on display all the time, helplessly ogled and unable to defend himself as a breast, at the mercy of a world both obsessed and disgusted by female mammaries.[24] It is a problem which David now seems to understand from both sides.

But there are not really two sides—not when it comes to understanding the processes of female socialization whereby bodily shame is inculcated, *hurt*, into her. The breast screaming for "cunt" on its nipple is not a liberating polymorphous perversity, much less an awakening lesbianism, as Roth makes clear, but a patriarchal entitlement which in its crude shamelessness is foreign to the women in the novel.

Indeed, what makes the breast's mutation a crisis of sexual meaning is precisely the fact that it is merely imitative of female form. Intriguingly, this is also something that women artists have spoken of going through, with a hyperawareness that they must question their performance of gender at every turn. At times nothing can be taken for granted, no matter how seemingly innocent or routine. Antin, according to Lucy R. Lippard's 1975 essay "Making Up: Role Playing and Transformation in Women's Art," "thought herself 'in drag' when she wore a skirt for the first time in two years."[25] "'How others see me' and 'how I see myself' are two of the basic themes that lend themselves"[26] to women's art, because for women these issues still often represent literally claiming a subject position in relation to themselves that is not automatically given.

Certainly it is eminently possible for men, now more than ever perhaps, to suffer anxieties over body image; but dishevelment, for example, is still often a gender-coded (and oddly moral) judgment. As has been pointed out by many, there is no female equivalent to sexy facial stubble. In defiance of this, Adrian Piper's *Catalysis* series

> involved her appearance in public looking "mutilated" in some way: riding the subway in clothes that had been soaked for a week in a mixture of wine, cod liver oil, eggs, and milk, or with her clothes stuffed with Mickey Mouse balloons; in the Metropolitan Museum blowing gum bubbles and leaving the remains on her face; in a library with tape-recorded burps going off every few minutes. At the time of the action she neither talked nor provided any explanation to passersby for her bizarre conduct....[27]

There is a special defiance in the "actions" where she, as a then-art student, allowed herself to appear disheveled and therefore potentially incompetent within an academic or artistic setting—those kinds of settings where women historically endured an extra burden of proving themselves capable. Similarly, when I saw Patti Smith perform at Three Rivers Arts Festival in 2007, she wore her usual white button-down shirt, black necktie, trousers and jacket, with every item of this clothing noticeably stained. ("Good for her," a woman said admiringly when I told her about this.) Although "dirt" can be sexy and naughty, it is, in a feminist context, usually a discouragement of sexist exploitation: the implication is that the woman in question will not "stay in line" or remain a tabula rasa for men to write (their own stains) upon.

Lippard writes: "Transformation is also the motive for cooler variants in which body is subordinated to art, exemplified by Martha Wilson's *Breast Forms Permutated* (1972), in which nine pairs of breasts stare out of a grid, wondrous and humorous in their variety...." Perhaps Roth's *The Breast* suggests an extreme and circuitous way in which even a male character who is in some ways traditionally sexist (Kepesh) could come to view the female breast non-erotically—non-psychologically, as a kind of interesting shape or a "mere" token of humanity.

This is a distinction which we will return to at other points, between the "psychosocial" and the "psycho-natural." The realm of the psychosocial is impeded, biased, conditioned; it obstructs the clear messages of the self. What we are in the psychosocial realm is a mix of semi-repressed instincts and learned behavioral codes. In the psycho-natural realm, however, we can postulate a relation to the self and to the world that is definitively pure of all control, except the ones which the subjective mind itself feels the need to impose. We have never been to the psycho-natural realm, at least not collectively—in some ways, the very definition of "collective" requires a set of psychosocial ground rules to be in place. For the individual, the psycho-natural realm is often mistaken for certain kinds of madness; and it is not accidental that, during most of its journey, the breast believes itself to have gone insane. In the end, we have a psyche that has been stripped down and re-built as thoroughly as possible. It still knows Rilke's sonnet to the ancient torso of Apollo, but it is living out the injunction to change rather than contemplating this from a serene mental distance; it has been absorbed into a wholly new culture of one—the psycho-natural—in which, among other things, the ego's voice grows less insistent, harmonizing more with circumstance and the inner voice of destiny.

These are the equivalent of baby steps, however. The breast seems to finally reject the need for the phallic ego to be unique and omnipotent, but at the same time can hardly accept "averageness" as anything but "monstrous, ludicrous,"[28] the inexplicable "*it was so*"[29] beyond which we give up trying to find ourselves unduly fascinating.[30] Lippard

4. The Dean's Laughing Fit

acknowledges that what is considered the search for unvarnished truth in male art (I am showing my naked body as proof of my honesty) is often dismissed as twisted and phony "narcissism" in female art.[31] But even as parody Lippard rejects, among other sexual signifiers, "bare breasts" in female artists' self-portraits, since these are "necessarily complicated by social stereotypes" and potentially pandering to sexist prurience.[32]

Just prior to the 1970s high point of French feminism, Lippard wrote: "One does not call oneself a feminist in polite art society in Europe unless one wants to be ridiculed or ignored."[33] The wave of change was not long in breaking, and it broke hard. For Lippard and numerous others, things changed radically overnight, just like Kepesh's transformation. "By the time the women's movement hit," Lippard has said, "I was feeling almost male. I lived alone with my kid in another country then, writing fiction, and when I came back, I wasn't ashamed of being a woman anymore. The idea of identifying with women's work was very exciting to me—the whole thing of caring."[34] Along with this shedding of shame came the chance for many women to explore what it would be like to feel public social power. This, too, had its expression in radical performance art. "Claudia," for instance, was the brainchild of Martha Wilson and Jacki Appel: "a composite person who exists in the space between ourselves, a fantasy self—powerful, gorgeous, mobile—who is the result of the merging of the realized and the idealized self."[35] Lippard writes, "One Saturday, six New York women who shared this 'fantasy of omnipotence' dressed up fit to kill and lunched at the Plaza as Claudia; then they took a limousine to the SoHo galleries, engendering admiration and hostility along the way. 'By manipulating elements from the culture to our own ends,' they discovered an expansion of the self, 'power over destiny, choice of and responsibility for one's own actions.'"[36]

Sometimes, a "mutation" such as "Claudia" can be occasioned by the do-or-die realization that we have but one life to live, and the fantasy selves we fail to externalize are doomed to eternal silence if we do not embrace them *at some point*. Ultimately, this is also the problem of eternity, albeit reconceptualized, that we saw in Chapter 2, specifically relating to man's slow, agonizing, intellectual digestion of the meaning of death as the final, permanent mutation. Here, the fear of eternity is not so much the endlessness of death as the rebounding verdict on a life that was stifled, undefended, badly lived. In this sense, it is exactly the opposite of Christian eternity, whose "heavenly" values of stasis and resignation one must anticipate before death. "Reflect upon eternity," the breast issues a Sphinx-like challenge, "consider, if you are up to it, oblivion, and everything becomes a wonder."[37] Why not try to become everything? Eternity is such a long time, after all, to be one thing and one thing only; to remain suspended in a single state.

We strain against this intuitive knowledge, and the challenge it bears, at every turn. Whether we view it as punishment, reward, or absolute nothingness, the true meaning of eternity is that it *reflects back* upon the lived or unlived temporal life. The breast learns to overcome human blind spots by seeing without literal eyes. This can only happen after the disaster of "oblivion," after the breast's objective removal from human time, when nothing, so to speak, is left to lose. Thus, Rilke's sonnet, which Roth chooses as Kepesh's epitaph: the sculpture, headless, eyeless, armless, legless, only a torso beginning at the neck and ending at the groin, is a fragment wondrous for having survived for centuries, even in mutilated (mutated) condition. In fact, it is what has randomly survived, what historic time has accidentally carved away, that seems most important to the poet, a wise view which naturally gives rise to the imperative to "change." Change, for you shall be changed anyway. Such is cosmic law and the law of history. As Roth appropriates Rilke's poem, he acknowledges that the last line "may not be so elevated a sentiment as appears at first glance."[38] Ashes to ashes, dust to dust, man to breast.

But let us get even more realistic: the passage of time denoted in the sonnet is only a matter of centuries, a millennium; eternity is still more inconceivable, still more unutterable. We humans, preternaturally obsessed with time (to such extent that we have no record of human existence that is not simultaneously a record of time), we who note the seasons and the years, we who work by the day and the hour

4. The Dean's Laughing Fit

and the week, we who want to possess what we love for as long as possible—we cannot begin to assimilate eternity into any of our meticulous structures. (Eventually the breast loses all need for calendar time.[39]) It is the central madness of civilized man, that the abstract, unempirical infiniteness of death would so overwhelm and transform the palpable, empirical definiteness and finiteness of life.

So, even as a man, before he changed, Kepesh felt "grim premonitions of extinction or paralysis or unendurable pain," a chronic hypochondria with which he has come to live in a kind of double consciousness: registering all the "telltale symptoms," while finding it prudent, as "a reasonable man," not to take them seriously.[40] Naturally, when his medical problem overtakes him, it is something like the revenge of the worry that he has learned to deny and dissimulate. The primal worry, the eternity which can never be assimilated, takes shape, or rather, takes over *his* shape; we know that this is about death, because becoming a huge, disembodied breast is something that literally makes death seem unusually merciful. At the same time, the narrator still does not wish to die, reduced, Job-like, to every ruin and indignity; Kepesh nonetheless cleaves to the faith of life: "No, it is simply that having been terrified of death since the age of two, I have become entrenched in my hatred of it, have taken a personal stand against death from which I seem unable to retreat because of This."[41] "This," given its allegorical capitalization, could be a linguistic substitute for God, the whip that scourges Job's faith; but Roth does not make such endless perseverance believable, and instead seems to let the breast's thought stand as an irrational compression of humanity's sore dilemma: after all, why go through the pointless, dreary pain, why mutate again and again in life, why work, for example, at anything (jobs—why is this word in English nearly identical to the name of Job?—marriages, children, art, *anything*), when we only have to die, as always the final obscene, humiliating, irreversible mutation? Is that what the human is, finally? Faith in the inevitable mutation as something which reveals, if nothing else, "strength of character" and "the will to live?"[42]

We see this in the immigrant experience of Kepesh's parents, who ran a Catskills hotel for many years. Although they were the owners and employers of the hotel, the parents felt more like abused tenants, as we read in a disturbing passage that calls to mind the fear which Jews in Hitler's Germany developed of their own servants who had become Nazis and could turn their *ressentiment* of servitude into lethal betrayal. An Aryan menial could have his or her Jewish employer sent off to the camps quite easily. Kepesh's late mother, we are informed,

> put up with alcoholic bakers and homicidal salad men and bus boys who still wet the bed ... *Beasts,* she call them, *barnyard animals,* but always she went back to the kettles, back to the cleanser and the mops and the linens, despite the *angst* she endured from Memorial Day to Yom Kippur because of the radical imperfection of our help. Isn't it from my mother that I learned determination to begin with?[43]

It is impossible not to feel that these "bakers," "salad men," and "bus boys," with their various psychoses, are all goyim, as surely as the torment that begins with the start of the season on Memorial Day (a quintessential American-goy holiday) is never leavened until reaching the promised land, so to speak, of Yom Kippur. Clockwork, timekeeping, the management of eternity and its attendant, oozing crises, is part of the immigrant minority's assimilation, his or her ability to succeed within a hostile society: "Isn't it from her [my mother's] example that I learned how one goes on from summer to winter to summer again, in spite of everything?"[44] Forced mutation, due to perverse social conditioning, runs in this immigrant, working-class family.

In fact, the widowed and retired father still works, and with a similar sense of duty, Kepesh persists in memorizing recordings of Shakespeare, "for the same reason that my father answers the phone at my Uncle Larry's catering establishment—to kill time."[45] Mutating into a breast, however, has killed off time more completely and efficiently than any mindless job ever could, and perhaps this is the decisive element of the breast's final embrace of its now-innate passivity. In a society where the immigrant's only hope of assimilation is usually through hard work, there is no retirement per se; there is only the possibility of new ways of coping with extremity and of assimilating the absurd.

5

The Road to Kotka at Night

In Don DeLillo's novel *The Body Artist,* Lauren Hartke is a postfeminist performance artist who seems to rigorously transform her entire physical presence—body, face, voice—into different people, male or female, people from foreign lands and so on. Lauren's truth is radically empathetic. It is Rimbaud's societal, acted-upon consciousness, "I is another," but with a revelatory twist: perhaps this is not, as generations of male critics have pondered the aphorism, a thing of loss. If "someone thinks me," this may not be an impingement on my freedoms but instead a tribute to my harmonic interconnectedness with the world. To be or become another is perhaps only, in the last analysis, to survive, as in DeLillo's novel where Lauren turns to her austere art and mutational existence in order to get over her husband's suicide.

The novel begins with the couple's daily breakfast routine at their rented beach house. Rey Robles is an older man, a world-renowned filmmaker; Lauren is his third wife. Rey has decided to kill himself that day; he does not tell Lauren, although he gives hints that the reader interprets in retrospect. It is his final secret from her, not to spare her but (as she experiences it) to deny her, to shut her out. This lengthy opening is a masterful fugue in which strands of consciousness weave, come undone, repeat.[1] In DeLillo's layered style, some of these strands are attached to individual characters and some seem to be from a kind of zeitgeist, messages from social history itself. In fact, all through *The Body Artist,* DeLillo is perhaps more concerned than usual with foregrounding that sense in which a person at any given time is an intersection of instinctive response, pooled cultural information, and routine perception. As he states later in the book, "There's a code in the simplest conversation that tells the speakers what's going on outside the bare acoustics."² One must beware of what DeLillo terms the "unadjusted words"³; somewhat like domestic animals who can scent out generations of prior animal history in the rooms of a house—corners marked by fear and sickness, places sprayed with insecure warnings and self-assertions, territorializations, etc.—DeLillo's characters know themselves mainly by their ability or their failure to pick up on cues that might help them to survive. In his work, the triumph of humanity is not a matter of heroic transcendence or fanatical belief, though he gave goosebump-inducing portraits of such immense albeit delusional quests in *Libra* and *Falling Man*. Large events are, for him, almost ahistorical, interrupting the flow of a more familiar, intimate time which is actually the very essence of history itself, history lived daily.

So Rey and Lauren's last morning is built from mundane details— the water running clear or murky from the tap; the length of toasting time required to get the bread the right shade of brown—that are nonetheless fraught with the tension of inner life. That toast will soon become smeared with mashed fig and eaten as a kind of shared sacrament by the couple, and this, too, is a kind of art, not least because two artists are doing it. Lauren's body art (symbolically represented as the lean, mean art of the future, while Rey's cinema is a romantic-nostalgic art of the past) is about life and everyday identity grown porous and translucent through rehearsal and routine.⁴

The more life is emptied of conscious thought, the more it becomes comforting to Lauren and shareable. Rey is a restless adventurer, at home nowhere. This is the impasse they have reached as a couple, since the phenomenology of a marriage demands that neither partner retain a privileged or sequestered viewpoint, as we see from the moment in which Lauren groans as she bends to get something from the fridge, here absorbing her older husband's arthritis "in a manner so seamless and deep it was her discomfort too."⁵ At the same time, Lauren's need to merge with Rey touches on unexpressed problems in her marriage: Rey has sides of himself which he keeps hidden from her, and she is all too aware of this. He resists the marriage becoming that process of "someone thinks me"; and of course, Rimbaud's statement of symbiosis is at odds with Western imaginaries of a freestanding consciousness, a Cartesian I that dreams itself into sovereign existence in complete isolation. (It is also the Western, liberal I, whose legendary "bleeding heart" goes out to strangers half a world away.)

If anything, Lauren's sense of an interwoven domestic phenomenology intensifies after Rey's death, when she feels she must get back to a daily life of itineraries and tasks.[6] Keeping to an order, following schedules—these things do not denote blind conformism for Lauren but a way of caring for others, and for oneself. For Lauren marriage is Enlightenment orderliness, not Rey's Romantic messiness, and it is the strange conceit of DeLillo's novel that empathy is a function of determination and work, it doesn't just happen. It is intriguing to think about this in regard to Lippard's assertion that the "antilogical, antilinear approach ... common to many women's work" is linked to women's openness/"open-endedness" in general, what we tend to think of (perhaps somewhat stereotypically, although it's not commonly regarded as a *negative* judgment) as a kind of floating ethos of identifying, taking in, empathy.[7] Normally, we posit this zone of empathy as mushy and at peace, but what concrete, even difficult and necessarily stringent actions arise from it? What sort of labor is performed in its name?

Lauren makes her body a site of interactions, what DeLillo calls "daydream variation."[8] Mostly she slips into stories in the newspaper, identifying with others to the point of mimicry and extension, "doing another version of the story."[9] After Rey's death, her process becomes more aggressive, her intuitive imitations breaking into fractals as she seems to want to escape her own life more. At one point she encounters a strange man whom she sees for only a split second while driving her car:

> His life flew open to her passing glance.... She knew him. She saw into him ... in the barest blink.[10]

Of course, DeLillo is careful to paint Lauren's identifications as a possible reduction of experience; it is far from resolved in the novel whether routine or romanticism has a greater future, a greater purchase on artistic truth. "She saw and thought clearly," DeLillo writes, "which might only mean there was little that needed seeing and not much to think about."[11] For better or worse, however, such identification becomes habitual.[12] How does an individual consciousness function in a world where it is constantly impinged upon by every other consciousness, and is this, finally, the real art of the body, any body, to be able to go out on its reconnaissance missions behind enemy lines while preserving its own contours and internal coherences? Is it even possible to do this?

If we think of one line of the visual arts since the Middle Ages as being a progressive amelioration of the fear of lost bodies and also a progressive attempt to satisfy the utopian urge for immortality (portraiture, cameos, photography, film, digital images), then we may have reached its inevitable exhaustion. When images proliferate too densely, they lose value like any other commodity in a production-consumption nexus; or rather, the commodity form triumphs over the subject of the image: the physical presence that is being commemorated and preserved. The imagination, wearying of undefined things, adapts to its training at the hands of visual culture, and constantly trails off in search of new things. Virtuality expands existing taxonomies to the point of bursting, since search engines can now "hit" on everything under the sun, and webpaths (clicking from link to link) uncannily imitate the structure of neurological response. Put otherwise: we are living in a post-taxonomical age in which the limits of what the mind can collage together are no longer restricted by scientific logic.

We are also living in an age that is marked by lack of human eye contact. This becomes an explicit theme of *The Body Artist*. We have passed from the age of the meeting of eyes (presumably: souls) to the age of the void staring back. When we communicate via phone or text or email, we are not seeing or being seen; when we look at visual images, even motion pictures, we are looking at the eyes of people who cannot look back at us. Skypeing is live but protected and removed via electronic screens that reduce intimacy even as they provide access. We no longer have moments of spontaneous intimacy, or rather, such moments are no longer the norm of communication. If they do occur, they are more likely to induce fear than trust, to constitute an ending rather than a beginning.

We do not know how or when the age of eye contact began. As DeLillo writes, movingly:

5. The Road to Kotka at Night

> What did it mean, the first time a thinking creature looked deeply into another's eyes? Did it take a hundred thousand years before this happened or was it the first thing they did, transcendingly, the thing that made them higher, made them modern…?[13]

Nor do we know how long the age of voids will last. For all its liberatory powers, the Internet is where ancient inamoratas go to die. It is the logic of consumption: if one channel is busy or blocked, switch to another. It is not necessarily a special quality but random timing, dumb luck, a faster connection or better browser, which creates the initiatory spark, love's goofy illusion.

Of course, this is merely the current manifestation of a deeper ontological misunderstanding. We persist in believing that our links to other people are relations with the external world, when in fact they are primarily relations we carry out with ourselves. The world is our subjective perception; things and people are channels of our own imaginations; we pull our own switches and push our own buttons. As an abandoned spouse, Lauren, already obsessed with sensory details, especially those that are unnamed and uncategorized,[14] has the epiphany that we are trapped in a bad classificatory system passed down by a "Medieval scholastic" whose nose, it is implied, grew lazy and gave up.[15]

This passing observation is related to her inability to trust her husband. There are hints and traces of a different man, and these escape the classificatory system of an intimate, two-person union. The fact that Robles is something of a cipher is echoed by his official newspaper obituary, which acknowledges gaps and inconsistencies in the public record of the director's life.[16] But the mystique and ambiguity that are good for art are less good for the humble simplicity of domestic relations. Indeed, Robles' lack of a concrete, rooted identity is made to seem ideal for a filmmaker; in DeLillo's deftly written faux-obit, Robles becomes a whole sprawling *Guernica* of modern film, peripatetic, hardscrabble, transnational, literally meant to evoke an entire coven of cinema obsessives, starting with Nicholas Ray (Robles is called "Cinema's Poet of Lonely Places"), but clearly making passing reference to several others who knew exile, studio interference, and political strictures: Sternberg, Skolimowski, Polanski, Buñuel, Tarkovsky, Hellman. And, like cinema itself, Robles thrives on aggregates of names and places, a thousand tales in one body.[17]

We might recall Godard's description of Nicholas Ray's *Bitter Victory* (1957): "It is at once the most direct and the most secret of films, the most subtle and the crudest."[18] Rey is everything that we love about cinema, and also everything that makes us doubt it, for there is something undeniably troubling when so much evasiveness is supported by such massive technological prowess. For DeLillo, it comes down to the currency of emotional response. Somewhat like the routine life that represents higher consciousness, the affectless, blasé response is more truly human than the heightened displays of the movies: real people, for example, do not turn and stare apprehensively at ringing telephones.[19] In this, DeLillo opposes the hidden and finally obliterated Rey, disappeared inside his cigarette smoke and dreams, to Lauren, whose entire artistic medium is as tangible as the limits of her very body.

But what if someone in real life did suddenly turn and stare apprehensively at a ringing telephone? We would sense that this person had a secret, or was perhaps living in fear of receiving bad news. We would see what separates us from that person, or perhaps we would join in staring apprehensively. It is a different kind of empathy, of longing to know the other, more distant and controlled. This is perhaps why Rey regards anything he must repeat (an unheard question, a misunderstood hint) as a "self-diminishment"[20] since he identifies with film's more or less automatic recording of an already layered and unexplainable reality. Rey disdains clumsy attempts to facetiously resolve murky intersubjectivities, as if there were only one answer, one single way of apprehending anything. The recorded image is also, like Rey, frame-bound, fatalistic, and nostalgic. Lauren is more emblematic of what we call a "live feed" or "streaming feed"—events transpiring in real time and sent out over the Internet digitally. People can become hypnotized watching such live "cams" in action, even when the subject matter is an empty room, empty time, nothingness. The more one sees nothingness, the more one invests in the gamble of attention whereby one waits for the moment of change, of nothingness becoming something, afraid that after all our time spent staring we will somehow blink and miss it.

Indeed, the hypnosis of cyberspace becomes a refuge for Lauren

5. The Road to Kotka at Night

after Rey's death. One of the things she does in her grief is obsessively monitor a live computer feed of a lonely road near Kotka in Finland. The famous flattening or shrinking of the world is here tangibly evoked, with the last fantasy of human involvement shed: what draws Lauren is precisely that the road is mostly depopulated, silent, Zen-like in its tranquil non-action. She makes it a completely passive, absorbent witness to her mourning, a happening as private and nearly imperceptible as a muscle spasm.[21] This intimate transaction harkens back to Rilke's insight (quoted by the breast) that he is *visible* to the torso of Apollo, even though it is eyeless, inert, and mutilated—or rather, because it is all these things, it reaches out a feeler from some clipped shorthand of eternity.

Drained of sense-memory, Kotka is minimalist spectacle, "an act of floating poetry [that] made her feel the deep silence of other places...."[22] It is technology finding a way to serve that meditative, imaginative calmness and connectedness which we associate with pre-technological times (when people sang songs or told stories by candlelight). What Lauren likes watching most is "just the empty road in the dead times. The dead times were best."[23] This is Kotka's strange consolation. With these "dead times" she does not have to wonder anymore if life is something other than how it appears; its isolation, a priori, grants it a symbolic truth, an inability to dissimulate its own coordinates. Where nothing happens, there can be none of the omnivorous paranoia of what is "really," secretly happening, since utter nothingness is not distracting enough to make for a good cover. It is an alibi for dodging that weary social contract whose terms have become more difficult to negotiate; the fear of malevolent intentions is so strong that if you do not behave in a completely paranoid way around others, you can easily cause them to become paranoid, thinking that your confidence must mean that you are the one whose arrival they have been dreading, the one who already knows what they mean to hide and against whom they can have no defenses.

Lauren's art-critic friend is astonished by her convincing transformation into a man in the middle of lunch in a restaurant and describes it in a magazine piece:

I'm not sure what she's doing. I can almost believe she is equipped with male genitals, as in the piece, prosthetic of course, and maybe an Ace bandage in flesh-tone to bleep out her breasts, with a sprinkle of chest hair pasted on. Or she has trained her upper body to deflate and her lower body to sprout. Don't put it past her.[24]

Lauren seems to lose some measure of sisterly trust in the shrewd, telling phrase, "Don't put it past her": isn't this what people say when someone is impressive but in a rather fearsome, shameless way? It is different from *The Breast,* whom everyone feels sorry for, embraces, caresses, and weeps upon—the bosom of the world, so to speak, gathering its children in. Lauren is a loner; her talent emerges from a sense of isolation from others. But she is finally not, as DeLillo's title might suggest, an heir to Kafka's "Hunger Artist." That role is fulfilled by Rey, perpetually dissatisfied, disliking the taste of every food that is offered, making a deal of letting Lauren eat most of his meticulously prepared fig-toast on their last morning together. Lauren eats literally all through the novel, even when she doesn't seem to want to. When she is prepping for her performance, not eating only occurs to her as an afterthought, prompted by the idea of Rey.[25]

DeLillo's spare novel *is* like a retelling of "A Hunger Artist," but from the point of view of the "young panther" who comes to occupy the Hunger Artist's cage after his skeletal body has been carted away:

> Even the most insensitive found it refreshing to see this wild creature leaping around the cage that had so long been dreary. The panther was all right. The food he liked was brought him without hesitation by the attendants; he seemed not even to miss his freedom; his noble body, furnished almost to the bursting point with all that it needed, seemed to carry freedom around with it....[26]

Kafka does not blame the panther for being young and vigorous; neither does Rey blame Lauren, for Rey is not only the eclipsed Hunger Artist but "the most insensitive" and jaded spectator who cannot help but find the panther "refreshing." And none of this is really lost on Lauren. Indeed, she is like that panther if it had loved, in some obscure but elemental way, the Hunger Artist whom it replaces; put otherwise: if the panther had been aware of following in the wake of a great, misunderstood genius, loving him as a kind of precursor, and taking pos-

5. The Road to Kotka at Night

session of the cage as if to celebrate as well as exorcise the remaining traces of this love.

The panther knows, too, that traces are never wholly expunged; to its powerful nose a scent that has been scrubbed long past human detection still blazes forth brightly as a lighthouse. Scent may, in fact, be the thing that animals have which corresponds to human feelings of sacredness over the thought of distant time. Rey is, typically, the more animal-like within the couple, on their final morning scenting his own end, his time to go, even as he makes the remark, cryptic at the time, that Lauren "eats and sleeps and lives forever."[27] Nothing is as isolating as the feeling that one has an entirely different relation to time than one's partner, even though it is often part of the tribute which lovers pay each other, that they need do nothing special to attain eternity or immortality, that even lying there, drowsy and unkempt, they are making history for their appreciative partners—the beautiful hand which does nothing is mightier and perhaps less alienated than the hand that lifts pen or paintbrush or chisel to craft something potentially enduring. (Giving up on both eternity and love, Rimbaud writes, "La main à plume vaut la main à charrue.—Quel siècle à mains!—Je n'aurai jamais ma main. Après, la domesticité mène trop loin. [The hand with the quill is equal to the hand with the plow.—What a century for hands!—I will never have my hand. When it's over, domesticity carries us too far afield]"[28]).

At the end of *The Body Artist,* Lauren is more alone than ever; one possible interpretation of DeLillo's stark last paragraph is that she hurls herself out of a window. Yet it is more in keeping with Lauren's survival mechanisms that this ending is a classically Kafkaesque image of stretching or sprouting, Lauren left savoring the ever-changing "flow of time in her body, to tell her who she was."[29] Her aloneness *is* her physical capital, and her most productive mode. Even at lunch with her best friend, Lauren is distracted, angry, noncommittal, noncommunicative, and she runs out before the check arrives. Revisiting that Martha Wilson/Jacki Appel art-piece, it is as though one of the empowered Claudias had stood up in the middle of their power-lunch and said, "You know, I think I'd rather not be here after all."

Whereas the breast is never either abandoned or abandoning,

always succored or succoring. The ending of Roth's novella is the point where Kepesh *enters* the world, history, and language—fully as a breast. Whereas Lauren by the end is going nowhere fast, defined more by what she has failed to incorporate and assimilate into her body art than by what she has managed to overcome. She is still holed up in the rented beach house, still monitoring the road to Kotka: "In the mirror she waited to see someone who is classically unseen, the person you are trained to look through, bled of familiar effect, a spook in the night static of every public toilet."[30] Like *scum*, an invisible, often nearly nonexistent, but germy, communicable residue, and also the word we use for social outsiders whom we fear and disdain: Lauren's self-diminishment is a slow, protracted insult to the self, a stubborn pursuit of balance through teetering, as if she were finally asking to be allowed to strive, in her own way or time, to reach a psycho-natural rather than psychosocial self-understanding.

The breast accepts itself as a fragment (in the sense that Lippard speaks of the fascination for fragments among women artists[31]) and in so doing unites with a spiritual and aesthetic history that exalts the fragment as a record of what has survived the predations and random hostilities of time. The torso of Apollo in Rilke's poem is ascendant (and transcendent) in spite of the fact that it seems a helpless mutilated fragment: in reality its true inner meaning shines forth in its reworked, shattered physique. And the breast is a fragment, a mutilated remainder: it is alone in the final pages of the book, turning inward, an internal voice and little else. Lauren, similarly, embraces her own fragmentation and ends in lonely wholeness, comparing herself with the two elements that are most directly altering of form: "sea tang" (which evokes *The Tempest*'s decaying "sea-change") and time. The end denotes the closed circle of that animal life which, again, relates her to Kafka's young panther, and which Bataille specifically states "comes entirely from the movement of the seas [even as], inside bodies, life continues to come from salt water."[32] Like these wild forces, Lauren verbalizes little, while absorbing every change to the breaking point if need be.

6

The Aesthetics of Limbo

Cyberspace has fulfilled the central trope of Jorge Luis Borges' story, "The Book of Sand," about a fabulous and accursed tome whose contents are forever changing. You can never open it twice to the same page; nothing you remember reading is still there, rather everything has been replaced by something new. The book's owner, on the verge of losing his sanity, comes to see the book as "a nightmarish object, an obscene thing that affronted and tainted reality itself."[1] Finally, he takes the book of sand to a public library and buries it on a back shelf.

There it waited for decades before blossoming into: the Internet.

For the Internet, too, is filled with pages that cascade into and out of each other, so an initial search for one thing can lead the searcher along a hybrid path. Content can literally change, pages once accessible can become unavailable, one can scroll in vain looking for a link, a posted message, something that you know you saw once but somehow cannot find again. The terror experienced by the book of sand's owner, that knowledge was ultimately destructible like matter, has become a way of life in the virtual world.

Superficially, this is neither good nor bad. We are rapidly becoming used to the idea that cyberspace is a place of imaginary matter which feeds off the concept of the human. Or rather, what remains human is only what has not been finally assimilated. A photo (called an avatar, or avi) might or might not be the person whose online profile it represents; however, it is a photograph of *someone*, and if it appeals to us, we might become "involved" in the life that it conjures. Such logic admits no room for doubt or skepticism, even if one would rationally think that no other response is possible. Far from futuristic, the net beckons backwards to pre-technological eras in which you might sit spellbound for hours over stories told by a returning traveler, having to take his or her word for things you would never actually see for yourself (all that mattered was if the stories were good); eras in which you might fall in love with a painting of a famous stage star and take on faith that it was an accurate likeness. You might never see the actual star performing on a stage, and even if you did, there was no way of being absolutely certain that it was the real star and not an impostor.

Such verifiability has an impact not only on knowledge but on physical capital. Verifiability turns knowledge into capital, something which can be equated with specific value, held up as evidentiary proof. The book of sand dispenses unverifiable knowledge, knowledge that cannot be definitively owned, like those archaic traveler's stories of remote lands or the fanciful painting of the stage star. It is knowledge that floats in a heady atmosphere of gambling, charisma and irrationality. In the end, all you can do is describe to someone, second or third hand, what you remember having seen, and the stories, the descriptions, get reowned, reused, retold again and again. Put otherwise, one's own physical capital—a good memory, a convincing voice, articulateness, attractiveness perhaps—must be summoned into play to support the knowledge. Facts require no physical capital apart from the inanimate references which support them, e.g., a real book rather than one made of sand. But faith is a completely different matter; faith demands inordinate amounts of physical capital from its seller-believers and buyer-believers. This is the anarchic danger of the book of sand: you cannot say whether you are exerting change upon it, or vice versa. "What good did it do me to think that I, who looked upon the volume with my eyes, who held it in my hands, was any less monstrous?"[2]

Far from being a place where the soul gains ascendancy over the body, religion is all-body. It originates from a culture that has reached, in a way, the exhaustion of the generic body. Paganism worshipped the divine in the generic body; sex was a frequent sacrament of pre–Christian religions. There was no incongruity to this, because right and wrong were also largely physiological phenomena. "Right" was personal satisfaction blended with appropriate compassion and love for others, felt as a glowing of the body; "wrong" was a destitution of

6. The Aesthetics of Limbo

the senses blended with the breaking of the heart. There is no eternity yet; the dead are simply bodies of another place, another realm, who may yet find their way back to us.

Monotheism corresponds, probably, to a shift in which the body as an ideal Platonic form had become wearisome, depleted, and was ready to be traded in for a hierarchy of specific bodies, every man for himself, so to speak. Hence, what is generic about the body seems tarnished or fallen; exceptionalism comes through things which do not automatically exalt bodies qua bodies, but instead through meanings imposed by tendentious narratives, sagas of abnegation and sacrifice.

Christ becomes the last variation on centuries of pagan myths in which gods appear on earth in human form. For the pagans, the gods came to take pleasure from our human bodies, and this was not a degraded thing: to be marked out by a god for copulation and procreation was a unique destiny, the explanation for how certain people stood out as possessing markedly excellent qualities (Hercules was a mixed spawn of god and human, as was Perseus). Often the seducing god took on animal form. When the same scenario happens to Mary, the form of the myth remains—"God" appears to her as a dove—but the body is now missing. She is chaste, and the dove only wants to talk.

And yet, albeit drained of pleasure or sacramental mystery, the body nonetheless becomes an even more potent locus of obsession, but now demonized and blood-drenched. The end of the body, like an end of innocence, means no longer being able to look upon it in a simple, undivided way. Punishment, pain, etc., are brought into line with pleasure a priori. Physical pleasure is no longer a birthright but the token of a hard endurance. Indeed, Christ does not come among us for pleasure but for unspeakable agonies. (Likewise, in the Hindu religion, Ganesh is decapitated before being resurrected as the elephant-headed god.)

Thus, we might say that Christ is the ultimate Western emblem of physical capital in crisis mode: are we ever not aware of his tortured flesh, and is it not an alienated labor that he enacts for us, endlessly hanging on the cross, endlessly dying in the slowest and most painful ways imaginable? Each crucifix seeks to eternalize these agonies. It is even the limbs—the hands and the legs being employed most often in manual work—which are singled out by the special torment of being *nailed down*. Feeling sorry for himself and seeking consolation, Rimbaud thinks of the labor of hands (plowmen, poets) and writes, scornfully, defiantly, "I will never have my hand." Rimbaud, the great renouncer of physical capital (in his poems anyway: his life was, of course, far more complicated), the one who realized most clearly that passion-plays were always a kind of scam. Though he or she might give unrestrainedly, *give our whole life every day*, the worker is not valued as a physical being; he or she waits to be used up, hung out to dry. Finally, the reason why labor can be taken for granted, exploited, has everything to do with the example of the tortured body; it is because everyone is potentially *equal as a soul*. Bodies cannot be equal, as they seem to have been for the pagans. Through Christ and the Christian doctrine of repentance and salvation, physical capital enters Western civilization as something which divides the body from itself. The pagans took for granted that their bodies were prized possessions to the gods; the Christians will take that certain luster and ascribe it to the soul. The body that is left will be voided of its meaning and turned into physical capital, and this capital, whether it is skill, labor power, or attractiveness, becomes the worldly referent or proof of the unseeable soul. Moveable type and the printing press enabled knowledge to have a body, to have physical capital; and increasingly, as material progress came to interlock the intuitive metaphors that arose from a world fundamentally made in the intimate image of our own bodies (including, as it had always been, the world of deities, gods and goddesses) bodies became the moveable physical capital of the soul, advertising the emotional life within and converting followers to causes left and right.

Let us return to DeLillo's *The Body Artist*, for there is an aspect of this complex novella which I deliberately obscured in my earlier analysis. After Rey kills himself and Lauren moves mentally into inhabiting cyberspace, she encounters a stranger inside the beach house.[3] She maintains that he is a real person, a kind of derelict outpatient who has mistaken her residence for his own. Yet, even from the beginning, he occasions in Lauren an unaccountable, backwards dislocation

6. The Aesthetics of Limbo

of her own inner sense of time and space.[4] Even as she comes to live with the alien presence and communicate with him, he creates time-continuity problems for her. In fact his main characteristic is that he does not exist in earthly or human temporality. "She thought maybe he lived in a kind of time that had no narrative quality."[5] He is "here and there,"[6] a hologram-revenant akin to both her real life—he has qualities which suggest Rey, perhaps when he was younger, before Lauren knew him—and to her own life in cyberspace. "She amused herself by thinking he'd come from cyberspace."[7]

Like an apparition from cyberspace, he is shaped to her yearning, internalized a priori and thus in some ways rigged to seem more real than what is really around her. The man keeps her poised toward an amorphous future characterized by endless waiting. The wait itself becomes the life, the future, as when one looks up to realize the time after spending hours in some chat room where nearly nothing has happened; it is one of what Lauren calls her "dead times" online, staring at the road to Kotka, numbed by long sips of the eternal. Life (such as it is here) waits out of sight, tingling on the edge of consciousness, to be rediscovered again and again in its familiar yet ever-changing form, as much an ontological obsession as the Book of Sand is for its hapless reader: "At night, in the meager intervals my insomnia granted, I dreamed of the book."[8] What lurker in chat rooms has not experienced this somnambulistic drag, refreshing pages to watch the grains of textual sand drain and shift? To fall inadvertently into limbo, or what Nietzsche calls "the problem of those who are waiting,"[9] is part of being abused physical capital in a mass society. Such limbo ends in death after an unfulfilled life. One patches into cyberspace to escape the blandishments of the physical world,[10] only to find that one has not truly escaped anything. Cyberspace seems to be where matter enters its protected zone: nothing can ever be destroyed, no trace evidence can ever be completely expunged or, for that matter, definitively apprehended beyond any hoax-like suspicion of doubt. Yet one still ages inside this void, and there are even diseases here: beset by viruses, our computers become our portraits of Dorian Gray, as it were, putrefying and falling apart in penance for our online "sins."

The seeming aleatory of cyberspace is nearly always an illusion. Online, you have always chosen your coordinates, not only through the place where you have gone to at the moment, but through all the web paths which place in your vision sites (sights) that have been suggested based on your own browsing history. It is not quite like having an index to the book of sand, but it is something like the breadcrumb trail through the witch's forest. You encounter other "users" whom you have pre-selected; you get "recommendations" to purchase items similar to ones which you have purchased online in the past. Online desire is a mutation of various pre-fixed and interchangeable phantoms, a Derridean "monstrosity" patched together from innumerable, small desires that have not been truly satisfied epiphenomenologically but rather by the conjuring of something wanted but not there.

Adapting oneself to the Net can feel like discovering some special innate or higher skill-set, the mark of future man, someone who can live in two places at once, with multiple minds, multiple memories. "Time is flexible on the Net," Steven Shaviro writes:

> Sometimes I must read and type extremely fast to keep up with rapid-fire chat room conversations. Other times I have to hold myself back as I wait for pages or files to download.... My body is pulled in several directions at once, dancing to many distinct rhythms.[11]

The nature of those "many distinct rhythms" is that they often feel as though they are literally happening to one's body while online. It is the lonely phenomenology of drug-taking, where one feels intensely but cannot always connect that sensation to the world. The concern is that relationships will flatten and attenuate into "relationship status," the choice of cached emoticons denoting "happy," "sad," "mixed up," "angry," etc. There is a quickening of what the songwriter Robyn Hitchcock once called "emotional metabolism,"[12] in the sense that now one can spontaneously digest and summarize the kind of conflicts that people used to linger over, or hash out together. Can relations be sustained that resort so easily to this kind of reactivity?

Marcuse's *one-dimensional man* becomes, now, not a malapropism or even a metaphor, but a matter-of-fact descriptor of something: the avatar, the emoticon, the status update as it appears on a flat screen. Lauren's cyber companion stammers when he speaks and even seems to flicker in space like pixels or molecules not quite settled.[13] He is a manifestation of "the hidden [...] around you..."[14]; a blinking cursor "elusive" with the "thinness of physical address."[15] He shares the same indeterminacy with the original seller of the book of sand: "Dressed in gray ... he had an unassuming look about him." The man who purchases the book sees him as an old man, then a young Scandinavian with pale blond hair—at any rate, a "foreigner."[16] This foreignness is not a matter of nationality but of matter itself. Through his own physical indeterminacy, the seller introduces the buyer to this staggering and uneasy new concept of unverifiable knowledge, knowledge without physical capital, and wholly self-created desires. Lauren's pixel incubus in *The Body Artist* performs this same function. And it is clear in both texts that the apparitions are taking on forms to make themselves recognizable to the ones they are appearing to. They are emissaries of antimatter who have come to meet the human world halfway, and in doing so, expose its human limitations (Lauren's lonely neediness; the book collector's acquisitive desire) and perhaps offer a kind of remedy—the potential reconfiguration of physical needs as virtual, metaphysical ones.

In this sense, they both possess strange agency. Lauren's apparition is not entirely anonymous, he has a kind of personality, however imitative and limited, even a charismatic personality, because of "the air that rushed from his lungs into his vocal folds...."[17] We are familiar with these mutated voices emitted not by mouths but by flesh-like folds or layers. In Roth's novella the breast is said to speak faintly from within "flaps" of adipose tissue.[18] The breast also gains a certain bullying dominance over some of the humans around it, although it lacks most senses and all appendages: consciousness vies with physical capital as coin of the realm, and in fact in cases of extreme mutation, it is consciousness which must assume the role of physical capital. Like a schizophrenic who hears voices coming from inanimate objects, we anthropomorphize relentlessly, solipsistically, narcissistically, as we do online, where the many Babel-like strands of ironic, disembodied activity—odd random timing, phony pictures and screen names, partial conversations, intimations, winks that can either appear generous or sinister—must be converted into something comprehensible or left as an inexplicable, alienating phenomenon.

For Shaviro, this sociopathic process is built in to the net itself, where "the vampiric flow of blood is reduced to 'nothing more than a flow of information.' As such, it can be calculated and manipulated, just like any other packet of bits." As Shaviro writes, Dracula is ground zero for the huge leap toward alienated labor in the time between feudalism and Marxist formal subsumption under early industrial capitalism: "Dracula is a feudal master and not a capitalist, but for all that, his ravages are captured by, and brought within the scope of, the capitalist world market."[19] Something similar happens in *The Body Artist*, which is not without its own hyperlinks to vampire lore. The stranger from cyberspace seems shaky and undefined, but as Lauren begins to succor him in her imagination, he becomes more of a tangible entity, an allegory of the way people only truly come into existence for us when we lend them our powers of creative sympathy but also a reminder of how vampires retain their ageless, powerful bodies. Indeed, his "thinness" overtakes his host and seems to alter her own physical dimensions.[20]

At first he seems to be preventing her from working, while prompting speculative and meditative inner journeys; however, it turns out that this *is* Lauren's work, preparation not only for mourning and finding closure but for her next performance. There is no job description in our culture for a cybernetic muse; there is barely a name for such a mutation. Indeed, what manner of physical capital is this? He is described as dressing like a workman.[21] Yet he operates largely through passively getting Lauren to respond and reach out, drifting in indeterminate ether, both strangely candid and affected, someone who, in seeking one's attention, simultaneously claims some semblance of intimacy, sickly and demeaned, but still enough to break open the heart.

There is a torso with the face scratched out (like some tawdry imitation of Rilke's torso of Apollo); there are ownerless, disembodied genitals. Throats and chests without breath; their chat like a message scrawled on the beach before the tide. But we must not miss the point: what is hoped for among consumers of cyberbodies is a sort of aggregate-

6. The Aesthetics of Limbo

ideal, the perfect form of a body which exists conceptually prior to, and even long after, any real body. "From the faces of four hundred male American students, one obtains the typical face of the American student."[22] It is not the particular which is sought; as Bataille notes, "each individual form escapes this common measure and is, to a certain degree, a monster."[23] Desire is deadened by always being fulfilled by the same thing in the same way. We do not need to know as long as we recognize; we do not need whatever is missing as long as it is not essential to the instantaneous recognition. What is missing might even disturb us, thus seeming monstrous rather than attractive. Bataille speaks of the uncanny feeling occasioned by the presence of someone who makes one feel both malaise and sexual arousal: "On a practical level this impression of incongruity is elementary and constant: it is possible to state that it manifests itself to a certain degree in the presence of any given human individual. But it is barely perceptible. That is why it is preferable to refer to monsters in order to determine it."[24]

Who does not wish to appear—or be conversant with—the typical if only as a refuge against the doubt that comes from living in an ostensibly post-typical (post-stereotypical, post-prejudicial) world? Standards of appearance grow tighter in order to take up the nervous slack occasioned by no longer being able to judge on any other basis; "taste" gleefully makes room for some of that immoral bias-profiling which social ethics can no longer condone. Technology subverts individual faces into a totalizing reduction, what Bataille calls the "superior principle," "which this servile reason would be only too happy to establish above itself, in order to speak like an authorized functionary."[25]

Adorno points to this problem of subjectivity within Hegelian dialectical thought and its nature of "abhorring anything isolated."[26] Dialectical theory has been an important repository of critical thinking, but Adorno acknowledges that this is equally true of basic "common sense," while adding that dialectical theory's "lack of passionate commitment makes it, all the same, the sworn enemy of such [critical] thinking."[27] He advises us to search for "what might be called the waste products and blind spots that have escaped the dialectic."[28] Put otherwise: mutations. There is hardly a dialectic into which we can fit the breast in Roth's novel, for example. It has taken an extreme and *sui generis* route of escape from the entire reciprocality of social relations; it has neither kin nor antipode. It has desires, but no way of satisfying these or anyone else's. It reveals all conscious bodily life as an unattached term without a dialectical reciprocal or other, in this case not even the normative body, since we see how the breast's longings and frustrations remain incredibly standard and familiar. A body is a body is a breast.

Already we have seen how much this has to do with physical capital and alienated labor, but it also stares down the impasse of total pessimism to which dialectical thinking brings us when it comes to the unique problem of intersubjectivity. Fredric Jameson writes:

> But even in the case of the we-object, the collective "being" which I shared with my fellows was that of my materiality, my objective quality, and not that of my subjectivity: a world soul, an interfusing of minds and subjectivities is clearly an impossible and contradictory notion.[29]

Did Marxism abandon this "world soul" from the beginning, even though its early thinkers must have realized at some point that this world soul had to be the goal, that no communism would ever work if people remained within the oppositional realm of materiality and of dialectical materialism? Self-interest arises to implacably defeat collective bonds. Yet that self-interest can never be wholly satisfied alone, and leads inevitably to death's lonesome sting. "Now it may be clearer," Jameson writes, "how the Utopian instant, or indeed the Utopian eternity, if it cannot abolish death, may at least rob it of its sting" by offering "a perpetual present in which there is a specific, yet total ontological satisfaction of every instant. Death, in such a world, has nothing left to take; it cannot damage life already fully realized."[30] Jameson, here, comes down on the side of Hendrix's "Let me live my life the way I want to," by linking "death and the present instant"[31] against the unempirical claims of eternity.

In fact, this potentially fully realized life is also completely outside of dialectical thinking, although Jameson does not present it as such. There is no tension of opposing forces since nothing is opposed, and no remainder, since everything has been said and done, and no dominant share, since nothing is left to take. There is not even the sense

6. The Aesthetics of Limbo

that death is the opposite of life, no lingering delusion that the incommensurable can be brought into line with a mode of thought that is completely based in measuring, dividing, comparing. What one feels overwhelmingly in the following passage by Bataille is a valorization of Jameson's "world soul" in immediate, daily, and practical terms:

> If it is only a matter of recognizing diversity in identity, or identity in diversity, if it is only a matter of admitting that what is diversified does not necessarily remain identical to itself, then it is useless and even imprudent to invoke the authority of the Hegelian dialectic.[32]

The only problem is that, with practical socioeconomic reforms still in need of being made, identity differences can not yet wholly disappear in what Bataille terms "an *a priori* fog of universal categories."[33] But again, we are in a zone of unprecedented questions and answers, since everything that we have already reasoned and attempted has failed spectacularly, so there is the need to get as far away as possible from former ordering principles. What is needed is something like the "new temporal reorganization of experience" which Jameson refers to, claiming it as the potential basis for a revolution that will be waged on behalf of something *more* than "practical consequences."[34] This is because it is reasonable to assume that what has kept us from finding lasting and real solutions, even after a long string of vital, committed and well-intentioned revolutionary actions, is that the problems of practical life cannot have entirely practical solutions, since they come down to things that are already vast and unknowable: individual consciousness, death, time. There must be absurdity in revolution as well as scientific rigor; the world that is to be improved for the sake of more sustainable living must also be partially abandoned as well.

7

Window Babies

Was the window the first artistic enterprise of man?

What we now understand about many ancient cave paintings, as beautiful and elaborate as they are, is that they were not intended to be *looked at*. They were placed not only within dark caves (as opposed to in the open, in the light) but often within the most unreachable, remote places within those caves: grottos that could only be reached by crawling through claustrophobically narrow tunnels, or the walls of the tunnels themselves. This is the opposite of what we would call a *view*; it is an anti-view, and we must liken cave paintings more than anything to a kind of buried treasure. But it is the "buried" aspect that is most significant. Rather than decorative, these paintings were most likely functional: intended as figurative embodiments of human and animal lives, symbols of the dead passing away from sight and needing to be contained, confined, in an undisturbed sacral place; recorded and honored but also kept at bay, unable to wend their way back to the living.

Aside from this concrete memorializing function, the cave paintings cannot be called "art" in our sense of the word because they lack any element of framing. The window, on the other hand, with or without glass, was an automatic frame, and an aesthetic decision. It isolated a single distinct view, within which information (the content of the world) could be contemplated in a digestible, indeed picturesque fashion. This was precisely something to be looked at—as in the memorable scene from Jim Jarmusch's *Down By Law* (1985), in which cellmates draw a window with chalk on their jailhouse wall and look "at" rather than "through" it. We can say that the frame predates painting-as-art; moreover, the concept of the frame is what gave rise to art, which is still struggling, centuries later, to break free from that ruling primal

7. Window Babies

concept. For example, even performance or environmental arts, spontaneous and seemingly unbounded, are committed to posterity only through photographs and films, which serve to place sometimes arbitrary frames around them.

Thus, artists are window babies. They are the ones upon whom is cast, from the very beginning, the shadow of a frame. And all manner of windows, various frames, have proliferated in our time, through television and computers and iPhones and iPads, everything comes to us via some enclosed quadrilateral, some view whose meaning has been defined a priori by its set dimensions. Likewise, we might expect that what cannot be mapped or bounded is inevitably more like mysterious raw existence than premeditated art. Modern houses can now be built almost entirely out of glass, thereby becoming one enormous window, a symbolic merging with the environment that is not a totalization of art but, ironically, a denial of it. The lack of a frame denotes the refusal to delineate, which art on some level always requires. But windows are not always strictly material, as when artist and philosopher Stan Brakhage calls cinematic vision "a large gift from some elsewhere."[1] There is the conceit that some windows can be nearly invisible gateways into metaphysical realms; one captures only the threshold, only the shadow of a more distant space. As with the elaborately hidden-away cave paintings, the aesthetic experience at its most spiritually heightened can require that the object be almost completely removed from earthly sight.

In Brakhage's films, windows hold a kind of privileged place. They appear often, as frames within the cinematic frame. Brakhage has described filming on the New York City El before it was demolished: "It had glass that was so old that it rippled everything. As you moved along, it rippled." He called this "incredible magic" and compared it to visionary moments from childhood.[2]

Camera frame and window frame become inter-metonymies. In *Burial Path* (1978), there is a shot, taken through a window, of backyard greenery, and the camera lens is reflected in the window glass. Later in the same film, looking indoors this time, Brakhage films a mirror through a window. Such window shots prime us to understand the idea of framing when, again in *Burial Path,* there is a shot of the sky with birds flying in and out of frame. The camera does not move to follow natural life as it moves; instead, the frame establishes itself *around* natural life and then becomes the fixed, contextual limits of that life. The birds become like brushstrokes on a canvas; as if they were already mere representations rather than living things, we learn nothing about them except what occurs within the pre-set frame.

This idea of the cinematic frame abides throughout Brakhage's work, where each block of a celluloid strip is sometimes treated as a discrete canvas, to be literally painted on, for instance. Brakhage credits two female filmmakers, Maya Deren and Marie Mencken, with helping him to understand strips of celluloid as plastic objects; they unlocked his sensual awareness of what it meant to hold the negatives up to the light, to let them drape lightly against one's hand.³ He developed that into the idea of film as a series of miniature canvases. Godard suggested that film was truth at twenty-four frames per second; with Brakhage, the frame is truth, thus in every film there are twenty-four truths per second.

An important strain of visionary documentary originates with Brakhage, for this truth of the frame is not merely in the facticity of his subject matter. Although Brakhage often filmed "real life," he brought to it a discerning, revising eye which often expresses itself precisely through issues of framing and of angles of sight. For example, in 1959 Brakhage made a movie of his wife giving birth to their daughter; this film is entitled *Window Baby Water Moving.* This was long before people routinely filmed the birth of a child as a family video record; plus, Brakhage was not merely recording the events out of sentiment (although sentiment is very much part of the final film, as the title tells us: the last word, "moving," denotes both physical movement and internal raptures). This is, in fact, an oneiric film, with some of its most poetically resonant images composed seemingly on the spot.

The first image is of the wife's pregnant stomach, bulging and nude, with a cross-shaped shadow upon it, seemingly coming from

7. Window Babies

the framework of the window (there is also natural light coming from the same direction). Brakhage holds this striking shot for only a few seconds, planting a seed that will bear fruit in the film's unfolding birth process. Bringing visual referents together, the superimposed frame on the woman's belly about to give birth marks the belly itself as a frame, an artwork, a window which will soon let us see: life.

This is not the physiological seeing that eyes do; this is the conceptual seeing that frames or windows do. Brakhage, behind the camera, frames the frame in order to assert his rationale for why we need to see through frames to begin with. We begin to be born in these openings, these privileged spaces. Like the shot in *Burial Path*, where birds fly in and out of frame, the window marks a continuous sight, which exists prior to whatever vision it contains. It existed, conceptually, prior to the life it takes in. In this sense it is metaphysical, as Brakhage has said, representing the ability to see "both the inside and outside of something,"[4] or to see, perhaps, with eyes of God.

Windows also play a role in less organic forms of birth or creation within Brakhage's cinema. In *Crack Glass Eulogy* (1995), he has a tracking shot that pans from a large recessed window to a mirror leaning against a wall, finally up to a skylight, which sort of "dissolves," in a rather low-tech way that recalls the primitive stop-action magic tricks of Meliès, into a panoramic view seen through yet another window. This is followed by an epic tracking shot across a city skyline: what builds up this entire world, seemingly out of nothingness, must be the guided looking-at of the series of frames which Brakhage has presented in a series of superimpositions and fades. It is almost like a kind of psych test, in which one is shown a picture of a man, a picture of a woman, and then a picture of a baby, to see how many subjects will immediately conclude: "This is a family." With Brakhage, frames are subliminal (or blatant) progenitors of visual reality itself. Just as they are alike or similar, so they group like with like, or rather, anything they happen to group attains that imitative, subconscious resemblance which is mutational, an act of radical empathy.

What formally arranges content is not the idea of a temporal progression, then, but simply the fact that it begins and ends somewhere (physically). There is a naïve (and somewhat counterintuitive) longing for eternity in this reduction of vision to the contours of a frame. This became an incipient lesson for the later cinema of contemplation: to create physical limits through static set-ups was a way to heighten, point to and exalt a suggestion of temporal limitlessness. One is already missing so much that takes place out of frame, with every passing second, that one grows used to the idea of a boundlessness that can only be detected through a fixation of the visual field on arbitrary events. This kind of image may have an aura of transcendence, but it reveals cinema as being merely pregnant with a sense of the eternal which it cannot literally bear.

There is nothing in the human imaginary—even eternity itself—that does not possess recognizable contours, here in the sense that limitlessness must be glimpsed through the limited. This is probably because consciousness itself exists only within the contours of the body. It is like trying to picture space aliens: they always end up having a head, two eyes, a mouth, arms and legs. The psycho-natural body impresses itself spontaneously upon any kind of drifting sight or abstract thought. All art is, in so many ways, a mapping of physical being in altered or disguised form, in translation as it were, and thus an investment of the artist's own physical capital. In interviews, Brakhage has linked film and even the technical apparatuses of filmmaking to the corporeal, as extensions of the human body (and his own body): Super-8 "shakes with the pulse of a person"; films approximate "streamings of light within the body itself."[5] Like windows, we ourselves are freely penetrated by rays.

In his fascinating Gertrude Stein lecture, Brakhage identifies "inattention" as one of the main problems of human existence. Inattention is what causes people to mistake the moments of their lives as repetitious, and thus lapse into ennui and mechanical routine; in fact, each moment is gloriously different, unrepeatable by definition.[6] Borges echoes this: since "an almost infinitesimal particle of the universe is capable of such variety, we should lend little or no faith to any monotony in the cosmos."[7] But that endlessly variable particle still might require some extra concentration, some breaking free from the tendency to self-reify (here, I am extrapolating from Brakhage). Inattention may be more innate and deeply ingrained than its (necessarily trained) opposite.

Here, then, is the positive side of the Borgesian Book of Sand. It is never boring. It requires that one attend carefully to every moment as a fully sculpted, unique entity; it is the bibliophile's ever-spontaneous injunction to Be Here Now. Of course, it is designed to break the most precocious memories, but that's the point: one lets the information cascade through and away. To let each moment penetrate one to the core is good; to try to hold onto any single moment or make nostalgic sentimental journeys is very, very bad. One is reminded of the flowery speech in the film of Tennessee Williams's *Suddenly, Last Summer* (1959) of Mrs. Venable talking about herself and her grown son: "My son Sebastian and I constructed our days. Each day, we would carve each day like a piece of sculpture, leaving behind us a gallery of days like a trail of sculpture…." But the verbal tic of neurotic repetition is only an early symptom of what is being carefully repressed: the mother is a mad castrator and the son has been eaten alive by starving children. Even under the most optimistic of circumstances, mortal risks are endemic to the life of chance and attention—the life of sand—if only because one loses the sense for survival which comes with the arrangement of life into recognizable behavioral patterns. Repetition, usually a friend to science, here turns into the bewildering anti-guide, the undoer of sense, the eater of the breadcrumb trail.

Brakhage is an exemplar of Adorno's "lone eccentric," who refuses to adapt himself to an ailing world. If it is true, as we have been surmising, that the exemplary moment is all that can define eternity and thus inevitably mitigates against it, then cinema, its moving images themselves a kind of book of sand, has been one of the most important leverages against the eternal. It is composed of finite moments that shift and jar, unlike what Borges calls "the motionless and terrible museum of Platonic archetypes,"[8] especially Brakhage's cinema, which often uses rapid edits and disjunctive juxtapositions. The one film experiment that has maybe come closest to really replicating or upholding some sense of the eternal is the unedited long version of Warhol's *Empire* (1964). Brakhage in many ways defined himself against the New York underground film world, describing his cinema precisely as an impassioned quest for that lofty eternal, "the search for God."[9] But God is not a movie star: the serendipity of unreconstructed footage, the rapture of raw nature and life, all of cinema is basically the evidence of what is stirring and wondrous about immanence. Some have always looked at a tree and seen God; others have felt blessed just to see a beautiful tree.

There is very little difference, at bottom, between religious thought and human thought in general, religion being, for better or worse, humanity's master ontological narrative, with even atheism essentially stemming from religious thought, as its incomplete negation. As soon as one ponders one's own existence at all, one is resorting to a form of metaphysics—whatever answers one comes up with will presumably be meaningful enough to form the basis of a faith claim, since nothing metaphysical can be scientifically proven. As a creator of moments, the artist is caught in this contradictory bind: if the artist removes phenomenology from symbolic orders, there is no longer any need to actually produce artifacts. The epiphany itself is enough. If one continues to invest in symbolism which taxonomies the scattered moments (like an index for the book of sand), then the moments turn away from transcendence and become something more prosaic, like the traffic lights that help us get across a street without being run over. Such moments, merely mechanical and routine, are finally inattentive in the Steinian sense.

Does our own attention create the visions that we see before us? Are these visions universal, or sustainable, or even real? Brakhage seems to want to film epiphanies, to show how they work, while remaining oblique; his films are examples of active looking, a looking that decodes or creates, and this active looking is often inscribed within the films themselves. In *Cat's Cradle* (1959), a man inside an ordinary kitchen, filmed in close-up from several different angles, seems to be watching a woman entering the room, looking up, half-turning, swinging her arm in the air. But the woman is filmed directly, while the man, shown from various angles, seems to be looking somewhat "off" to the side. Is this even the same kitchen? The woman seems trapped in repeating movement—her reality becomes more dubious than the man's, who does not move at all. Is she being conjured by the man? At one point, the man looks away pronouncedly, and the woman disappears.

At the same time, the woman does not completely disappear; she returns to the film at a later point, indeed she anchors its vision. As *Cat's Cradle* progresses, the editing becomes more and more frantic with synaptic fits, but Brakhage allows his shots of the woman to linger. The longest shot of her, again in the kitchen, features a cat in the foreground, the same cat who has appeared throughout the film as an embodiment of sensuality and also of the woman. This visual stabilization seems to go hand in hand with a view of the woman as something more than a woman, something like the Eternal Feminine or a goddess power.

In terms of visual consciousness, *Cat's Cradle* is lovely and juvenile. It sort of gushes in a way that has few equivalents in formally experimental cinema. This is finally a kind of fulfillment of Godard's intuition that there were things that "worked" only in the cinema, things that would have been nothing on the page or in a play but which penetrate directly into the autonomic nervous system when presented as filmic images and sounds.[10] Brakhage himself seems to have been a seeker after universal forms, using film to incarnate all of the vast psycho-natural human consciousness that we posit as possibly existing before the psychosocial, or (today) against it. In the voiceover to Brakhage's *The Stars Are Beautiful* (1974), we hear: "The stars are entirely in the eyes of those who are looking at the sky. If no one is looking at the sky the stars are continually dark." Again, vision and attention *create;* this is as succinct a statement of ars cinematica as Brakhage ever gave. Meaning is therefore unsymbolic. It is a purely formal gesture, an action whose importance lies entirely in this spontaneous and unreconstructed creation of the world through looking— at a city, a childbirth, a landscape—and capturing that looking with a film camera. Art becomes, according to this ideal, functional, as it had been with the ancient cave painters, for whom it was a means of "putting away" the spirits of the dead; now it is a way of insisting or proving that something had existed if only in the moment when it was looked at by the filmmaker.

This creative looking is open to the possibility of an interrelatedness of all things. In *Window Baby Water Moving*, there is a shot which must have occurred to Brakhage more or less spontaneously, since it occurs within the real time of his wife giving birth: the baby's dark head, shiny with lanugo, crowns in the open vulva, and this is composed in such a way, and in immense close-up, that we feel as though we are seeing a round eye on the side of an animal's head, a horse perhaps. Brakhage clearly inscribes his creative looking within the film: in the final shots of *Window Baby*, Brakhage himself, after his daughter has been delivered, looks into camera for a close-up in which he shows joy and relief, astonishment even; cut to the mother and the new baby; cut back to Brakhage, again looking directly into the camera and displaying the emotions that are natural to a new father. This disjunction of look and object, similar to the kitchen scene in *Cat's Cradle*, where the woman seems to exist only in the space which the man is looking at, is a deliberate invocation of creation myths. And creative power is redoubled, since this new father is also the maker of the new film.

Such limbo looks flourish and multiply in cyberspace, the realm of window babies. It is not the thing itself, but the attention paid to it; not the image, but the look that is given (and recorded in the form of "hits," cookies, likes and dislikes). The look precedes the image. We click on a link because we desire to see the image cached, embedded, coded in that link. Looking is active; it disembeds, even decodes, in cases where the caching is particularly hidden. In this sense, we feel that we have created the contents of the image, or at least selected them, having willed them into appearing and being. There is nothing more jarring, disappointing, or humorous than opening a link and finding something radically different from what one has anticipated, especially when it is a large image that takes a long time to fully display.

7. Window Babies

For Brakhage, creative looking was innocent and straightforward, at least relatively speaking. Whereas our limbo grows more sticky, since it teems with virtual beings: each person looking becomes the proverbial "Father of You All." Photographed, edited, and manipulated bodies begin to function like the ancient cave paintings, as substitutes for lost bodies and as ways of fixing them in a kind of eternity. The hard drive is the burial ground of living forms, often ones who have only existed for us as electronic images, and it is loaded with the superstitious hope that the image will cause its living referent to stay put, to remain under one's control, or to stop haunting us.

Window Baby Water Moving is a kind of earthy conception of "heaven," a heaven of sweat and placenta and blood, out of which life re-emerges; the Internet is more like that heaven of the ancients, a furtive rite deep inside a cave, where image-bodies collect to neutralize the fear and the hope that *no life is coming back.* This is, of course, the most primal and irresolvable of death's terrors, as it must have been in primitive ages before we understood the medical and scientific realities of death—on one hand, that we missed the dead and wondered where they went to, but on the other hand, that we could never be completely, empirically certain that they would remain dead or for how long—and as such the complex emotion survives in us. *Burial Path* begins, significantly, with a pale, overexposed shot of what appears to be a flat hieroglyph or cave drawing of a bird, with stick legs and a border around it; in the next shot the focus or the negative itself has changed and we see that this is actually a real bird lying dead inside a shoebox.

However painful it still feels, our modern grief is stylized. It is difficult for us to imagine the things of this world definitively "running out," everything becoming void. Yet think of what even one death would mean to a ragged, sparse tribe struggling to survive, in which several were needed to subdue one beast, babies were nursed by any woman who had available milk, and one had only the same handful of people with whom to converse for one's entire lifetime. Brakhage uncannily and tenderly evokes this feeling of the tribal; the Internet spawns its own kind of tribalism as a luxury, a fillip, rather than a need. I am on a cloud, leaving vaporous traces; my avatar is how I wish to be seen; you on your own separate clouds are singing different melodies, not quite a chorus. The default background of some chat rooms used to be a blue sky with clouds: a cartoon version of Rimbaud's "eternity at a glance." "Everything is happening at once," Brakhage tells us in *The Stars Are Beautiful*, "but the sky is a clock and it makes it look like things are happening one at a time." Moments chew into the idea of eternity as "glittering maggots" (stars) eat into "the dead, decaying body of God" (sky).

Thus, when Brakhage cuts into his shots with other shots, intershots, superimpositions, and double exposures, it is an affirmation of the chain of being as a series of substitutions, not a static, flat line; when he employs a sudden burst of color after extended periods of washed-out desaturation, ghostly overexposures, translucent afterimages, it is like a sudden restoration of physical capital through transformation. Moreover, Brakhage connotes this kind of flux in the very titles of his films, which at first sound cryptic until one realizes that they are actually quite literal, since they frequently contain descriptors of meshes, interweavings, transformations: "molten," "net," "cathexis," "commingled," "intercourse." Such words spell out the synaptic ambitions of the films purposefully enough. Kaleidoscopically, Brakhage's films are records of dynamic change, dazzling images that "labor" frantically as if to break out of the filmic body, the frame itself. Super-8 stock is made to perform incredible feats of multitasking, the same master negative being run through the camera again and again to accrue different layers of images. The filmic body's physical capital is pressed to give more and more of itself until it mutates under the pressure. Not only *Window Baby Water Moving*, but all of Brakhage's films could be said to be meta-birth-processes. He demands miracles, demands to have his life changed by what he photographs and thereby creates; a more active (but not necessarily less hysterical) version of the verdict imposed on Rilke by the torso of Apollo. Those obliterated eyes whose "ripening" we can never know, in Rilke's sonnet, are fully in bloom in the synaptic spirituality of Brakhage's cinema.

8

Surplus and Sacrifice

Money is endlessly fictive; as such, it is a story that needs someone to tell it and someone else to listen. Capitalism makes friends with this proposition. It philosophizes and narrates money, a thing of no fixed value, into a series of temporary values. This is in order to expand it, exactly the way Scheherazade invents epic storytelling to preserve and extend her own life night by night. It is, in other words, a highly serious game, where someone will be left amused and someone else's head may get chopped off. And to the poor, of course, for whom almost no amount of money, however small, is insignificant or valueless, the game can seem like a heartless one, this spellbinding manipulation of values, this protracted suspense and false climaxing of money.

But even in the legend there is a strange reversal: it is really the tyrannical King who represents poverty. Forced into passivity, nearly beaten down, lacking the will to change or end his own voyeurism of the delirious means of production, those flashing and cascading tales which charm and hypnotize him, the King is rendered poor; while Scheherazade, less and less a victim, represents capitalist energies of elastic renewal and distraction. Dependency is really what is at issue; if the King did not care about the twists and turns in Scheherazade's narrative, if he took back his power-by-fiat to confabulate his own end to the story, as it were, there would be all supply and no demand.

What we have currently in U.S. capitalism is a system where supply has outpaced demand and attempted to radically alter it. Whatever you needed yesterday is no longer good enough; what you will need tomorrow has not been "rolled out" yet; and the prices climb like the numbers of software versions or the levels in a video game. The economic narrative itself has been sapped of its power to make us suspend our disbelief in so much shoddy manufacturing, so many Ponzi schemes, so many buyouts and bailouts, while money goes on babbling to us, exhorting, whispering, making its strange commands. We buy things in order to hysterically rid ourselves of this money, this thing that will not shut up, this lying thing that is not even a thing. It is always only a mirror that takes its value from whatever we choose to assign to it. We might think of it as a worker of sorts, synonymous with all the tasks it can perform, and thus it is the only entity which closely resembles the physical capital of the laborer. It is the only way of measuring that physical capital, and in their reciprocal relation, physical capital conjures new money in an endless pursuit.

Literally endless for the Calvinists, since the fate of the pursuit determined eternity itself for them. If you died with a lot of money, your place in heaven was assured; this was not because places in heaven could be bought and sold outright, per se, but simply because having money in this world was a sign of being blessed, and a portent of future blessings in the world to come. The money hoard nearly deserves consideration in Canetti's *Crowds and Power* as a symbolic crowd which bears its owner through the pearly gates like some entourage. Money not only substituted for physical capital, it was expected to perform double duty, as it were, extra feats of symbolic prowess simply by being there. The fiction of money in that society, bound up with narratives of guilt and faith, was that money spoke loudest and best when being saved: the saving of money equaled the saving of souls. Interest on savings accounts is a trace of Calvinist fury in our world: those pennies and dimes that get tacked on to the end of monthly statements on the one condition that you do not touch the money. If you sit like the King, on his side of the room, and stare into a space vaguely occupied by the sound of falling coins, you will hear Scheherazade's faint promise to pay it all off tomorrow.

This was the opposite of Georges Bataille's sense of economics, which centered around "the need to destroy and to lose."[1] No accumulation here; in fact, one cannot ever be bereft enough. This, too, is a fiction of money, one in which "ostentatious loss remains universally linked to wealth, as its ultimate function."[2] Vomiting Beluga. Smashing bottles of Dom Perignon against the wall. Cracking up Lamborghinis.[3] These subversive ecstasies have never played that well in the U.S., which remains, in its national DNA, deeply Calvinist. (Schizophrenically, the U.S. is often reckless on a national and international scale, but devoid of much sympathy for the same profligacy in *individuals*.) Nietzsche observes, "One cannot erase from the soul of a human being what his ancestors liked most to do and did most constantly ... for example, assiduous savers and appurtenances of a desk and cash box...."[4] Instead, these problematic ecstasies become nightmares and fall to the working class and the poor, who might burn up an entire month's income on a weekend binge of some kind, not because money is endless and valueless to them, but because it is always too finite and too little. It reminds them too much of how oppressed they really are. (This topic is well-covered in Morrissey's trenchant 1989 Top 10 U.K. single, "Interesting Drug.") Again, capitalism feeds off self-destructive tendencies, as when people who are denied access to financial security begin to feel undeserving of it and then finally destroy their own chances.

Of course, the poor mainly put what little funds they can get toward their daily subsistence and that of their families; but the other phenomenon, the profligate poor, the addicted poor, certainly exists, not as proof that the poor truly are undeserving of help but as a symptom of their beleaguered state, their lack of a sense of future or a horizon forcing them back to insistent present needs. Indeed, we could identify any vicious cycle of *self-expenditure* among the U.S. poor as a tragically sovereign act.

Bataille writes about potlatch ceremonies among the native populations of North America: "Emblazoned copper ingots, a kind of money on which the fictive value of an immense fortune is sometimes placed, are broken or thrown into the sea."[5] These were the sovereign acts of real kings; the potlatch of the poor in the current U.S. has a more petty, vindictive quality, mainly because it cannot help but understand its own self-destructiveness. It is not about having too much, but about needing less. The destruction of material wealth can be a blessing only to those who hold something higher than material wealth—this is the subtext of Bataille's fascination with potlatch—and it goes without saying that we do not.

There is a dramatic link between material destruction and spirituality. "Cults," Bataille writes, "require a bloody wasting of men and animals in *sacrifice*. In the etymological sense of the word, sacrifice is nothing other than the production of *sacred* things."[6] Just because we worship money so all-consumingly does not mean that we hold it, or anything else, as a sacred thing. For this to occur, money must have a *collective* meaning, as in communist societies. It cannot be a story that bedazzles and hypnotizes the poor who wait helplessly for a conclusion which never comes. It cannot be fictional but must instead be fixed in value. Then the sacrifice of something does not fill the spectator with a sense of dread and loss, but rather with a sense of comfort, or specifically a sense of *surplus,* since the value of the sacrificed thing never stops growing in fictive-economic terms.

But this is inadequate, for comfort is a base refuge; it has not risen to the appallingly meaningless level of the true sacrifice summoned forth by surplus and identical to it. For Nietzsche, this was a matter of the highest honor, that is, the matter of how to honor someone or something: "It is the *powerful* who understand how to honor; this is their art, their realm of invention."[7] Bataille perceives this in the potlatch ceremonies, which link gratuitous power with the honor entailed by sacrificing or wasting material wealth. There is meaning in that meaningless waste: the same meaning as the broken heart, offered as a token of love, perhaps.

And yet this honor is essentially missing from how we understand surplus and sacrifice, which move too quickly from the materialist physical realm to the abstract, into a zone of superstitious faith, with all sorts of conceptual eternities as the ultimate surplus, either to be hoarded or cast away. "The locusts' wings say 'throng, throng'; well may your sons and grandsons be a host innumerable."[8] We wear buffalo masks to make more buffalo come, we dance like rain to make more rain. There is always a more or less "cheap" end to the means at hand, when in fact the means themselves are boundless, ineradicable and irreducible. No sacrifice is too great for the sake of "surplus energy—the accursed share—and the requirement that it be wasted."[9] Thus, surplus and sacrifice are not opposing movements of a dialectic but in fact a long, sinuous shudder of the capitalist body, an identical process of absorption and waste, pain and pleasure, guilt and redemption, death and renewal.

We need to reach a place—strange, remote, nearly forbidden—where reality itself is no longer something up for sale.

8. Surplus and Sacrifice

There is a need to put flesh on the bone, so to speak; indeed, most attempts to refute dialectical thought have stemmed from its bindingly abstract quality, the fact that it recognizes no limit to its power to make the subject disappear, as it were. There are Hegelian extremes of abstract reasoning that take us too far away from the ability to evaluate lived reality. The tension between revolutionary praxis, which must be flexible, and a foundation in the kind of philosophical system-building that casts its long post–Enlightenment shadow was always evident; one thinks of Engels's designation of the concept of "imaginary quantities" as being a complete absurdity.[10] And certainly an unhelpful one if what you are after is precise *values*. "But the time for this is past," Adorno wrote. "In his relation to the subject Hegel does not respect the demand that he otherwise passionately upholds: to be in the matter and not 'always beyond it,' to 'penetrate into the immanent content of the matter.' If today the subject is vanishing, [then there is a] duty to consider the evanescent as essential."[11]

Is the evanescent, properly speaking, social? Can it be given a social weight and presence, or is it, by definition, the implicit destruction of the social? What do we even know or can say with certainty about that fleeting, changeling state? Bataille: "A man who finds himself among others is irritated because he does not know why he is not one of the others. In bed next to the girl he loves, he forgets that he does not know why he is himself instead of the body he touches."[12]

The social is the last place, perhaps, where the dialectic hides, refusing to admit that everything wants to be irreducible in itself, that everything resists being broken down into constituent parts. However, it is in social interaction that all of the philosophical monologues in the Western tradition become like the elephant startled by the mouse. In the ancient dialogue tradition, philosophy was already social, even when it wanted to be anti-social and disagreeable, and thus the social itself could be reasoned out; whereas today, a chasm opens between any problem and our ability to rationalize it as a problem, as a source of irresolvable disagreement. The underlying plague on our attentiveness is not that we are too one-sided but that we are too reflexively many-sided in our thinking; politically, the collective has split down the middle (superficially, right and left) not to arrive at real difference but only to further certify its terminal rights as a collective in an age of rampant uncertainty. Right and left have become two sides of a fictional reality which gets sold and re-sold on a daily basis by the same merchants.

This is perhaps perceptible only when one steps outside of the network, outside of the marketplace. Many of us who are non-religious have, of course, repeatedly noted the eerie sameness of warring religious factions, because they reach the same conclusions about the world and its people albeit via nominally different belief systems; they are reflections of the same collective thinking, defined mainly by what they exclude. Political doctrines are now much the same, as well as cultural tastes, and what used to be called, in journalism, human interest stories. Everything has the same rooting interest; everything is shut down a priori, in the very process of telling its story, unraveled by cynical exposés while continuing to be milked as a novelty by the same entities who do the exposing. Scheherazade would now be a "Scheherazade type" and we would endlessly refer to how this type has fared in the past, what she should do now, and so on. Everyone would have advice to give, including the "haters," those whose chronic attack posture against anything and everything is the single valid proof anymore that something exists at all. There is nothing now in the (mediated) landscape which has not become a symptom of the paralysis of collectivist thought. Beneath the bickering, there is only a single numb acceptance; we are presented with every phenomenon and expected to accept it purely for what it is purported to be. This is why something can be belligerently hated now without ever being critiqued rationally. Indeed, it has become an unusually offensive act of rudeness to point to the specific ways in which something that is clearly destined for success fails to fulfill its potential on any level. One can call for heads on platters; to kill something is the flattery which one accords to something that is briefly seen to live. One cannot engage with the same thing productively; dialectical synthesis fails even where it could still prove useful, to move us forward into new perceptions and new responses. Phenomena do not emerge today in something like the birth process; instead they "break" upon the world, and shatter without ever being properly tested. The fact that they are witnessed at all, or noted in the vast ethers of cyberspace, is considered enough. Everything comes to a final fruition, a fulfillment of narrow ambition, in the public sphere. It cannot be otherwise. "Too big to fail" now describes the bankrolled, mediated world in its ultimate throes of repetitive and cyclical failure—there is an uncanny proportional relation between the fact that nothing bankrolled ever loses money anymore (at the highest level of investments) and the fact that we are increasingly unable to generate new ideas or, indeed, new forms of capital existing outside of money.

So, we still wrestle with the problem of the collective, the same problem which Adorno wrestled with, namely the draining away of exceptional, individual, human experience from life. Never has a cultural framework been so predigested, so thoroughly *shared out* among its constituencies. There is a way of "doing" Twitter, of "doing" Facebook, of "doing" the office and the gym and everything else; all of these petty sciences are essentially folklore that has been asserted with dulling obstinacy by professionals whose entire reason for being devolves upon the endless mediating of what is already mediation. The will to power now expresses itself in public only as a tiny checkmark in the margin of a nonexistent world. It has taken only a few decades for the mediated world described by Marcuse and Adorno to go from trying to hide itself from our awareness (if they were even right about that, and I'm not certain that they were) to now blatantly instructing us on how to see it more clearly, and how to live within it as the only world.

Scheherazade grows nervous and stumbles over her words; the plot twists must come faster and be more deranging, the information must be reduced down to the thing that can only be screamed: what you need now, the best and the worst of today. As with computer technology, the goal is fitting more information onto fewer gigabytes. When everything is a cri de coeur, mass-produced, able to be assimilated and imitated by anyone, then the real cri de coeur becomes self-parody. Everything is expressed in numbers; one watches the frenzy of gathering anonymous followers on social media sites and can only think that the dizzying astronomical totals of twentieth century genocides are now being lovingly stroked and welcomed home as pampered pets. First as tragedy, then as farce. Nothing underscores the death of the

Marks of Toil

individual as a force more than the way people strive to turn masses into extra zeroes on the end of long sums, and to enshroud as many as possible under the canopy of bland and total support.

Adorno wrote that "in an individualistic society, the general not only realizes itself through the interplay of particulars, but society is essentially the substance of the individual. For this reason, social analysis can learn incomparably more from individual experience than Hegel conceded, while conversely the large historical categories, after all that has meanwhile been perpetrated with their help, are no longer above suspicion of fraud."[13] He was never closer to dialectical despair than in these and other pages of *Minima Moralia,* a book which, dedicated to Horkheimer, Adorno's erstwhile writing partner separated from him by fascism and war, reinvents the dialectic as something irreparably broken (thus ripe for radical overhaul). The fragments resist synthesis, cry out as forgotten or crushed allegiances; one longs for an irreducible whole, even if only in illusion, and this illusion is associated with a lost noblesse, the image of a humanity that had not yet stooped to having to assimilate Auschwitz or Hiroshima, where even the act of mourning itself is tainted, "no longer above suspicion of fraud," by being asked to help us sweep something impossibly huge and filthy under the rug.

But let us open a window on this train of thought, as Nietzsche might say. We can no longer seriously imagine that Adorno himself remains somehow outside of the collective anymore—beyond the reach of that cooptation which he found everywhere. Anyone can argue this cooptation case against capitalism, even the capitalists themselves are versed in it: they know enough about it to mock it, or even fret about it when it suits them. We have not learned from and embraced their ideas as readily as they have ours; this is the innate disadvantage of feeling convinced that one occupies a unique moral high ground. One is already resistant to that particular dialectic by which they, the capitalists, acknowledge in so many ways that they need us, as obstacles. Nietzsche understood that external obstacles make up the entire wholeness of a developing organism, since they give him or her the reason to find an

8. Surplus and Sacrifice

inner strength to overcome them; in civilized man, when many of the physical obstacles disappear, new ones must be constructed and the instinct for dogma becomes perversely overdeveloped. Capitalism, like socialism and fascism, subsists only through its creation of enemies: when it runs out of constructed enemies, the market's capitalist sellers turn against their own consumers, all along the perfect fatted calf. *Something* must always be sacrificed to create the sacred hoard of invaluable lost things which is synonymous with the sense of surplus itself.

At any rate, postmodern Marxism has already moved beyond the faith that Marx himself placed in society as a subject-force in the changing or making of history. "'Society' is not a valid object of discourse. There is no single underlying principle fixing—and hence constituting—the whole field of differences."[14] This would seem to indicate the need for a synthesis that is more extreme and more organic than the dialectical synthesis of opposing forces, perhaps an a priori awareness of what Bataille calls "an *experience lived* by each human being. Through this, the terms of dialectical development become elements of real existence."[15]

Zygmunt Bauman has defined what he terms "postmodern ethics": "No universal standards then. No looking over one's shoulders, to take glimpses of what other people 'like me' do. No listening to what they say they do or ought to be doing—and then following their example, absolving myself for not doing anything else."[16] This is strikingly like Nietzsche's sense of the sovereign individual, whose ethical selfhood, along with everything else, must be built from the ground up. In the case of ethical behavior, one of the most slippery of Nietzsche's main concerns, this refusal to be modeled on existing axiomatic patterns is what saves it from mere altruism or compassion, which are themselves nothing but manipulated, degraded forms of the will to power, in which power stoops to conquer, so to speak; what Nietzsche called "moral narcotics."[17] Or rather, more precisely, this refusal of modeling is what elevates the ethic to something that can be both flexible and ubiquitous, intuitive—a universal *sui generis*, as it were, and an authentic response vis-à-vis the world.

For if a true ethic is to be arrived at impartially, it cannot be tested in a vacuum. Jeffrey T. Nealon writes: "Ethics, if it is to be of any use at all in a postmodern context, has to be precisely an ethics of response *both* to the concrete other *and* to the emergent other—the unforeseen other, the wholly other."[18] Ethical behavior always presupposes a rapport with an other; this is true even if one imposes an exercise program or a diet, say, on one's own body—the body becomes almost separable as the object of (self-)ethical will. Ethics are themselves what alone gives rise to the need for dialectic, the need to see two parts as bearing reciprocal responsibility toward each other. Hegel's sense of the State and the individual is actually an ethic, though it is neither presented nor resolved as such. Put otherwise, what Hegel saw as "pure idea," revolutionary in its dialecticism, was left to be ethically interpreted, or misinterpreted, by others. Indeed, once it became codified as the schema of political struggle, this dialectic tended toward the most brutal interpretive extremes, playing a leading role in both modern fascism and modern totalitarian communism, and now in global capitalism.

Let us look at this more closely. What should have taken place mainly under the aegis of ethics (Hegelian dialecticism) became merely a rhetorical ploy. Again, ethics begin in an awareness of dialectic, the reciprocal responsibility of two parts. But this is just what we might call the explosion at the base of the rocket, what initially launches it into space. Once on its trajectory, the rocket cannot remain invested in the parts of itself that have boosted it higher and then fallen away. What begins as dialectic should end as something more organic than the forced synthesis of opposing forces who remain unconvinced by each other, unassimilable, locked in conflict. Originating truly for the first time only from the dialectic, ethics should abolish the dialectic as they go; because they would ideally convert conflict and struggle into solutions, and promote a world in which the awareness of unsynthesized differences will no longer present a lingering, staid, moribund condition. Ethics are proactive dialectics, in which the dialectic, in whatever form, gives rise to the action that will put it, finally, to rest.

This is what Nealon recognizes as "critical responsiveness": "For there to be an ethical subject, I have to give up my dreams of mastery and recognize my cohabitation with the other, aspiring to become …

'a self that works on itself to develop critical responsiveness to that it is not.'"[19] And yet it is wrong to assume there is no mastery here. In fact, a major part of the conversion of dialectic into ethic, although this is still somewhat utopian, is that everyone will become master rather than slave; for ethics blossom, and dialectical oppositions wither away, when everyone is an equal master, and slavery does not even exist in the picture conceptually. Dialectics signify that nothing can be unthinkable or unthought, that indeed the thought of one thing must be imbricated with that of other things; ethics signify that what is no longer helpful or fair in human terms can be allowed, encouraged, to pass into unthinkability, beyond "eternal struggle."

Ultimately, then, we see that the problem with dialectical thinking is that it serves no ethic, or rather, by its very insistence on shifting to make room for everything within definable mental enclosures—dialecticism has the greatest physical capital of all philosophical ideas—that it can serve *any* ethic. This is, of course, what led Adorno, reeling from the horrors of World War II, to view Hitler's Wehrmacht as a ferocious, sour triumph of Hegelianism: raw power had elicited from the abstract possibilities of thought an unprecedented life of its own. "Had Hegel's philosophy of history embraced this age," Adorno writes, "Hitler's robot-bombs would have found their place beside the early death of Alexander and similar images, as one of the selected empirical facts by which the state of the world-spirit manifests itself directly in symbols.... 'I have seen the world spirit,' not on horseback but on wings and without a head, and that refutes, at the same stroke, Hegel's philosophy of history."[20] It was a frequent cri de coeur of Adorno's that the same dialectic which had emerged in the Enlightenment as a seeming prospect of balancing unequal social relations had been reduced to a brutal principle in which everything must be sacrificed to the totalization of systemic power for its own sake.

It is precisely where Marx, and also Hitler, conceived the "elevation of an end to the higher level of meaning"—the idea that humanity and history wait to be brought to a state of completion by our actions (complete destruction or complete perfection)—that Nietzsche diverges from both. As a disbeliever in final states of Being, Nietzsche would have been completely opposed to fascism. I believe that he would have seen through it: in its hard-edged, solemn certainties, its bureaucratic efficiency, its sense of itself as a culmination or final stage, he would have regarded it for what it is, a grotesque affront to human dignity and value, and a foreshortening of human potential. Hannah Arendt makes a similar point: "Whenever we hear of grandiose aims in politics, such as establishing a new society in which justice will be guaranteed forever, or fighting a war to end all wars or to make the whole world safe for democracy, we are moving in the realm of this kind of thinking"[21]—which is to say, that of fixed Being as a resolution of (false) dialectical synthesis.

To Marx's sense of material value, then, must be coupled Nietzsche's sense of human value. As soon as we do this, we see that Marx himself was engaged in an epic transvaluation, in which the worker's body was finally to be valued more highly than the labor he performed or the product he produced. This sort of value speaks to both the economic and the philosophical-aesthetic-ethical meanings of "value" (for both Marx and Nietzsche, the same German word: *Wert*). Because Marxist thinking remained so relentlessly materialist, it did not serve to promote individualism a priori, only the rights of "classes." Over time, the same dialectic became used (in the U.S.) as a weapon of reaction. Defeated in the name of socioeconomic and political equality, the wealthy, as well as whites, males and straight people (all of whom are possessed of humanity and must be accounted for in any world that we intend to inhabit), all began to squeeze through the loophole in dialectical thought, which is to say, the need for continued opposition and the essentially cyclical nature of modern post–Marxist historical truth, which favors the defeated in any struggle. This is because what the dialectic guarantees is not a solution but an endless perpetuation of the same problem, the same struggle of opposing sides: an inside and an outside, a hollow and a full, a triumph and a loss.

In place of dialectical materialism, we need a transvalued materialism, which is to say, after everything, an *ethical materialism*.

9

This Animal Which Is Not One[1]

A cage went in search of a bird.—Kafka[2]

I think you are making your own little totalitarian society, Rey told her once, where you are the dictator, absolutely, and also the oppressed people, he said, perhaps admiringly, one artist to another.—DeLillo[3]

The universe does not really want us earth-trodders, at least not as we are. Yet we do not strive to become worthy of its vastness, its strangeness, its randomness; we seek only to follow the rules as they are given throughout the ages, on stone tablets, in college textbooks, on bathroom walls. The words of prophets are not revered and memorized because the prophecies have come true, but simply because someone had the gall to assert them in the first place—and someone else was sufficiently frightened or impressed to pass it along. The psychosocial has replaced natural instinct (with its rough and ready form of scientific method) with superstition, in order to cower contentedly in cages of its own invention.

What is lost is the possibility of growth, chaotic and painful but also vitally necessary. Throughout *The Will to Power*,[4] Nietzsche inveighs against the idea that the universe, much less human existence, could ever find its way to a final state of being; it will, must, reach complete destruction before it reaches anything like a state in which the organism gains some total understanding and mastery over itself. (And the annihilation itself will only be a form of renewal, a new prelude.) This frustration of means and ends, a frustration of truly measurable progress, has led to the creation of dogmatic ideologies, which attempt to account for our origins and purposes. Nietzsche redraws the cosmic map so that consciousness is moved, as Copernicus moved the earth, from the center to a kind of dark meteorite stuck in fusty orbit. He writes: "In comparison with the enormous and complicated antagonistic processes which the collective life of every organism represents, its conscious world of feelings, intentions, and valuations, is only a small slice. We have absolutely no right to postulate this particle of consciousness as the object, the wherefore, of the collective phenomenon of life."[5]

The malleability or downright insignificance of human consciousness is a constant motif in the screenplays of Charlie Kaufman. If there is such a thing as an individual human consciousness; if so, what is it, in essence? This is the same as asking, What is a human being? Always behind this question is the inescapable fact that human beings are literally *created* by other human beings, and not only physically, through the birth process, but behaviorally, through lifetimes of shifting imprinting and indoctrination. "I'm inside your head, too, I'm you," Dr. Mierzwiak (Tom Wilkinson) tells Joel (Jim Carrey) in *Eternal Sunshine of the Spotless Mind* (2004). Consciousness is colonized; it cannot awaken from this process without feeling its own paralysis, its own inability to defend itself from being invaded and usurped, as happens with Joel when he is undergoing his memory-erasure operation. The brain, like a hacked computer, yields its info indiscriminately, to anyone who can find the unlocking neural pathway.

Thus, consciousness, for unhappy, unfulfilled people, like the lovelorn Joel or like Craig (John Cusack) in *Being John Malkovich* (1999), is "a terrible curse." This is more or less because it always comes into existence only at a point where it is less than free, compromised, conditioned, triggered. It is first compromised and conditioned by an idea, such as "love," which is amorphous but which gains incredible power over an individual as soon as it is invested in *another individual*. The psychosocial purpose that we have given to love is already a way of hierarchizing human relations and creating means of control. But this allegorical function of psychosocial conditioning applies to many other, less obviously storied abstractions, notably "wealth" and "fame," which we might think have less of a human claim than love but which

9. This Animal Which Is Not One

operate in exactly the same way. We are instilled with the abstract longing; later, we come to love or despise people in whom this longing seems fulfilled. So Craig, a failed street puppeteer of enormous ambition, despises Derek Mantini, a famous puppeteer; also, Chuck Barris (Sam Rockwell) in *Confessions of a Dangerous Mind* (2002) is driven by the wish to be rich and famous, and has a love-hate relationship with the numerous people whom he exploits to attain his wish.

Social status, then, instead of being merely a construct, must be regarded as something intrinsic to consciousness, for better or worse, simply because it occupies consciousness. Just as people do not attain to the same level of social status, so they do not attain to the same level of consciousness, although status and consciousness are not strictly reciprocal in this sense. But status can sometimes purchase or steal certain advantages which consciousness alone is not guaranteed to possess. In addition to being a product of social and scientific conditioning, human consciousness is also a product of entrepreneurial engineering. One of Kaufman's favorite (and most subversive) tropes is the corporate office setting that is a front for bizarre hidden agendas. This forms the core of *Being John Malkovich*, in which floor 7½ of the Mertin-Flemmer Building masquerades as a "filing company," but is really a carefully maintained, secret passageway into the consciousness of actor John Malkovich (played by Malkovich); the boss, Captain Mertin (Orson Bean), plans to use this passageway to gain personal immortality. In *Confessions of a Dangerous Mind*, a series of inane and mercenary TV game shows airing from the '50s through the '70s are exposed as a cover behind which Barris, their creator-host, conducts assassination missions as an international anti-communist spy.

Kaufman constructs elaborate fantasies about the secret lives of celebrities, businesses, entire industries. In addition to being centered around himself, a Hollywood screenwriter named Charlie Kaufman (played by Nicolas Cage), *Adaptation* features the character of a famous and respected *New Yorker* writer, Susan Orlean (Meryl Streep), who is, in "private" life, a drug connoisseur and Internet porn model. Work, no matter how exalted or well-remunerated, is always only a means to an end; all labor is essentially meaningless, needing to be self-justified by extrinsic processes and purposes which matter more than the perfunctory labor itself and which are frequently subversive of systemic order. It is while doing filing work that Craig stumbles on the portal into Malkovich's mind, for example. Busywork is forever complicating itself into brain-teasing quests—and the opposite movement also occurs: legitimate brain-work (writing, medicine) is forever collapsing into the kind of fleshy, dumb pursuits that are seen as incompatible with the conformist formalities of professional life. In *Adaptation*, Kaufman visits his agent (Ron Livingston) to discuss a new script, but the agent is more concerned with filling Kaufman in on the women in the agency whom he has either slept with or would like to sleep with.

This need of humans to escape their normative functions is a special concern of Kaufman's. Like a Third World magic-realist, smuggling political protests past censors in the guise of fantastical physical transformations, Kaufman does not simply present the individual life-crisis as a drab neurotic exercise whose contours we are all too familiar with; instead, this crisis takes place in a frequently delirious realm where body and mind themselves are literally reorganized, reprogrammed, through invasive means. In *Eternal Sunshine of the Spotless Mind*, Lacuna, Inc., is a business that people hire to erase bad memories from their brains; its founder, Dr. Mierzwiak, explains about a client that she "was not happy and she wanted to move on. We provide that possibility." But who would we be without our shares of bad memories? It is a problem of consciousness that people do not always know when it is truly broken and in need of being fixed, or when it is merely aggravated and in need of being assuaged, assimilated or overcome.

This forms the theme of *Human Nature*, in which some of the characters believe that animals should be coerced into evolving human traits and codes, while other characters believe that animals and animal-like people should be left alone to do what comes naturally to them. Dr. Nathan (Tim Robbins) is busy trying to convert a man who thinks he is an ape, Puff (Rhys Ifans), into a human being, replete with polite manners and a taste for reading Melville. Needless to say, Dr. Nathan is defeated in the end, the "animals" win even on human terms, because the conditioning itself is skewed and flawed. Dr. Nathan denies his own "animal" nature, which is non-monogamous and territorial at the same time.

9. This Animal Which Is Not One

As the offspring of this bad conditioning, Puff ends up having all of Nathan's faults, including a fickle heart and bad choices in relationships. Sex and love, although indoctrinated as abstractions, are also wild cards in the conditioning mix, since they often assert and attach themselves anarchically, in defiance of social-systemic cohesion. Indeed, problems of human consciousness are particularly related to problems of sex and love, since love is itself an invasion and colonization of one consciousness by another. Love becomes a metaphor for any vicious cycle of interdependent exploitation, whether corporatism (*Being John Malkovich*), medical exploration and advancement (*Eternal Sunshine of the Spotless Mind*), political espionage (*Confessions of a Dangerous Mind*), or the role of the media in creating fantasies of escape (*Adaptation, Being John Malkovich,* and *Confessions of a Dangerous Mind*).

In *Being John Malkovich,* love is said (rather hopelessly) to be about "being inside someone else's skin, seeing what they see, feeling what they feel." Kaufman's scripts are dizzy with love triangles that divide and redivide and subdivide again. There is no trauma without love, and this is not even a dialectic of sides in tension, or even a cause and effect, but instead a case where love and trauma are in fact synonymous. They come into being at the same moment; they are two names for the same emotion, as in the first "Duino Elegy," in which Rilke speaks of beauty as the beginning of terror. Dumbstruck, shaken love arises from the fact that this lethal beauty *could* exterminate us, but does not.

The feeling of adoring and unrequited love is, thus, formally the same as the relation which the individual bears toward society: we are never allowed to forget it can kill us yet it is all that we know and all that we have to give us what we call our lives. The social contract in all its various rhetorical incarnations marks a situation in which we as individuals have attempted to argue, persuade or seduce the abstract society into giving us what we need, and ourselves into the temporary delusion that we are not essentially cheated, lonely, anonymously rejected a priori. It is from a mercy which is not even given as such (for the angel of the elegy barely knows that Rilke exists, as society can never account for all its members, especially its fringe, disenfranchised ones—the scream invoked in Rilke's first line does not reach that far, or, we imagine, only sounds like the flapping of a butterfly's wings in some outer ozone). We contrive the idea of romantic love, since the isolated organism ventures out of its shell only because of this emotion which it calls love, knowing in advance that the emotion is part of that interaction with the world that is already feared as being categorically traumatic and unjust.

We recall that Nietzsche said that no collective social institution can be founded on love. But we see the subtext clearly enough: no successful institution can be sustained without love's *illusion*. The ceding of individual rights to the collective must be an act as desperate and impassioned as the giving of one's heart to a beautiful, scornful inamorata. It must be that insanity which takes place in the moment that one realizes how helpless one is against the lure of throwing everything away on a last-ditch effort to *prove* the validity of a rejected emotion. This insanity is the rocket fuel, so to speak, by which societies progress by absorbing the fruitful manias of individuals, as we see in the historical recreations of obsessed orchid poachers in *Adaptation*: specifically, a man driven to endure starvation and "dysentery" in his pursuit of the ultra-rare "ghost orchid." He is eventually murdered before he can find it.

Love summons the totality of human will, but does not always use it up or destroy it. Sometimes the effort pays off, but perhaps only when that effort is no longer tied to individual glory or destiny. One individual with a mad passion can turn that into an enterprise which outwardly seems humdrum and workaday, but which secretly fulfills a far greater destiny. Again, as in Kaufman's films, entire corporations are "fronts," founded and kept running to serve the immediate libidinal needs of their CEOs (and sometimes their employees). This is an allegory in which the growth of a business mirrors a certain kind of outlandish love which must be leveraged by an individual's sheer will. How long can one wait, and how far can one go, to amass the needed (physical) capital? In *Being John Malkovich*, Captain Mertin, once he has successfully used the passageway to gain entrance to the "Malkovich vessel," and achieved a younger body, finally marries Floris (Mary Kay Place), the pushy secretary whom he had worshipped from afar.

9. This Animal Which Is Not One

Eternal Sunshine of the Spotless Mind is something of a fugue woven from the central riff of the secret sexual life of corporations. Lacuna, Inc., serves as a way for Dr. Mierzwiak to seduce Mary (Kirsten Dunst) by erasing her past and filling her mind with romantic thoughts of only him. And in the sleazy apartment where Lacuna, Inc., carries out its memory erasures, even the technician underlings (Mark Ruffalo and Elijah Wood), as goofy as K.'s two assistants in *The Castle* and just as disturbing, get in on the sexual perks of the job. The law and order of labor, of physical capital, has broken down: no amount of money can compensate someone for a business job that is soulless, or mind-numbing, so the worker negotiates his own contract, so to speak, paying himself off in embezzled sexual currency, or other forms of physical capital. Thus, in *Being John Malkovich,* Craig and his rapacious coworker Maxine (Catherine Keener) exploit the portal to the Malkovich vessel by selling rides in the movie star's brain at two hundred dollars a throw. Malkovich is the ultimate physical capital: he can be exploited without his knowledge or consent. For most of the film he does not realize that he is being exploited, his body and consciousness rented out to others in something that is made to resemble prostitution. Skulking "average Joes" queue up outside the after-hours office in order to take their pricey turns inside the movie star. These are parasite-host relationships; we even sense that Malkovich is being altered, manipulated, by the presence of each new lurker inside him. More specifically, customers inside the Malkovich vessel seem to get Malkovich to do the things occasioned by their own psychical needs.

There are numerous examples of this. Craig, who worries about the economy and yearns for artistic acclaim as a street puppeteer, first occupies Malkovich while the star is grumbling through the *Wall Street Journal* over breakfast, and then, moments later, when he gets harangued by a cab driver (Kevin Carroll) who insists that Malkovich was great in a role that he never played. It is not hard to see this as a consolation to Craig's anxieties about missing out. This is money and fame (and the headaches that go with them)—still want them? Lotte (Cameron Diaz), Craig's wife but an incipient lesbian/transsexual, inhabits Malkovich in the shower, where she is thrilled to feel (through him) what it is like to have a penis. As he steps from the shower with Lotte inside his consciousness, he stares into his bathroom mirror, as if her fascination with changing her gender (again, through him) has taken over Malkovich and prompted him to ask, "Who am I?" One of Craig and Maxine's first customers, a lonely, self-confessed "fat man" (W. Earl Brown), slips into Malkovich while the star is indulging a late night craving for cold Chinese leftovers. It is as if Malkovich gets into the situations that would be most fulfilling to his parasites, and in so doing, unknowingly ameliorates the guilt that they feel about what their hearts most desire.

This is not so different from what actors do, or are expected to do. They project private fantasies and make them permissible, even possible. Often these fantasies are explicitly romantic and sexual. For example, Malkovich facilitates the romance between Lotte and Maxine, who begin to use his body as a go-between so that Lotte (through Malkovich) can seduce the skittish, bi-curious Maxine. ("Only in Malkovich," Maxine tells Lotte, in a sardonic '90s retort to "We'll always have Paris.") In this, we see a bold, vertiginous glimpse into the way movie stars, as incarnations and reflections of libido, represent forms of sexuality and sexual experimentation in an extrapolated acting-out by proxy. Kaufman's train of thought, here, is more subtle and knowing than the creepy brothel of surgically altered celebrity lookalikes in *L.A. Confidential* (1997); I am not talking about literal sex with celebrities (or even fan-fiction masturbation fantasies per se) but rather an aura of attraction and imaginative play.

This is what makes *Being John Malkovich* such a tribute to the actor as human palimpsest, enduring the use of his insides as a wall for strange graffiti. In the scene where the Malkovich vessel gets drunk in a roadside bar and gets into a fistfight (which he loses), it is partly Craig inside him, mourning his imminent loss of Maxine, but it is also, on another level that is not lost, some version of "Malkovich" needing to clear his head of its detritus. When the Malkovich vessel looks at himself in the mirror, his face bruised up, there is an instant when Craig has just vacated his body, a few seconds before Captain Mertin moves in, shaking Malkovich's body as Mertin in turn takes possession of it. That interval of a few seconds, in which Malkovich qua Malkovich sees himself and exults, "I'm free, I'm back," is all that he has in between these long stretches of being occupied by others. "*We're* Malkovich?" he says quizzically, as if learning a new line, a new part.

Again, we see that consciousness is a game that any number can play; one may feel exceedingly lonely, but two is surely too few, since others insist on barreling in anyway, and the would-be nuclear couple must learn to accommodate them, however painfully intrusive. Indeed, in each of Kaufman's numerous love triangles (and quadrangles, and pentangles), the same handful of people keep getting reshuffled in and out of each other's emotional and sexual lives. There is an element of sadomasochism here, especially in the character of Maxine in *Being John Malkovich,* in the sense that love is defined by what some choose to inflict and some others choose to put up with. Kaufman seems to channel Nietzsche directly in his assertion that unrequited love is the same as requited love, not because it feels like the same love to the lover, but because a simultaneous repulsion is latent in every attraction. When love goes unrequited, it reaps the currency of being able to complain (legitimately, without guilt). Also, the satisfaction of need remains intensely private no matter how fulfilled and consummated the love becomes; in its most minute particles (where Kaufman's savage operettas often play out) consciousness is always elsewhere, elusive, and therefore never entirely on the same page. Kaufman is hardly the first modern artist to suggest that sadomasochism is the inevitable outcome of the realization that whenever a hand is placed upon a knee, it is a matter of sheer blind luck or soft coercion if the knee is already primed to welcome the moment.

Nietzsche dissects relationships in telling terms: "The weaker vessel"—and we recognize this unisex word from the sci-fi terminology of *Being John Malkovich*—"is driven to the stronger from a need to nourishment; it desires to get under it, if possible to become one with it. The stronger, on the contrary, defends itself from others; it refuses to perish in this way; it prefers rather to split itself into two or more parts in the process of growing."[6] The lover who gains the upper hand is the one who physically dominates and humiliates the other two in the triangle, thereby revealing the angles of the plurality, the mismatching: we see this with Craig when he takes Lotte hostage, or with Lila (Patricia Arquette) in *Human Nature* when she locks Nathan and his assistant Gabrielle (Miranda Otto) in the same cage where they have been holding Puff.

Or, as in *Eternal Sunshine of the Spotless Mind,* the one who "forgets" the other first is the dominant one. This dominant forgetter reveals the guilt of the other and condemns it by being the first to acknowledge the presence of a problem. The power of rejection elicits nihilistic dependency from the one who knows himself to be always already abject and guilty. Nathan, the behavior-controller, cannot resist Lila after she has spurned him and taken up with Puff; her decision to side with his own lab experiment against him causes him to fall to his knees and praise her scent as "dirty and powerful." "The instinct to cleave to something, and the instinct to repel something, are in the inorganic as in the organic world, the uniting bond," writes Nietzsche. "The whole distinction is a piece of hasty judgment."[7]

In *Human Nature,* the love triangle seems to want to take us back to nature, where dog eats dog on a daily basis; yet the vengeance which the lovers wreak on each other lacks the pride of true natural predators, and instead reveals man's complete inaptitude for the natural world. Indeed, we see that it is a misnomer to speak of going "back to nature" or making a "return to the wilderness" (as Puff vows to do, although he ends up running off with the Über-faux Gabrielle). Nature has never existed concretely in or for us, so it is never something we return to; we flatter ourselves in thinking that we once had a place in it (perhaps during the instinctive drives of childhood, or the head-swimming possibilities of first love, or even further back, in some ginned-up primal collective memory), but the best we can summon up with nature is, again, an inflated, illusory déjà vu. It looks and feels the way we always wanted it to look and feel; finally, we clamor for more credit for the perverse human imagination even as we hope to shed ourselves like so much baggage and attain a freedom that would probably prove to be messy and distasteful in the end. We make out the a priori world of nature to be our invention; we are all betraying lovers in the face of the natural world—and, of course, in the face of everything that constitutes the interpenetrating "reality" of other people's subjectivities: that fabric of the psychosocial which we jealously or paranoiacally regard *in others* as being somehow psycho-natural. In fact, this is where

9. This Animal Which Is Not One

the pain of sexual jealousy comes from: the idea that the psycho-natural realm belongs to others who inhabit it more freely than we can. Other people are instinctual, spontaneous, unconflicted; we ourselves, to ourselves, are the ones who struggle with complex coded rules that we can truly defend only in a moment of blustering outrage when we secretly *admire* someone else (always a rival) breaking them. In this paranoia that comes on the heels of the feeling of freedom in love's crazed euphoria, nature splits down the middle. "Our" natural functions are ungainly and shameful precisely for being natural, raw, unpreventable; while others' natural functions are graceful and lovely in spite of their being as innate and generic as ours. Again, the loved one's choice to reject us is the ultimate power to unmake or remake the lover's consciousness. The rival represents the community; the rival's requited desire is validated and therefore becomes, in the rejected lover's eyes, less free and pure, even though it is the same fulfillment which the rejected lover claims to have sought for himself. Needless to say, this denigration of fulfilled love is also an emotion which cements the lover ever more firmly into the collective system even while it appears to be setting him on an individualistic quest: unrequited love is not rebellion but a resigned nostalgia for communal law.

All of this is because man is an animal who does not think, know, or believe that he is one. More precisely, man is the animal which is not one. Actual animals do not think, know, or believe themselves to be animals, either, or anything conceptual for that matter. Humans are animals with conceptual minds and self-regarding, ontological consciousness.

This tension has never been resolved; more to the point, for Nietzsche, this tension has been continually dissimulated, throughout the ages, by puerile and self-glorifying rationalizations offering Man as higher being, as child of God, as spirit and finally as judge of an externalized, objectified, "othered" world. "As a matter of fact," Nietzsche writes, "it was Christianity which first induced the individual to take up this position of judge of all things. It made megalomania almost his duty...."[8] Specifically, this megalomania is as unnatural, at least theoretically (Nietzsche hopes), as any of the societal superstructures that have been set up as barriers around "we halcyonians"; along these same lines, we can think of alienated labor as being indictable as yet another artificial and false rationalization for man's existence.

This is what fuels Lila's life in the woods in *Human Nature*. "Animals," she says, "have eyes that do not judge." Animals react but do not pretend that there is a moral system behind these reactions; reacting is contingent, judging is categorical. Judgment is a perversion of instinct, but it does not affect the way animals live; instead, it points toward a lacuna—that strange blank space where we might look for "human instinct" if we only knew what to look for.

In *Human Nature*, Nathan's parents remorselessly associate any instinctuality with animal life, which is abhorred as unclean and inferior. Nathan's mother (Mary Kay Place) smirks acidly: "I *love* nature—as long as it stays in the zoo where it belongs." In Kaufman's cinema, we find again and again this tortuous fear of losing control. In humans, particularly ones who are considered highly successful, the special art of life is wholly describable as finding the means to lose control in highly controlled, secret, remote ways which manage not to touch upon respectable life. So Nathan's reformed ape, Puff, can finally go out to dinner without trying to hump the bemused waitress (Mary Potser), and can dance respectable tangos onstage with Gabrielle, but after he collects his applause and his pay, he stalks down dimly red-lit alleys where hookers perform fellatio on him in dissociative, tranquilized, ashamed passages of self-obliteration. Like Dr. Moreau in *Island of Lost Souls*, Nathan is guilty of making his "son" Puff in his own guilt-ridden image: "duplicitous, anal, thoroughly out of touch with my surroundings"—*like father, like son*. What is the law? Are we not men?

Likewise, in *Adaptation* Susan sneaks off to a forest cabin to have stoned sex with an old reprobate and master of Id, Laroche (Chris Cooper), and then brings her inspiration home to the city to write "sprawling shit" for *The New Yorker*. Complete gratification is what must be kept separate and hidden; whereas forms of "regressive" anality can be practiced shamelessly in public, like the scene in Buñuel's *Le fantôme de la liberté* (*The Phantom of Liberty*, 1974) where wealthy dinner guests sit on toilet seats defecating around a table, then one by one excuse themselves to a tiny room where they guiltily consume food

9. This Animal Which Is Not One

that has been left there for them. The social illusion is the same in both Buñuel and Kaufman: gratification, as long as one does not take responsibility for it, can be palmed off as a triumph of the instincts in a human world that has all but repressed the instincts, particularly where it could not control them and channel them into exploitative production. It was a unique human distortion of nature to allow ourselves to be proud of our consumption and exploitation, while ashamed and deceitful regarding the fact that we create waste that we do not know what to do with—how different history would look if these aspects were reversed! Isn't the exalted and warlike whole of humanity nothing but an insane attempt to claim the right to eat without shitting, as if this were possible? Some day the history of the world will have to be seen as the story of those often unsung, noble spirits who embraced waste and thus found a way to live freely and wholly all the time, not just when no one is looking. And we should not be surprised, in Kaufman's work, that this furtive state of "no one's looking" becomes the neurotic obsession of people who are otherwise always being looked at in some way or another: Nathan, watched too closely by his strict parents; the movie star Malkovich, constantly accosted by strangers who mistakenly feel that they know him through his roles; Orlean, whose glamorous book jacket photo becomes a masturbation aid for Kaufman in *Adaptation*.

The worst crime of those who seek to control or condition humans is that they believe they can define and quantify, even inculcate, that human instinct which we know to be undefined, something brought into being through a still-impossible process of living in complete freedom, of Becoming. "What is best in us," Nietzsche asserts, "we do not know—we cannot know."[9] This is the same as what I have been referring to, at certain points, as the psycho-natural, that impossible state of psychical existence prior to, or beyond, any social conditioning. Like the state of nature itself, it is a state that we cannot return to (although the very distant and exotic past holds clues to it, because the social conditioning was different then and largely unimaginable to us) but instead one which must be cultivated and learned from the ground up, so to speak; one which we must *move toward* without knowing exactly where or what it is.

The lie is pretending that we do know. The grizzled old cop at the beginning of *Human Nature* humorously groans and checks his watch when Lila starts into her tell-all confession: "It all began when I was twelve...." But this reversal of cinematic formula is revealing. The great human lie arises in saying, existence begins *here* (with a birth, of life, of consciousness, of love) and ends *here* (with a death). And yet there is no way of managing existence without these oversimplified, misleading timelines. It is like the writer's nervous breakdown in *Adaptation*, trying to write a script about Darwin and feeling that he must start at the very dawn of time, with the Big Bang and the first feelers of life on earth. There is a horror of endless origins, of origins before memory; among other things, they are like the flashback in general, a poor ruse of often talentless writers; "oops, I forgot." They defy Nietzsche's Becoming by placing too great an emphasis on an earlier phase or stage. Why can't experience always be crowning, like the baby's head in Brakhage's *Window Baby Water Moving*, whose dark round pate confuses us into thinking that it might be a horse's eloquent, alert eye?

David Thomson points out that Kaufman's narratives begin bewitchingly and then have difficulty finding endings that are not in some sense a compromise or an anticlimax[10]; but Kaufman is clearly so enamored, in theory anyway, with all the dazed, déjà vu entropy of eternal return, that his ideal film would probably begin all over again at the beginning. It is like Nathan's afterlife in the white room in *Human Nature*, where he narrates the story of his life, believing that he is auditioning for either heaven or hell. In the end, he finds that the telling of the story is all that matters: "What, I just stay here ... and tell it again?" Put otherwise, there is no *moral* here, which would amount to a judgment, or the impossible definition of a final state. Kaufman sometimes underscores his disbelief in such a judgment by having his characters quickly transform into something else at the end of the film: Craig gets trapped in the consciousness of Maxine's and Lotte's young daughter (Kelly Teacher); the death of Kaufman's twin brother Donald (also played by Nicolas Cage) gives way to time-lapse flowers blossoming at the end of *Adaptation;* the young madcap posing as a TV host in *Confessions of a Dangerous Mind* suddenly becomes, in the film's final sobering shots, the real Chuck Barris, aged and seemingly suicidal, dwelling morbidly on endlessly relived regrets.

9. This Animal Which Is Not One

Similarly, in *Eternal Sunshine of the Spotless Mind*, memory is already a form of reliving, or in narrative terms, flashbacks unfold in present tense exactly like "new" memories. It is Borges's horror before the sleepless eternity, the Book of Sand, both of which undermine the pretense of narratival control. Eternal return would seem to make all stories into one story, all destinies into one; yet it is as lonesome as unrequited love. For Borges, eternal return was a pure flowering of Nietzsche's own will to philosophical power: he "disinterred the intolerable Greek hypothesis of eternal repetition, and he contrived to make this mental nightmare an occasion for jubilation. He sought out the most horrible idea in the universe and offered it up to mankind's delectation."[11] The result was a kind of patent-jumping, in which "the eternal recurrence of things is now Nietzsche's and does not belong to some dead man who is barely more than a Greek name."[12] Kaufman seems to want to jump Nietzsche's claim in turn, in our time and for film audiences (in a number of his films, his characters quote Nietzsche directly).

Granting that Thomson has a point about Kaufman's anticlimaxes, I would say that Kaufman grasps that endings are narratival *forgettings*, whether inside or outside of narrative tradition, and as someone obsessed by the impossibility of ever forgetting anything, he dooms his endings not to work. The paradox of memory in *Eternal Sunshine of the Spotless Mind* is that whatever we try hardest to forget is what haunts us forever: even the words of forgetting themselves, those undoing spells, come back to the forgetters in the form of cassette tapes of their pre-erasure application interviews. Moreover, there is no "pure" memory to begin with, so the only thing that could be forgotten is merely one aspect, one cubist angle that presented itself in an impulsive flash one day and then receded into other, broken planes.

But what eternal return implies, again only theoretically, is that even for the great forgetters, there are privileged memories which remain encrusted to the soul. There is always a key back into the labyrinth, or rather a reminder that we are still inside it, just as there is always another recurring point at which we forget (for sanity's sake) that we are really in a labyrinth in the first place. For Borges is correct in his harsh estimation of the implications of Nietzsche's eternal return, which Nietzsche himself describes as the fulfillment of the "will for ruin," "the desire to perish," the humans' "right to cancel their existences—the great disciplinary thought."[13] It is the depleted universe as serpent swallowing its own tail in an apocalyptic "conservation of energy"[14]—the waste is still not embraced, confronted, dealt with, but hidden away inside the excreting body, which it poisons. In its certitude that some meaning (however hopeless) will come from the imposition of limits on something which is all too open-ended (consciousness), it is also the singular leap of faith which replaces Judeo-Christianity in Nietzsche's thought, a gloomy, single-minded reconstruction of that self-defeating moral labyrinth which Nietzsche elsewhere demolishes.

Kaufman's affinity for self-engorging monomania could be the darkly absurdist refutation of Bataille's sovereign lust for waste and kamikaze economics, since if anything we now live in a time that has seemingly embraced waste, and disastrously so. One can view the entire Wall Street collapse of 2008 in this crazed light: generations-old financial institutions bankrupting themselves for short-term quarterly profits, buying up each other's toxic assets in displays of surplus absorption-powers, and finally offering their business failure as a grandiose enterprise deserving of reward in the form of bailouts and CEO bonuses. We could see this as a dead-end, low-level exercise of Bataillean sovereignty and Nietzschean power, but it is something that is not condoned by a probing reading of Nietzsche, for example. In fact, Nietzsche knew those bankers: their tyranny represents what he called "the rule of shopkeepers"[15] writ large, mediocrities who may have made some profits under certain rigged conditions but who fell far short of the vastness of human potential. We would be wrong to see them as beings who confronted, in peaceful and healthy ways, their own waste. The investment bankers' potlatch-like ventures were only for the benefit of making us overlook their greed; they had certain secret guarantees. The cultural shame remained attached to the usual capitalist suspects: working people, disabled people, and poor people.

Nietzsche writes that, for the powerful, the "masses must be converted into mere tools (that is to say, into the most intelligent and flexible tools possible)."[16] Here, we have a sense of Nietzschean sovereignty which, for us, does not fall neatly in line with dialectical materialism so much as defy comfortable distinctions between the powerful and the powerless. The powerful are superior beings; their "tools" must be superior beings as well. But at that point, would they still remain tools? We can unriddle a kind of unfinished or undeclared proposition latent in Nietzsche's compressed logic, for at what point does a tool, in its mastery of superior qualities, cease to be a tool and become sovereign in his or her own right?

This is similar to Nietzsche's dictum that the time of kings has passed because people are no longer worthy of them. We can only have kings if we ourselves are kings. We halcyonians can only be "tools" if we can continue being halcyonians; this is only to say that the definition of "tools" must change to augment the contentment and fulfillment of the one who serves and, in doing so, establishes his or her own worthy power. Is this not an attempt to abolish alienated labor through an elevation of man as a species to the point where no motive would be greedy, no work would be grubby, nothing would be an affront to man's soul? It seems simple on its face: instead of abolishing the powerful, abolish the powerless! Power could be human, could emerge from within and take any natural form; it could be rewarded simply for existing. Could this even be the lost psycho-natural, the unknown "best" in humanity which has never been brought out before? In *Human Nature,* Lila identifies her biggest self-betrayal as the selling of her soul (to Nathan), and this occasions a Kaspar Hauser variation, in which the unrepentant, nonconformist wild child is not murdered by the frustrated civilizers but instead turns vigilante against his or her human captors. The human attains to higher humanity partly by becoming the animal who will not be caged.

Here is Nietzsche's humanism, in what is easily one of the most stirring passages in all literature:

> [N]o one is responsible for man's qualities; neither God, nor society, nor his parents, nor his ancestors, nor himself—in fact ... no one is to blame for him.... The being who might be made responsible for a man's existence, for the fact that he is constituted in a particular way, or for his birth in certain circumstances or in a certain environment, is absolutely lacking.—*And it is a great blessing that such a being is non-*

existent.... We are not the result of an eternal design, of a will, of a desire ... and we are just as little the result of a mistake on God's part in the presence of which He ought to feel uneasy (a thought which is known to be at the very root of the Old Testament). There is not a place nor a purpose nor a sense to which we can attribute our existence or our kind of existence ... and let us say it again, this is a great blessing, for therein lies the whole innocence of our lives.[17]

Human beings, or at least we halcyonians—we who have, shall we say, an instinct for the instincts—really just want to be left alone. This is because humanity has much to figure out. We want to be left to do that figuring in peace, which is precisely what has never been done. We have been rushed—have rushed ourselves—from one lunatic frenzy to another, one dogma to another, and in thousands of years have only begun to barely guess at the greatness of our potential, which Nietzsche states is as concrete and particular as the five senses, and simultaneously as limitless as "the whole universe."[18]

Nietzsche himself provides the perfect use of metaphor to connect materialism with the stunting of human potential: "A division of labour among the emotions exists inside society, making individuals and classes produce an imperfect, but more useful, kind of soul."[19] This sentence could stand as a missing link between Marx and Nietzsche, whose incipient political awareness has been noted by a number of Marxists, such as Steven Shaviro and Étienne Balibar. Although not organized as a formal political ideology, Nietzsche's disdain for democracy and collectivization forms, as Balibar notes, "an analysis and a genealogy which lay bare the mechanics by which hegemony is constituted and consensus engineered."[20]

What Nietzsche uncovers is that humanity has a kind of instinct; it is simply there, not confected, but natural. It can be refined and heightened, or weakened, through degeneration. But it can only be justified by instinctual life itself ("the justifying principle must be one through which life itself speaks"[21]). A wolf justifies its need to run quickly by simply running quickly; the expression of power and freedom is identical with the specific being's need for it. But this is not yet true freedom and Nietzsche knows this. A bird in flight, for example, may seem the embodiment of freedom to us on the ground; in fact, it is performing a kind of work, but one arising from innate attributes. Whatever is natural to an organism cannot feel like the extra burst of "freedom" generally associated, in humans, with stepping beyond one's nature or routine. But what is natural to the human being? What instinct of the human corresponds with the bird's instinct to fly? It is still hidden from us. Wherever it shows itself, it must be nurtured, as only an instinct can be, until it achieves that unconscious self-justification as the wolf's quickness. We do not yet know what a "man" really is, Nietzsche is saying, but first we must grant him the truth of this simple mystery without containing, controlling or judging him.

Therefore, since freedom is the only power that can lead to happiness,[22] what is closer to true freedom, as Nietzsche comes to define it, is only measurable in the lack of resistance to maintaining one's power or one's freedom.[23] This is not necessarily about aggression and counter-aggression; it can be a "positive power"[24] in which the world certifies and recognizes one's power and freedom and thereby increases it. Naturally, this would mean an extension of equal sovereignty to everyone, but since Nietzsche is explicit that there can be no such thing as equal sovereignties, it also means a long, undetermined waiting-time during which "weapons of war are converted into weapons of peace (out of scales and carapaces grow feathers and hair)."[25]

Ordinary human nature must itself evolve; and here, somewhat surprisingly, the anti–Darwinist Nietzsche seems to credit evolution as a slow process of species-improvement, as long as the results (feathers and hair) are worth what has been sacrificed. (Then there is a further twist, in that even hair must sometimes be sacrificed, as when Lila states in *Human Nature* that she sacrificed "her beliefs, her body hair" for love of Nathan.) There is a hint that modern physical capital—that of our birds as well as our hominids—is a matter of progress in terms of learning how to do more with less: less mass, less density, less aggression perhaps. "Weapons of peace," unless I am guessing wrongly, is a suggestive phrase in which Nietzsche manages to have his beloved strength and at the same time a kind of ethic, or at least a tempering of his usual contempt for any disguised or dissembling forms of power.

It is important to note that Nietzsche did not despise Darwin

Marks of Toil

because he thought Darwin was entirely "wrong"; in fact Nietzsche himself espouses an essentially evolutionary process in nature, particularly for the lowest orders of life, such as the pseudopodia,[26] because of the enormous will required for the formless to attain form, and then to attain higher and higher forms. However, Nietzsche seems to envision a break, at which humanity was no longer forced to exert its physical will as strongly and thus contrived, through language, through religion, through customs and all the elements of culture, to secure survival whether we were technically fit in every sense or not.

What had been physical will became physical capital, quantified, domesticated, and able to be finessed into ever more skewed and unequal advantages. Man is the reverse of the animal kingdom: in the latter, strength does denote the ability to survive, and strength is the rule; whereas in the former, the rule is that one survives mainly through weakness, obeisance, deception, mediocrity, hypocrisy—and uncommon strength, because it is now unnecessary and risky, is the exception.[27] The cliché "Only the strong survive," would have been transvalued by Nietzsche as "Only what survives is viewed as being strong, *whether it is truly strong or not.*" Ultimately, strength is attributed to those qualities which the social order, the realm of the psychosocial, wants to see advance and proliferate.

This guilty secret of conditioning is what separates us from the animals, and what makes us ashamed (when we are) in the presence of nature. Nietzsche was the first Westerner to point out that the practice of anthropomorphism is essentially an injustice to animals. In many cases, animals are stronger and more "individualistic" than people, without self-consciousness or manipulative hidden agendas; it is a rare person of great strength and directness who bears comparison with an animal.[28]

We could say that what we have described as a kind of "universal sovereignty" (my reading of Nietzsche's idea that all people must become like kings in order for there to be kings at all) has a correlation in a kind of universalizing of eternity itself. This is, naturally, the only kind of eternity which Nietzsche wants: where nothing is lost or

9. This Animal Which Is Not One

wasted, and we never properly leave the consolations of world and human temporality. "I seek an eternity," he writes, "for everything; ought one to pour the most precious salves and wines into the sea? My consolation is that everything that has been is eternal: the sea will wash it up again."[29]

This eternity is not sober, but drunken on "uncertainty," the delirium of many created worlds, and work we can be proud of.[30] It is not like Rimbaud's drunken boat, however, which does become intoxicated on pure liberty but which finally lives and dies as a boat; even as it dissolves in open water, it calls out to its lost boat identity. Nietzsche's eternity of universal Becoming is more reminiscent of a Kaufman trope, from *Being John Malkovich*: Captain Mertin's achievement of immortality by "leaping from vessel to vessel" over the centuries. And we also note that Mertin is not greedy: he brings a number of friends with him on his journey. It is part of his (socialist) ethic to want to share the physical capital represented by the Malkovich vessel (even though this physical capital is hijacked from Malkovich in a way that resembles colonial exploitation).

The film's deep-seated anti-elitism is also expressed in the real Malkovich's astonishing lack of ego in allowing himself to be so central to the film's Nabokovian humor. His performance in *Being John Malkovich* is a milestone in the growing openness and elasticity of everyday social identity. There is no such thing as an automatic human identity—all being is in flux—and this gets back to Nietzsche's quarrel with Being as such, its imposition of mental absolutes on the free flow of existence.

All absolutes must be regarded as means to an end, and therefore not as absolutes. "Supposing, however, that the ego be absolute, then its value must lie in *self-negation*."[31] It is merely superficial and reductive to say that this is because it can obviously brook nothing higher than itself, including itself. The more subtle and positive meaning might have to do with removing barriers between oneself and the world. Just when it thinks it has risen to a peak of mastery and control, the ego must shift, must become something different all over again. We might also say it tests and challenges itself, as athletes do when they train. In part, one's power—or one's freedom, as Nietzsche would say—must prove itself by finally turning against oneself.

There is selfishness in this self-negation, yet another degraded expression of the will to power; however, we must also see that sovereign self-negation also exists, in a sense, beyond power: as the ultimate fulfillment of Nietzschean Becoming. It is not the fault of energy that it can only be made visible through what Bataille called expenditure—just as it is not the fault of fossil fuels that we overuse them in the U.S. and jeopardize nature's future as well as our own. Whatever is must not remain what it is; this is stagnation and degeneracy. It is not to properly see oneself when one looks in a mirror—the height of power is merely a vantage point, and not one on the objective world per se, but on oneself, one's inner life. We can certainly understand this better if we read power as "freedom," as Nietzsche wishes. What good would it do to statically "be" free if this is not reflected in the world of dynamism: e.g., if one does not "feel" free or if one cannot "act" freely. This is why Nietzsche sees all being as illusion; true, healthy being is a verb, a motion, a process of Becoming.

For Nietzsche, Becoming is an ethic, and also an economy. What is at stake is loss of human value, the value of a person's mental, physical, social, and emotional energies. If we apply this to materialism, we see a slightly new and more holistic axis beginning to form. Dialecticism, which pits one set of human energies (wealthy or oppressing) against another (working-class or oppressed), is itself a "degenerate" devaluing of human energy as a goal worth striving for. One is left with two equally unsatisfactory options: revel in the powerlessness of workers as the (dis-)embodiment of a higher moral principle (saintliness, say, or resignation), or else attempt to do away with human energies altogether, by making everyone weak to the same degree.

Nietzsche's bone to pick with socialism is precisely this: it should be about "*making many* [free] *individuals possible*"[32]; instead, he viewed socialists as deceiving themselves about this goal, because the "individual" (in the abstract) had become an end in itself, an ideal which had to be invested with a certain prosaic "purity." Hence, the inevitable resemblance of so much political and even radical-political thought to the fixed dogmas of religion, which calcify the human potential of Becoming for the dubious status quo of a progress which is not genuinely progressive. Such progress, in socioeconomic terms, might well be material: we could redistribute wealth, for example, but without a redistribution of the energy of power/freedom (or rather, an initial *distribution,* since it is far from clear that simply having wealth or even governmental power leads to an enlightened state of free Becoming), it would be an empty gesture. It would lead to what Nietzsche calls "the rule of shopkeepers."[33] The totals would add up in the ledger books, while people remained tidy and dull, taking inventory of the same storehouse. This would not be progress at all.

Of course, dialectical materialism was never incognizant of the fact that class structure damages both sides—the rich are themselves kept stunted to the same degree that they force the poor to stay stunted. The nature of any dialectic is to show that the parts are essentially indivisible, even as parts, and that what happens to one part also happens to the other, since the larger organism (made visible through synthesis and structuralism) is the same. But merely to assert this truth was never to resolve it, and the expected synthesis of dialectical meaning was often proof that a certain blunt reductiveness could be performed even on areas of the greatest nuance. In fact, I would argue that it is precisely the lack of synthesis which Nietzsche contributes to dialectical thinking. He deliberately separates the terms of every conflict. He massages every incommensurable idea. Walter Kaufmann, Nietzsche's great interpreter, says as much: Nietzsche "considers the belief in opposite values an inveterate prejudice ... and insists on a scale of subtle shades, degrees, and nuances."[34] Nietzsche will give, on one page, an exorbitant, overheated declaration in which something is clearly being left out; the declaration begs for balance or qualification. Then, several pages later, he will throw in that counterbalancing "other term," but without direct reference and certainly without apology. The synthesis, if it is even possible to speak of one (for the idea of synthesis is largely overthrown by Nietzsche's writing—but perhaps only to make us miss it and thus set about refashioning it in a more probing way), is left for the reader to perform.

This technique reaches its expressive height, for better or worse, in *The Will to Power,* in which the constant Nietzschean motif of the truth being hard or ugly or "immoral," is taken up again. *The Will to Power* is the end point of a rigorous line of thought, and one feels throughout the book a fitful, nervy sorrow, as if the philosopher were demanding that someone challenge him and try to prove him wrong. His very assertiveness seems to demand, not followers, but antagonists. He tells his difficult truth in the utterly hopeless hope that someone will be able to forestall or reverse the destruction which that truth portends. At the very least, he hopes that his work will be only a beginning, something which others will willingly take up and extend: we see this in the utter humility of some of his book's subtitles, *Prelude to a Philosophy of the Future* (for *Beyond Good and Evil*) or *An Attempted Transvaluation of All Values* (for *The Will to Power*). Something else, something not yet existent or fully known, is required to complete the dynamic which Nietzsche sets in motion.

In fact, as history shows, Nietzsche was right: European culture was bent on an epic confrontation with its own self-destructiveness, and this occurred in the first half of the twentieth century. What Nietzsche was most correct about was that the baser elements of man would come to fruition, because it was easier for them to do so, long before nobler, higher ones could be cultivated; in particular, sociopolitical solutions would amount to an enormous casting away of freedom, a clichéd (or "all too human") pouring of lemmings over a cliff. Bataille and Heidegger were caught in the middle of this awful fruition of philosophy's vision; it was left to Sartre, after the war, to try to reassemble certain pieces of that vision, but it was obvious that classical philosophy was beyond resuscitation. It had to make an exit, not because it had a hand in the slaughter of the two world wars, but rather because it was revealed as a mad Cassandra who had seen the murderous bureaucrats coming and been unable to stop them.

It is difficult to find any philosophy today which embroiders originally and directly on humanity itself, without interposing textual references as the main context—we are struggling in this age with the fact that it has become a form of hubris, where once it was conventional, to inquire generally about humanity, e.g., mainly to try to bring philosophical perspective to the *suffering of others*. In any era where the suffering of others becomes taboo to speak of, coupled today with the inane shibboleth that emotional closure after trauma is categorically impossible, the humanities creep back to religion; as in the Dark

9. This Animal Which Is Not One

Ages, the churchmen enjoy a monopoly on being able to address Humanity as a whole entity, *as if they were once again the only literate ones;* they only want to hold Humanity back with dogmas that have not changed one bit since the Dark Ages.

The only point of certainty is, perhaps, that Nietzsche had many readers, some of them seeking prior justification for their own hate and violence, and others more attentive, more humanistic—in a word, more truly *Nietzschean,* for Nietzscheanism was the last original branch of humanist philosophy, as well as the least abstract one, directly intolerant as it was of what Spinoza called the "sad passions." Everything that came after would regard narrow sociopolitical circumstances as a founding principle, rather than something merely contingent. Everything after would be *partisan*—inhuman and doomed.

Some of Nietzsche's best readers were founding members of the Frankfurt School, which attempted an unofficial merging of Nietzsche with Marx. Negative dialectics are, to an extent, Nietzsche without exclamation points, and with the synthesis placed ahead of the dialectical terms so that it is essentially a synthesis of negation, a double negation of possible terms. Nietzsche was dealing with weakened nation-states; Adorno, by contrast, with all-powerful totalitarianisms. Totalitarianism is the perfection of the dialectic, and also its consummate undoing. In totalitarianism, as the word itself implies, all sides are forced to become one in effect if not in intention. Today we cannot pretend to Nietzsche's "innocence," if this is even the right word—but to think about Nietzsche at all is to think "like" Nietzsche, this was his seductive greatness. He was the consummation of classical, which is to say, pre-totalitarian philosophy. But it is far from certain that there has been any real philosophy *after* Nietzsche—only a series of increasingly nihilistic anti-propositions about philosophy itself.

We long for our old "types" back, flawed and inadequate as they were. Totalitarianism absorbed the degenerate and the anarchist long ago and continues to make a sock puppet out of freedom, intellectual and otherwise. What becomes clearer and clearer is that we need a return to that branch of philosophy considered by many to be most dusty and recondite: ethical philosophy. Just as we can read Nietzsche and Adorno as predominantly concerned with the ethic of being human, human value, and the conundrum of how to remain a free individual within a social collective system, so we can also read Marx's analysis of material values as essentially an ethic. *Capital* is the great modern work of ethical philosophy, precisely because it presupposes a materialist ethic, an ethical materialism, if you will; and Marx—*our* Marx, only passable as a hardcore economist, better as a social historian, and ruinous as an idealogue—emerges as the greatest modern ethical philosopher. Following from this, we can say that ethical materialism, simple yet massive, has only one real tenet: the flourishing of the human body and soul in its liberation from the tyranny of eternity and other unempirical rationalizations, and in its fulfillment of Nietzschean Becoming.

10

Dialectics at an Impasse

There can be no more damning evidence of the spectacular failure of dialectical thinking than the way that neoconservatism has been able to read the Marxist dialectic of the capitalist and the worker *against* the worker. A follower of Hayek, Robert Nozick in his book, *Anarchy, State, and Utopia,* presents a case for the "exploiters" in the Marxist dialectic of exploitation. Where Marx was a lover of workers (and we must ask again, can one genuinely "love" a generalized mass of people?), Nozick is an unapologetic lover of capitalists, or what he euphemistically calls "entrepreneurs." Marx's humanist identification was with the workers; Nozick's is with the entrepreneurs.

However, although the objects of identification are diametrically opposed, the quality of identification itself is the same. Like Marx, Nozick wants to humanize the otherwise abstract object of his affection by depicting him as a beleaguered soul who is forced to struggle—against who else but the workers, who are demanding, short-sighted, incapable of steering themselves to success without the priceless help of the entrepreneur. Where Marx "demonized" capitalist exploiters, Nozick demonizes workers as essentially too lazy and dumb to go out and accomplish what the entrepreneur does.

Nozick imagines a world in which workers control the means of production:

> The workers may lack the entrepreneurial ability to identify promising opportunities for profitable activity, and to organize firms to respond to these opportunities. In this case, the workers can try to hire entrepreneurs and managers to start a firm for them and then turn the authority functions over to the workers (who are the owners) after one year. (Though, as Kirzner emphasizes, entrepreneurial alertness would also be needed in deciding whom to hire.) Different groups of workers

would compete for entrepreneurial talent, bidding up the price of such services....[1]

A strange passion is unfolding in those above sentences of Nozick's. It seems on the surface to be all distance and controlled logic, every human figure an abstract group (except for "Kirzner"); people as such are defined more as "functions" or "services" than as anything tangibly human. But this zone of mechanical functionality is already the zone of Nozick's passion, which betrays itself in these descriptive words: "entrepreneurial ability," "profitable activity," "respond," "alertness," "compete," "entrepreneurial talent," "bidding up the price." These words attempt to charm, giving an idealized, flattering view of the entrepreneur as someone of superior skills and reflexes. The masses trudge through a sleepwalking existence, but the entrepreneur is awake and ready; the masses merely labor in a way that does not even seem particularly active, but the entrepreneur is constantly in the midst of a fray, competing, responding, bidding up.

Where there are slaves there must be masters, in the eyes of power anyway, and in the eyes of dialecticians. If we are struck by the fact that Nozick cannot envision a world in which there are no entrepreneurs, cannot even compose a sentence in the above passage that does not contain the word in one form or another, then we must allow that dialectical materialism *cannot do this either*. There is no way of avoiding laborious strain and cut-throat competition in any dialectical model, whether it is left-communist (Marx) or neoconservative (Nozick). Both models preserve the vision of sides in tension, of winners versus losers, of profits versus losses. This vision is extremely one-sided in the case of both models: either the workers must win *because they deserve to,* or the capitalists must win *because they deserve to.* Each side (no surprise here) is prepared to say that it struggles more, works harder, contributes more, is fundamentally more vital to the system as a whole; and each side is willing to use an essentially dialectical mode of thought to assert this.

What would we see if we stepped off the wildly seesawing dialectic? First, the goal of a truly meaningful communism might be to create a world in which there was no competition for profits, in which the energy of labor produced only the equal energy required for sustaining,

10. Dialectics at an Impasse

and thus was conserved. No surplus, no sacrifice. This might be communism, but it would not be dialectical materialism, since exploitation or subsumption would suddenly be out of the picture. Put otherwise, the power that is currently invested in maintaining dialectical tension and opposition could be reinvested into the individuals themselves, who would be free to be neither exploiters nor exploited. Marxist materialism would be freed from its bad influence of Hegelianism, and thus would not leave communist solutions open to the charge that they have simply misread the dialectic from the biased perspective of the workers; Marxism would take on a larger, irrefutable dimension, by which it would trump capitalism by no longer being conjoined with it, as it were, in the sense of two mirrors presenting reversed images.

But beyond this general unwillingness to imagine a world that was not somehow invested in the struggle of opposed sides, there is, again, a kind of fevered love for the auction block and the skirmishes surrounding it, for this individual, the entrepreneur, with his hidden desire flashing, his pleasure in economic combat. Nozick gets headier still:

> It's risky starting a new firm. One can't identify easily new entrepreneurial talent, and much depends on estimates of future demand and of availability of resources, on unforeseen obstacles, on chance, and so forth…. Often people who do not wish to bear risks feel entitled to rewards from those who do and win; yet these same people do not feel obligated to help out by sharing the losses of those who bear risks and lose. For example, croupiers at gambling casinos expect to be well-tipped by big winners, but they do not expect to be asked to help bear some of the losses of the losers.[2]

The wish to be with the "big winners," inside the simmering atmosphere of a casino—this is vaguely James Bond stuff. It has a certain aura, the high roller, the international man of mystery, the one who tosses a chip to the smiling croupier in a gesture of magnanimous authority which the croupier, though he may have helped the player to win, can never quite achieve. We are led to believe that the menial worker is born to work, the winner born to win.

This is a dumbing-down of Nietzsche's and Bataille's statements about kings and lords possessing a true generosity, which plebs depended on and which became the substance of a kind of cross-economic "love." However, this misses the larger point made by both Nietzsche and Bataille in their depiction of feudal models, which is that the aristocrats did not resent the plebs, who were designated precisely as the most deserving beneficiaries of largesse—for whom else would the noble generosity of the aristocrats seek out and give to? There was sovereignty in the acceptance of gifts as well as the giving of them; it wasn't a bitter token tossed to a sweating lackey who stands while you sit, who must bow and scrape, who must be ingratiating.

Nozick overturns the chess board, as it were, when he nastily brings up the supposed unfairness of having to tip the croupier after you have won big, even though you have no expectation of the croupier reaching into his own pocket to reimburse you after you have lost. This is an early knell sounding for the death of any kind of simple, strictly Marxist reading of class dialectic. The assumption is that the high roller is really just a worker too: he may wear fancy clothes, he comes and goes with large amounts of cash or credit, but in the end he sees himself as a hard worker trying to get ahead, trying to score something for himself—a bone, a bonus. He is an equal agent in the casino, looking for a payday. He views all of society in this way, as a kind of playground where, if he applies himself, he will snatch rewards out from under other men's noses. No matter how much he attains and owns, wealth will always be someone else's to wrest away. The game is under suspicion precisely because it is run by someone else, someone employed by "the house." This, too, is the struggle of dialectical materialism, devoid of any ethical content and with a sense of bitter pleasure in the idea of constant warfare. It is like going to a restaurant and automatically treating the waiter and the chef as one's enemies; it is destructive of the social contract, a refusal to honor the human potential of others.

Indeed, Nozick's rather stagy metaphor of the casino tip becomes full-blown in the 2008 banking failure. There, the banks were like those high rollers, riding the crest of a streak until, suddenly, bust, and the rollers were down by amounts plunging faster and faster. The risk-takers shirked any responsibility—it was the fault of the investors who expected a profit, it was the fault of the money for being in the wrong

10. Dialectics at an Impasse

place at the wrong time. There is some lingering sense of Calvinist judgment against profligacy or laziness in this biased and inflammatory conception that the people who hold the daily-grind jobs are consumed by selfish opportunism, always trying to get something for nothing. It is a strange denial of the actual circumstance, which is that the ones who work (for an hourly wage and tips) are generally more patient, more selfless, more industrious that the "high roller" who hopes to strike it big all at one go, at an activity that is more like fun or adventure than labor. Always we return to the deeply ingrained U.S. Calvinism, which seems to say that the worker who lives from paycheck to paycheck is guilty and inferior, or else God would have lifted his economic burdens. Whereas the rich man has been blessed by God, and thus has a kind of mandate to do anything.

Whom, besides the rich man himself, would support such a claim? Only a person who *loves* the rich man would be so submissive to his sense of entitlement. Again, we think of Nozick's defense of the entrepreneur as if he were some kind of god on Earth, and we realize that this kind of neoconservative economic thought stems from passionate love for entrepreneurs, just as Marxism stems from passionate love for the workers. On each side there is the sense that burdens are unequal, that some matter of extreme pride is being questioned. It is difficult, needless to say, to combat such love where it exists. The attempt to fight against it is often seen as a highly personal affront, an infringement on emotional rights. This is why the U.S. has become so dysfunctional, its infrastructure in disarray, its public schools abandoned, its prison industry booming, its culture now nothing except news talk shows which belabor the crimes of individuals while remaining silent about the systemic crimes of the people at the top as they reap the benefits. Conservatives like to say that we should simply let business regulate itself and it will grow; that we should encourage every working-class and impoverished person to become an entrepreneur, and if people work hard they will succeed. The problem with this is that business success has never been a simple function of hard work; it is the wealthiest enterprises—the investment banks and hedge fund managers, big pharmaceuticals, big oil—who understand this and long ago stopped competing on level playing fields, instead marshaling all of their lobbying power to get laws passed (and even wars started) in their favor. For "grassroots" politicians to try to hoodwink small businesspeople into thinking that they, too, can have a stake in these grandiose machinations is a deliberate distortion of the truth. The independent, small entrepreneur, whose business, if it does not succumb to the odds and fail completely within the first year or two, will likely take a good ten years of investment and growth to see any profits, is being held up as the nominal object of pro-business political agendas that will, if anything, make life that much harder for middle-class businesses, since, by favoring the multi-national conglomerates, these agendas cause prices and taxes to go up. Capitalism, its defenders claim, encourages ingenuity and creativity, but this is simply not true: we are not in expansion but contraction mode, all successful companies are leveraged and bought out by consolidated financial interests who find it easier to acquire the ingenuity of others and then run it into the ground. Money is made only from money today. All of capitalist existence is now a cynical casino, as we imagine it was, perhaps, in Europe prior to the two world wars; a place where life and death are cheap, won and lost on a toss of the dice.

But in any successfully functional system, there are not sides in competition as much as interdependent Nietzschean "units"; this is what dialecticism, with its ability to justify any configuration of oppression through the synthesis of necessarily opposing forces, tricks us into forgetting. The logic of dialectic, too, cannot be ameliorated even when one side does win. All syntheses are only temporary. The movement of history waits to recontextualize everything. Pure dialecticism has something in common with Nietzsche's valorization of Becoming over the moribund impossibility of merely being. But at the point where dogmatic philosophy demands some final reckoning of the dialectic—in Marxist revolution, say, or in deregulated laissez-faire capitalism, both of which attempt to safeguard the position of their respective sides—there is, again, a forgetfulness about the fact that as long as the dialectic remains defined by its sides, so backlashes will inevitably occur. So, when entrepreneurs are riding high, it is not long before their dealings bring enough economic misery that the tide of popular opinion turns in favor of business regulations. And likewise, when work is plentiful and incomes rise, it is not long before the wealthy class begins to get corrupt designs on the subsequent socioeconomic surplus, and workers begin to be depicted as "ungrateful."

The solution would be, of course, to equalize relations between the high roller and the croupier. Note that there is no ordinary chumminess or cooperation in Nozick's casino: the big winners do not tip heavily because they are happy or appreciative; they sourly pay out after getting dully tapped. It is like what Bataille called capitalism's "deliriously formed ritual poker": "But the players can never retire from the game, their fortunes made; they remain at the mercy of provocation. At no time does a fortune serve to *shelter its owner from need*."[3] This, too, is part of the individualistic love, charisma and adrenalin, for it is the playing of the game that really matters here. We all remain at the mercy of provocation, that economic imp of the perverse. One must keep testing one's blessing of luck in case it was not genuine, because our spectral Calvinism places so much at stake. No single win can defeat the endless need to win, or the endless terror of ending up one of the "losers," one of those whom God has predestined for an eternity in hell.

A review in *Harper's,* blurbed on the back of the first paperback edition of *Anarchy, State, and Utopia,* says: "No contemporary philosopher possesses a more imaginative mind, broader interests, or greater dialectical abilities than Robert Nozick." At that time, 1974, Nozick was a Harvard professor of philosophy. The reviewer was not far wrong: we may not like what Nozick's mind imagined, but it is a valid and in some ways strikingly original use of dialectical thought. If we dismiss him out of hand as heartless, for example, we miss the point: dialectical thought *is* heartless. If we on the left would seek a philosophical basis for our compassion toward the working class, we would be better off looking for it elsewhere than in the Hegelian dialectic or even its Marxist-materialist revision. More to the point, we cannot return to dialectical materialism and continue to use it for our own purposes without acknowledging that it can, in effect, be wholly absorbed by the opposite purposes.

Thus, we see that Nozick's imaginary casino is still going strong in the U.S.; the risk takers have figured out that if they gamble with other people's money exclusively, or with things that only appear to be actual money (derivatives, junk bonds, toxic assets), they can have the thrill of playing forever and ever and effectively never lose. The "croupier" (the private citizen) now does pay them back for their losses in the form of bailouts with taxpayer money as well as the raiding of employee 401K funds. The charisma of risk is a hollow illusion, yet it cannot be dispelled, again because it carries the connotation of superstitious predestination and the musk of blind, all-forgiving love. "Why do some feel they may stand back to see whose ventures turn out well," Nozick asks, "and then claim a share of the success…?"[4] The selfish little people in the shadows, sniffing around, ready to rain on the parade, ready to take credit for the high roller's insatiable "luck": this is dialectical materialism *from the other side.*

Adorno offers this childhood memory in *Minima Moralia,* a kind of first exposure to and loss of innocence about class warfare: "In early childhood I saw the first snow-shovellers in thin shabby clothes. Asking about them, I was told they were men without work who were given this job so that they could earn their bread. Then they get what they deserve, having to shovel snow, I cried out in rage, bursting uncontrollably into tears."[5] Adorno tells this anecdote without embroidering upon it, but we can see two striking insights here. First, there is the helpless, hysterical rage against the brutality of an ordering system which treats its neediest members the most harshly: this rage, boundless and bitter, can find no immediate object beyond the needy workers themselves, since the system as such is concealed behind a kind of folkloric "that's-how-it-is" wisdom about life. It is less awful, in some way, to single out individuals for abuse than to condemn an entire system for being wrong. The system itself teaches us how to do this, by example. The men "were given this job," somewhat like Cain received his marked brow. The extreme embodiment of need is already a judgment which rationalizes harsh treatment and isolation in a vicious circle.

Second, Adorno's response of demonizing the workers is attributed to "early childhood." Put otherwise, it is itself an expression of

10. Dialectics at an Impasse

human immaturity, a tendency to quick impulsive judgments, lashing out, and so on. Experience has not yet offered an alternative, thought-through way of processing these emotions of injustice, rage and guilt. Likewise, Adorno implies that, just as individuals experience a sort of childhood whose length can be indefinitely attenuated depending on circumstances, social orders can and do experience something similar, a kind of nursery nap, as it were. Humanism was a premature attempt to wake the Western child from its slumber; it failed because the child, while already centuries old, was still not ripened to the point where it could appreciate life without the need for one cause or side to always be pitted against another; for life to exist without a rooting interest, so to speak. Dialecticism, too, belongs to the intellectual childhood of mankind.

If there are sides, and if we can only love one of these sides, then we simply choose between them. The gridwork has been laid down for us, the arguments are all in place; they all emerge from the same dialectic, which no one, least of all the neocons, deny exists. Yes, there are all-powerful capitalist masters—exploiters and cunning, resourceful entrepreneurs—and yes, there are unfortunate, downtrodden people who work long hours at hard, menial labor, those sheep, those hordes who would be lost without someone telling them what to do. Schizophrenically, we all keep both interpretations of the same dialectic constantly in our heads at the same time; we have no choice. Once a thought has pranced out on the stage of provability (abstract or otherwise), we have no choice but to accept it into the family of the dialectic, so to speak.

It is a family without love, however, love being, as Adorno defines it, "the power to see similarity in the dissimilar,"[6] i.e., to void the whole idea of sides in the first place. The roof could be caving in; the family of the dialectic would fight in the dust of the rubble over who should be holding up the beams. Our impasse can be summarized in the extreme way that both the Marxist and the neocon identifies his or her enemy as some version or aspect of the State: the corporate state for the Marxist, the welfare state for the neocon. It is, in fact, the last fragile proof that the U.S. is still in some form a democracy that the State (which is really the people) can appear as so nefarious to both left and right. The people remain a kind of reality principle that is needed to certify ideology; hence, the current unprecedented mania for conducting nonstop polls. Ideologies suckle at ever-renewed (albeit skewed) realities like crones. But real reality eludes their definitions.

Let us look at this shared ideological enemy, the State—a state which both left-wing and right-wing ideologies, needless to say, want to control. Never before, and certainly in no pre-revolutionary nation, has there ever been such messy amorphousness in how to regard the interests of the State. For the Marxists, the State is corporate, owned by a privileged oligarchy whose financial interests it directly serves. For the neocons, the State is the welfare state of tax money being used for infrastructure and for people who cannot otherwise make a living. To say that the latter is a perverse and cynical misreading, and dismiss it out of hand, is only to prove that one does not accept or grasp dialectical thinking. For the neoconservative subsumption of the Marxist dialectic, albeit turned upside down, with the capitalist as hero and the masses as villains, is itself a valid dialectical stroke, a total and inevitable fulfillment of the terms of Hegelianism.

I have tried to show in this book that the central flaw of Marxism was its committed indebtedness to the Hegelian dialectic, which is an obstacle to real sociopolitical change rather than a synecdoche of that change or a means of applying it. Once there are sides in opposition, then either side can be championed, even in the face of common sense or moral reason. For the workers are beleaguered more often than the capitalists are noble; the capitalists are crooked more often than the workers are. Moreover, and most importantly, the rich are better safeguarded than the poor in every aspect of life. But these postulates, though we might be able to prove them rather easily from an empirical standpoint, get us nowhere, since we uphold hegemony in the very terms of opposition. As long as the dialectical thread still squeezes through the eye of the needle, the camel can come along too.

Likewise, dialecticism is not in itself the motor of revolution. In many ways, it is what must be *overcome* for revolutions to transpire.

10. Dialectics at an Impasse

Slaves who revolt are no longer slaves, they have already become something else, something which places them within striking distance of the masters. The pessimism of Marxist orthodoxy, especially as it is practiced in academe, is a great friend to corporatism because it preserves the propaganda that there always must be masters. For power preserves itself precisely through the dialectic that would theoretically seek to undo or reverse it.

In spite of its aspect of two sides held in tension, the dialectic is a model of thought as a fixed state of being. It is even an unusually anal and restrictive model: the ways are all blocked. The fact that the sides connect while remaining sides is a Hegelian riddle on the order of eternity itself; it stymies progress. It is like the boarding school in Poe's "William Wilson" where the wings and rooms are always shifting; it is like the white afterlife room in Kaufman's *Human Nature*, where the exit takes you right back in again. Hegel was a friend to power; he set up his system so that power would always necessarily win because power and winning were synonymous, thus it did not matter what provisional side was temporarily on top.

How much more interesting and vital Marxism would have been if Marx had jettisoned Hegel and joined forces with Nietzsche. For there is a way of reading Nietzsche almost through Marx (I have tried to perform it to some extent in this book) in which power becomes freedom, in which sovereignty becomes universal, and in which humanity as a whole evolves beyond the roles that have been carved out for it and which remain preserved, specimen-like, in dialectical thought. Both Nietzsche and Marx loved value or values, after all, and saw little evidence of these in social life: for Marx, a world where the physical capital of real people was stolen and used up for a pittance; for Nietzsche, a world in which the majority of people consented to think like slaves and thus became them.

What Nietzsche would teach to the reader is not something specifically geared toward one's a priori socioeconomic place. His sense of liberation is total and spiritual. Politics and economics are the means to an end, like anything. The way to end master-slave dynamics is to encourage everyone to evolve into what the master would ideally like to be, and what he may be only in the artificial and claustrophobic corridors of his constructed power: an epitome of nobility, and a superhuman force. But in achieving the goal of Becoming on such exalted terms, a "true master" need finally master nothing, for he or she would be all mastery, fulfilled by the unprecedented oneness of a universal, post-dialectical existence.

(In)conclusion: On the Evanescent

We have seen this before in Adorno's thought: responsiveness to the "evanescent," which is (in political terms) decentralized, anarchic, anti-systemic. It favors the tossing out of aphorisms over the building of overarching, hierarchical systems. There is humility in the intuition that, even in our well-entrenched traditional positions, the evanescent has something all-important to teach us: how to break free from the *expectations* of the past.

A parable is told in Godard's *Hélas pour moi* (*Oh, Woe Is Me*, 1993):

"When my great-grandfather had a difficult task to accomplish, he went to a certain place in the forest, lit a fire, and immersed himself in silent prayer. And what he had to do was done.

"When my grandfather was confronted with the same task, he went to the same place and said: 'We no longer know how to light the fire, but we still know the prayer.' And what he had to do was done.

"Later, my father, too, went to the forest and said: 'We no longer know how to light the fire. We no longer know the mysteries of prayer. But we still know the exact place in the forest where it occurred. And that should suffice.' And it did suffice.

"But when I was faced with the same task, I stayed at home and I said: 'We no longer know how to light the fire. We no longer know the prayers. We don't even know the place in the forest. But we still know how to tell the story.'"

Stories: the ectoplasm from forgotten spirit entities. The touchability of the void. Interruptive communications. Intercessional rather than direct. And the maps that trace forests which no longer exist.

But then again, this parable might not trace a divestment or diminution, but instead—an *evolution?* Toward more and more *independent* forms...

We need to address the predominant psychosocial meaning of *consolation*. Or rather, its psycho-natural meaning, since consolation transcends social structures to express the ways in which the individual derives from, conforms to, and in many ways understands himself or herself as part of the natural world. The body is nearly all that is left of this powerful connection between humanity and nature, which once inflected all of our decisions great and small. Sensitivity to weather and seasonal cycles, now considered a form of depressive neurosis, may be a lingering vestige of that all-consuming relation between nature and humanity. Indeed, most of our links to nature are effaced and weak today; our bad faith forbids us to either completely enjoy or completely disown this nature that we have so profoundly misunderstood. And we are also victims of nature: we are more certain today, in our man-made worlds, of what nature takes from us rather than what it still surrenders. Yet nothing else has been vast and preeminent enough to replace the loss of nature: thus, everything in our human world, everything attainable, is merely a kind of regretful, compromised, second-best consolation, no matter how necessary or fondly held. It is painful to acknowledge this, especially since it is not certain how we could ever finally establish a genuine bond with nature, when all our attempts to do this have been misguided and when, moreover, everything in the realm of the psychosocial mitigates against it. The strategy for accomplishing this would in itself be the solution, because it would have to come in the form of entirely new ideas which would immediately strike everyone who hears them with a sense of rightness. We do not yet know what those ideas would be, or we are not prepared to hear them. However, I believe this is where we need to begin in order to bring the human state to a point where it can start to train itself toward those unprecedented higher instincts now hidden from us by the fact that all we have for our existence is a program of pre-formulated responses to a set of incommensurable experiences.

What Nietzsche did for the study of human ethics was to once and for all free it from any need to reference morality. Moralities are narrow and time-bound; they come with agendas. Higher ethical humanity should have no need for them, because when it is discovered, the ethical instinct will transcend all of the merely social attempts to define what should and should not be. Marx tried to do the same for the study of economics, i.e., freeing it from the cyclical push and pull of politics. The ideal Marxist economic system would have no politics; it would not require politics to achieve its aims or to ensure fairness, indeed politics would only hamper it. If we say that the higher human instinct which is summoned by Nietzsche and Marx still remains unformed, then we can also say that those men's enemies, morality and politics, still remain the greatest barrier to what we would like to achieve in helping that higher human instinct to form, in the name of what I am calling "ethical-materialist philosophy."

Pericles and Plato were right: in the ideal, perfected world, there shall be no poets. They will simply disappear, along with all other dress rehearsals for the state of highest human nobility. It is not even that art will have nothing left to say (for we know that art often exists with nothing to say) but rather, no one will need to hear it anymore. Without ears, there is no speech.

Art is different from stories. What the highest human nobility and instinct will finally transcend is the image. Formerly, only gods were permitted to accomplish this transcendence. (All images are eternity in negative.)

It is likely that, when it comes to redeeming the past, images can only redeem the *guilty images* of the past, and then only by subsuming or quoting (repeating) the same images of the past into a perpetuity which would perhaps otherwise mercifully forget them.

(In)conclusion

The highest human task has always been to overcome any and all restrictions. This is not even primarily a physical overcoming, which takes place at the level of basic survival and subsistence, and which either occurs or fails to occur; it is only the foundation for an overcoming which is more difficult and intangible, a mental, psychical, spiritual overcoming whose goals and satisfactions wait to be discovered within the overcoming process itself. And whether or not an individual sees this as a single, finite movement in which something singular and worldly is overcome during the course of an entire lifetime, or whether he or she sees this as an "infinite" process of constantly overcoming and then overcoming the overcoming, so to speak, probably has to do with the individual's largeness of spirit, as Nietzsche suggested. We might also say that this largeness of spirit is partly a measure of one's immunity from suffering, or one's prior overcoming of that suffering, which is a completely different process that need only be accomplished once, if it can be accomplished at all. Then, with one's suffering defeated, one can proceed from each overcoming to the next, as if they were rocks in a stream whose danger has been "paved over."

However, it may be wrong to think of the overcoming of overcoming as a truly infinite, never-finished process, in the sense that one can never imagine actually attaining a final state of being. This is because the final state must be something unimaginable—that has never come before, that has never made itself visible before, that has never been uttered—something brought up from total darkness. We can never name the form that formlessness will take. Yet, like the sculpture receiving its finishing touches from the sculptor, the brushing away of the last traces of dust, it can happen that there will be nothing more left to do to perfect the form, and the only further change to occur will be when the statue's matter is destroyed, however and whenever this might occur.

Marx's Europe was one predominated by inherited wealth. It was a society without mobility, but it had always been that way. In the eco-

On the Evanescent

nomic development of the U.S., it could be said that this state of immobility was somewhat disrupted. Old World money gravitated toward the northeastern establishment, whose centers were New York and Boston, and thus inherited wealth staked most of the financial claims and reaped most of the financial rewards from the new resources of the U.S. However, there were also people who truly had come from nothing, who managed to get their foot in the door by farming or mining available land which often became theirs by default possession.

This was a messy business even where it seemed to fulfill the capitalist ideal of hard work rewarded. Criminality flourished hand in hand with the westward expansion that swept the northeast corporate interests to even greater consolidation of wealth and power, numerous independent self-starting businessmen to new wealth and power, and many, many others to complete destruction. Claims were jumped; the kind of wholesale slaughter visited upon Native Americans and immigrant populations could also be directed against business rivals of the same European descent. What was put in place was a superstructural form of panic and mistrust that has remained the strongest legacy of the unfettered frenzy which capitalism reached in its first gigantic playground, the American hemispheric expansion.

Unchecked, capitalism did not want rules or cooperation. By the 1920s most businesses were in the hands of a few: the monopolies and trusts. It was bad business to let anyone win at this game; mobility could be touted through a few examples, but the odds had to remain, so to speak, with the house. The same structure of inherited wealth was quickly put in place, and now in the U.S. we see that the main feature of our current crisis is the impacted mobility of our society. Once again, as it had been in Marx's Europe, the main form of wealth is inherited; the main guarantee of gaining wealth is its prior possession.

These are end games, and once they have been reached the game is technically over. That it never should have been a game, that it never should have yielded itself wholly to the cruel combat of winners and losers, is, of course, the point that cannot be lost. For capitalism is still going out in search of new wild-west frontiers, new unfettered play-

(In)conclusion

grounds. We have re-imperialized the process of making money, as Marx saw in the imperial Europe of his day.

Without dynamic mobility, capitalism is a lie. It remains congealed within the dialectic of oppressor and oppressed, capitalist and worker, ruling elite and impoverished masses. Class structure is deeply ingrained: it is probably a kind of human instinct. In animal packs and in primitive tribes, there are pecking orders based on dominance and aggression; this ancient sweat, this primordial stink in the nostrils, this pounding heart, can be found in mutated form in the capitalist logic of the markets, of insider trading, of derivatives. There is the hunt for a secret advantage to be pressed, a way to make the rules themselves friendlier toward conquest. The conquered are not people; they are numbers, sums, calculations. Put them in the shredder at the end of the day. Scan the map for hot pockets where the rules have not been written yet; where states of emergency and war preclude any rules at all. Take.

Is there a possible human instinct, whether innate or to be learned, that could override the deeper, panicked one that endlessly sniffs after the hunt, the prey, the leader born to dominate and the follower born to serve? This is what we need to cultivate. The final dialectical synthesis will be a dissolving of dialectical sides in a fluid, spontaneous atmosphere in which there are no longer sides; in which no one will be oppressed because no one will be oppressive.

It is natural that a collective social order founded on the idea of personal and individual freedom, however spurious and hypocritical this always was in practice, should reach a point where different, partisan conceptions of freedom become mutually exclusive. There is the freedom of people who wish to have easy access to guns; there is the converse freedom of people who would feel safer in a society where guns are controlled. There is the freedom of developers to pollute the environment in the name of profits; there is the converse freedom of those who do not wish to live with impure, carcinogenic water and food. There is the freedom of corporations to outsource manufacturing and customer service jobs to developing nations where they can save money; there is the converse freedom of U.S. workers who want to join the middle class. These freedoms are incompatible; in fact, they are directly assaultive of each other. They are like the unborn twins in the Nirvana song, "Drain You," in which the stronger of the two kills off his weaker sibling. This attack mode is not properly understood; it runs counter to so many generations of classic American optimism and pluck. But those who do not understand the nature of the preemptive attack are ill-equipped to deal with capitalism as it is practiced today in the U.S. We can say, looking at the above examples, that there are active and passive freedoms: these are the terms of the impasse, if not one of its prerequisites. The owning of guns, the polluting of the environment, and the outsourcing are examples of active freedoms; their converse in every case is a passive or idealized freedom. We would like to feel safe; we would like to receive clean drinking water; we would like to have career opportunities. It is always unfathomable that these things would be denied us, but that is the nature of the active freedoms' preemptive attack mode.

Things have reversed since the '60s, say, when the left stood for active rather than passive freedoms. Integration was active change, while Jim Crow and segregation were passive defaults; ending the Vietnam War was active change, while continuing it was a passive default; civil rights for women and African Americans was again an active change, while the white patriarchal hegemony was, again, a passive default. The karma of history is that whoever is passive (and defeated) in one era will return ascendant and active in the next, and vice versa. Why is this? *Because nothing succeeds like failure.* "The deepest human impulse is to wage war against the truth"[1]—but this is also the deepest impulse of the dialectic, which cannot distinguish between opposing viewpoints except to the extent that one gains precedence over the other. The intellectual honesty of the dialectic, of course, is that this precedence is only temporary at best, although this honesty does us little good in the material world, which remains the prize (and subject to massive amounts of dishonesty). There is no side, left or right, that cannot be justified either on its own terms or on the terms that it manages to impose upon the paradigmatic relation between itself and the other side. Thus, rationalizations and justifications trade off, my free-

(In)conclusion

dom is not your freedom, indeed it curtails and eradicates your freedom, but that does not mean that it ceases to be a kind of freedom: my own. This is only to say that I am automatically a target in all the places where I have become temporarily strong. *Because nothing fails like success.*

There was only one Achilles, and only one Achilles' heel. But for the multitude of Lilliputians with their tiny slings and arrows, the principle has become second nature and intrinsic to their survival.

Christian conceptions of heaven have always been vaguer than Christian conceptions of hell; the latter usually consist of vivid exaggeration of the worst pains that we know of as humans such as being burned alive, being whipped and flayed, profound regret and humiliation, and wishing for a death that does not come. It is never considered that our souls might require a different kind of torment from our bodies or even our inner spirits as we have known them; indeed, the pains of hell presuppose that we will still be bodies, with nerve endings, dermises, and a sense of space and time. Whereas heaven is prepared to exalt pure soul, and we essentially have no idea at all what this would consist of. Music—again, an entirely earthly experience of transport which presupposes, moreover, that our souls have some kind of ears— is generally the one constant trope in Christian depictions of heaven. The one thing that defines heaven is the absence of having to become, of having to sweat to impress the right people and climb a ladder of success; the hard-working, thrifty Calvinist mind could readily conjure up punishments for its repressed inner slacker, but when it came to heaven, it gave itself an unheard-of gift: a space where inaction could not only be imagined but countenanced. As the Talking Heads sang, heaven is a place where nothing happens—actually, the only place in the Western imaginary where such stasis is allowed. Yet it seems too good to be true, since we know how easily heavenly circumstances can change into hellish ones. Families, marriages, workplaces, schools— all can have promising beginnings and still grow odious with time.

Why was *this* element of earthly reality wishfully suppressed from the designs of the afterworld when first-degree burns or music were not? Eternity is such a long time to have to be pleasant and (in spite of everything) ingratiating, in order to prove that one truly does belong there. Isn't it natural to imagine that there is a lake of fire up there, too, in case the angels change their minds about us?

 This crippled, self-imprisoning world of humanity is a parable. Parables, even postmodern, deconstructionist ones, always attempt to grope their way back toward an ancient certainty, a substratum of truth beyond or before truth, which is to say a non-relative truth. Non-relative truth still exists, in a categorical and empirical sense, even if it has been erased linguistically by the philosophy of our time in ways even more devious and all-consuming than the sophists ever dreamed of. The sophists were finally like fussy headwaiters, rushing around, trying to convince a ritzy couple to be seated next to the rest rooms, trying to explain why they were out of one fish but could substitute another and you'd never know the difference. They dazzled with flashy cufflinks and an ersatz appearance of orderliness, tidiness (it all makes sense—it is so), which projects forward like a deep bow from the waist to the Second Empire or the Victorians.

 Today's sophists, by contrast, are barbaric and blunt, still with the same need to preclude others' convictions and inspirations, but without the same skill at finessing each conversational opportunity as it arises and arguing in that way which seems so often like barbed agreement—the hook of agreement that sticks in the throat of the flattered one. Now, there is no way not to be a sophist whenever we take up and use the instruments of philosophical culture. Of course there is no reality, only language, the better to render what we say both invalid and megalomaniacal; of course there is no ongoing history, only narrative(s), the better to doom what to do to inconsequentiality; of course there is no identity, only socially conditioned responses and functioning, the better to suppress whatever love or hate would have kept our ancestors going through their lean hard times. To fight against these points from even the simplest-seeming logical position is only to prove how deeply ingrained and hystericizing is this lack of reality and selfhood. It is what marshals one to defend reality and selfhood to the very death, as if something were actually at stake.

Something *is* at stake. Even the post-human has not found a way to vanquish the meanings of life and death, those meanings which art and philosophy (whether overtly didactic or not) still long for and tend toward. There is, after all, a kind of moral at the end of every story, even if the story is not quite a story, and even if the moral is not moral. The trope of mutation is a way of understanding this. Unless one can change the world (in art, the linear-narrative ethos perhaps; in life, political and socioeconomic structures) one must change oneself, in order to endure, and then one must live with the results of that change. Rilke's ancient torso of Apollo has never been more relevant, for the vanished and vanishing past cries out to us now from everything around us; we have never needed more strongly the urge to measure up to the greatness of the past, helpful even where it seemed to obstruct us, uncondescending even where it seemed to talk down to us, sovereign even where it seemed (most) oppressive. We have done much to expose the limits of the past; it was narrow, true, but it was rigorous. That rigor was not an endless supply or, as it turns out, a natural flowering of human evolution: it was something that had been worked toward, proudly, joyously, the opposite of the work of alienated labor. From Rimbaud and Nietzsche to the Velvet Underground, say, this was the crowning glory of humanism in recent history. We need the ethic of its undiluted rigor (which also includes ecstatic abandon, freedom) more than ever.

It is another way of saying that we still allow the brutal conquerors of history too much power in how we conceive of past eras. In the interest of "never forgetting," we view the twentieth century as the property of its worst criminals—Hitler, for instance. We punish the free humanity that could give rise to such a monster; and in the slow, grinding infliction of punishment, we become monsters. We must find a way to truly accept and process the lessons of the past, and then live *as if it never happened.* Or at least as if we were certain of it never happening again. In this cavalier-sounding proposal, we may yet find our way out of the maze of eternal return. Because, as we know, Hitler was neither the first nor the last of his kind. Even now, one is growing, looking at the shy freedoms of his brothers with resentment and envy, preparing to unleash his version of freedom: the crushing of others. What must be rooted out is this base destructive impulse, which falls far short of human potential; which feeds on wasted, stolen lives.

The higher human instinct, when it comes, will belong to an ethic that remains to be cultivated.

Chapter Notes

Preface

1. Mike Sprague, "Ex-Bumble Bee employee says major error must have caused fatal accident," *Los Angeles Daily News* online, accessed 15 October 2012, www.dailynews.com.

2. Julhas Alam, "Bangladesh Factory Fire Leads to Protests As Workers Demand to Return to Work or Get Paid," www.huffingtonpost.com, accessed 30 November 2012.

3. The Marxist theologian Bo Eberle was helpful to me as a sounding board in the early conception of some of the ideas in this book. I thank him for allowing me to babble at him on Twitter while I was gathering my head of steam.

Introduction

1. Fredric Jameson, *Marxism and Form* (Princeton: Princeton University Press, 1974), 235.

2. Friedrich Nietzsche, *The Will to Power: An Attempted Transvaluation of All Values, Volume II*, trans. Anthony M. Ludovici (London: George Allen & Unwin, 1924), 213.

3. Rainer Werner Fassbinder, *The Anarchy of the Imagination: Interviews, Essays, Notes*, trans. Krishna Winston, ed. Michael Töteberg and Leo A. Lensing (Baltimore: Johns Hopkins University Press, 1992), 135.

4. Ibid.

5. Quoted in Jeffrey T. Nealon, *Alterity Politics: Ethics and Performative Subjectivity* (Durham: Duke University Press, 1998), 171.

6. Arthur Rimbaud, *Oeuvres Complètes* (Paris: Librairie Gallimard, 1954), 184–185 [my translation].

7. Jorge Luis Borges, *Selected Non-Fictions*, ed. Eliot Weinberger (New York: Penguin, 1999), 126.

8. Hannah Arendt, "History and Immortality," *Partisan Review* 1 (Winter 1957), 35 [my italics].

9. Nietzsche, *The Will to Power, Volume II*, 184.

10. Ibid., 184–85.

11. Ibid., 190.

12. Friedrich Nietzsche, *Beyond Good and Evil*, trans. Walter Kaufmann (New York: Vintage, 1966), 222.

13. Representation, or the image, is not a slight or an incidental concern, however. As the body was being transformed into physical capital through industrial labor, it was also being commodified as representation by new and advancing, mid- to late-nineteenth-century technologies, such as photography and cinema, which had begun to capture physical likeness directly from the body. Modern capitalism could not have arisen in its present form without this confluence of reifications: the body as physical capital and the body as image capital. We can imagine a certain tipping point, although this exact point is far from clear in terms of when and how it came about, at which these two reifications began to merge into a single

Notes—Chapter 1

negation of the body as *anything except capital*. The human itself, in its essence as well as its surface appearance, became a matter of "marketing" in a way that I believe to be distinctly different from any other epoch, if only because this capital had less and less claim to imperishability. The ancient pharaoh's immense statues and ornate sarcophagi honored both the labor of creation/production and the image that was meant to be eternalized; the Bourbon kings or Napoleon still belonged to an age in which the image possessed a certain awe: one could view a painting of a Great Man without feeling as though it was a trivialization, and without feeling as though one knew or possessed that man. Roland Barthes' resonant revelation about the daguerreotype of "Napoleon's youngest brother, Jerome, taken in 1852 ... *I am looking at eyes that looked at the eyes of the Emperor*" (3, my italics) is essentially about this devaluation of image capital. The eyes that looked at the Emperor are not the same as the eyes that took the photograph (much later), and vastly different from our eyes, which can take another's physical capital, so to speak, freely and almost limitlessly. This is related to what Walter Benjamin called the "aura" of handmade objects versus those which have been mechanically reproduced, except that here we wish to apply it to people who existed prior to industrialization versus people who exist in its wake. The gap has become so vast that "aura" is perhaps no longer as precise or meaningful a term as it once seemed; after all, part of our adaptation to post-industrial technology is to imagine that we have rediscovered the lost aura in things precisely through hyper-technological manipulation, as when Blu-ray high definition is said to reveal the true aura of a film; it is not the aura that is gone, but the former requirements that it be attached to something unique and human. Perhaps it would be better to think of it as the same principle as the corruption and degeneration of data in software technology: the original programmed path to the data remains in place, traceable, but the data itself is unreadable encryption. We know what we are looking for, and though we never quite find it, we go on looking, going through the motions of the aura, of intimacy, with our eyes *that have never looked at the Emperor*.

14. Étienne Balibar, *Politics and the Other Scene,* trans. Christine Jones, James Swenson, and Chris Turner (London: Verso, 2011), 13-14 [translation slightly modified].

15. Fassbinder, *The Anarchy of the Imagination*, 196.

16. Theodor W. Adorno, *Minima Moralia: Reflections from Damaged Life,* trans. E. F. N. Jephcott (London: Verso, 2002), 200.

Chapter 1

1. Georges Bataille, *Visions of Excess: Selected Writings, 1927-1939*, ed. Allan Stoeckl, trans. Allan Stoeckl with Carl R. Lovitt and Donald M. Leslie, Jr. (Minneapolis: University of Minnesota Press, 1985), 124.

2. Ibid., 125.

3. Ibid.

4. Allan Pred and Michael John Watts, *Reworking Modernity: Capitalisms and Symbolic Discontent* (New Brunswick: Rutgers University Press, 1992), 12.

5. Ibid.

6. Steven Shaviro, *Connected, Or What It Means to Live in the Network Society* (Minneapolis: University of Minnesota Press, 2003), 167.

7. Rimbaud, *Oeuvres Complètes*, 268.

8. Richard Wightman Fox and T. J. Jackson Lears, eds., *The Culture of Con-*

sumption: Critical Essays in American History 1880–1980 (New York: Pantheon, 1983), xi.

9. The copious mutants of *Gulliver's Travels*, although pointedly satirical, do not imply a wholly broken, moribund system, but instead, broken *segments* of a vigorous, thriving system: odious factions, moralist groups, temporary tyrants, opinionated "yahoos," etc. The thrust of critique is on behalf of those who would govern or live *differently*. This is why one feels optimism in even the darkest Swift; he lived in times when political solutions still seemed not only possible but even potentially honorable. When "A Modest Proposal" gets rewritten in the twentieth century by Kafka, as "Letter to His Father," there is already a sense of hopeless stalemate, of jaundiced innocence flatly ruined, as if the Swiftian children were suddenly saying: "We understand why you must eat us; have no doubts that, in your situation, we would do the same."

10. Edgar Allan Poe, *Stories* (New York: Platt & Munk, 1961), 385.

11. *Oxford English Dictionary* Online, www.oed.com, accessed November 2012.

12. Poe, *Stories*, 389.
13. Ibid., 390.
14. Ibid.
15. Ibid., 391.
16. Ibid., 388.
17. Don DeLillo, *The Body Artist* (New York: Scribner, 2001), 37.
18. Shaviro, *Connected*, 7.
19. Poe, *Stories*, 389.
20. Ibid., 389. "This prisonlike rampart formed the limit of our domain."
21. Ibid., 389–90.
22. Ibid., 393.
23. Ibid., 394.
24. Ibid., 396.
25. Ibid., 398.
26. Ibid., 414.
27. Ibid., 414–15.

28. Ibid., 401.
29. Quoted in Kristin Ross, *The Emergence of Social Space: Rimbaud and the Paris Commune* (London: Verso, 2008), 75.
30. Rimbaud, *Oeuvres Complètes*, 101 [my translation].
31. Ibid., 102.
32. Ross, *The Emergence of Social Space*, 51.
33. Rimbaud, *Oeuvres Complètes*, 101 [my translation].
34. Bertolt Brecht, *Baal, A Man's a Man & The Elephant Calf*, trans. Eric Bentley (New York: Grove Press, 1978), 34–35.
35. Ibid., 92.
36. Charles Baudelaire, *Les Fleurs du Mal* (Paris: Flammarion, 1991), 185 [my translation].
37. Brecht, *Baal*, 34.
38. Rimbaud, *Oeuvres Complètes*, 102 [my translation].
39. Hans-Jost Frey, *Studies in Poetic Discourse: Mallarmé, Baudelaire, Rimbaud, Hölderlin*, trans. William Whobrey (Stanford: Stanford University Press, 2006), 123.
40. Balibar, *Politics and the Other Scene*, 28.
41. See Rimbaud, *Oeuvres Complètes*, "Les Ponts" (187), "Ville" (188), "Villes" (189–90), "Villes" (191–92), "Métropolitain" (197–98), and "Promontoire" (199).
42. Ibid., 268 [my translation].
43. Adorno signals this resurrection of the dialogue tradition in *Minima Moralia* when he prefaces the book by saying that it "bears witness to a *dialogue intérieur*: there is not a motif in it that does not belong as much to Horkheimer [Adorno's writing partner, separated from him by the war] as to him who had the time to formulate it" (18).
44. Pred and Watts, *Reworking Modernity*, 16.
45. Rimbaud, *Oeuvres Complètes*, 100.

Notes—Chapter 1

46. Ibid., 103 [my translation].
47. Ross, *The Emergence of Social Space*, 61.
48. Rimbaud, *Oeuvres Complètes*, 233–34.
49. Ibid., 283.
50. Ross, *The Emergence of Social Space*, 60.
51. Franz Kafka, *The Great Wall of China: Stories and Reflections*, trans. Willa and Edwin Muir (New York: Schocken Books, 1970), 131.
52. This makes the bridge-man kin to the Indian in one of Kafka's most poetic texts, "The Wish to Be a Red Indian," in which a Native American, galloping on horseback over the land, disappears piece by piece (*The Basic Kafka* [New York: Simon & Schuster, 1979], 242). What makes this brief text disturbing is that Kafka longs to be "an Indian" even as he describes the Indian's extinction, perhaps because the Indian achieves a kind of perfect velocity on the horse before disappearing. In fact, it is the Indian's excellence, somehow, which seems to cause him to disappear. But this answer is somewhat unsatisfactory to account for the koan-like, runic nature of the text: if extinction is the natural and inevitable reward for living excellently, why praise it at all? Why risk or achieve the sarcasm that emerges? There is a kind of gentle, whimsical "shaming" which every Kafka text and voice attempts to perform at some point or another, merely by describing the aggressive distillation of sacrifice between lower, weaker orders and higher, more powerful ones. This process ends politically even if it does not begin that way: ethnicities, genders, and classes are wandering names that we give to certain peoples in certain epochs to explain the ubiquity of sacrifice, its endless machinery, which would transpire in one way or another; the way chess exists as a game to be won or lost every time, no matter what two players are playing. However, once named, the onus of weakness becomes crucial, although its odd chipperness recalls a time when everything was all still *like* a game, a game that it might have even won had it been seated on the opposite side of the board. Shaming is an honorable, mensch-like tsk-tsking at the unfair workings of fate—more honorable than being a sore loser (an attitude that one never encounters anywhere in Kafka).
53. Kafka, *The Great Wall of China*, 131–32.
54. Deleuze and Guattari: "Kafka deliberately kills all metaphor, all symbolism, all signification, no less than all designation. Metamorphosis is the contrary of metaphor" (*Kafka: Toward a Minor Literature*, trans. Dana Polan [Minneapolis: University of Minnesota Press, 1985], 22). Just as nothing in Kafka's fiction is ever "dream." It might be, however, that Kafka kills off all these merely rhetorical devices by deliberately deluging the reader in them while not obeying any of the rules by which the devices could be comprehensible or congruent. Kafka's symbols, such as they are, refer to things that *do not exist yet*. His metaphors point toward a reality that cannot support them through cross-reference. At the same time, metaphor is the rhetorical thing-that-will-not-die, and is intimately linked with mutation for this reason. Signifiers drift in and out of metaphorical existence; literal objects, as Plato knew, are already metaphors for ideal forms. Metaphoric thought is like a scope that holds the target in its quivering gunsights while knowing that it can at best fire warning shots. Born of necessary bad faith, writing creates itself, exists, continues precisely because the target can never be hit *legitimately*, or at least not definitively, i.e., when the reader's back is not somehow turned.

55. Borges, *Selected Non-Fictions*, 363.
56. Deleuze and Guattari, *Kafka*, 58.
57. Ibid., 60.
58. Ibid., 56.
59. Nietzsche, *The Will to Power, Volume II*, 218.
60. Ibid., 187.
61. Ibid., 171.
62. Ibid., 227.
63. Friedrich Nietzsche, *Beyond Good and Evil: Prelude to a Philosophy of the Future,* trans. Walter Kaufmann (New York: Vintage, 1966), 203.
64. Arendt, "History and Immortality," *Partisan Review*, 21.
65. Ibid., 24.
66. Nietzsche, *The Will to Power, Volume II*, 175; 215–16; 220–21.
67. Rainer Werner Fassbinder, *Plays,* trans. Denis Calandra (New York: PAJ Publications, 1985), 64.
68. Arendt, "History and Immortality," *Partisan Review*, 24.
69. Deleuze and Guattari, *Kafka*, 15.
70. Ibid., 55.
71. Borges, *Selected Non-Fictions*, 503.
72. Deleuze and Guattari, *Kafka*, 13 [my italics].
73. Balibar, *Politics and the Other Scene*, 12.
74. Paul Goodman, *Adam and His Works: Collected Stories* (New York: Vintage, 1968), 27.
75. Ibid., 28.
76. Ibid., 29.
77. Ibid., 30.
78. Ibid., 28–29.
79. Ibid., 28.
80. Philip Roth, *The Breast* (New York: Vintage, 1994), 88.

Chapter 2

1. Bataille, *Visions of Excess*, 224.
2. Fassbinder, *The Anarchy of the Imagination*, 29.
3. Ibid., 144.
4. Ibid.
5. Bataille, *Visions of Excess*, 236.
6. Nietzsche, *The Will to Power, Volume II*, 177–79.
7. Ibid., 211.
8. Ibid., 177–79.
9. Ibid., 179.
10. Ibid., 230–31.
11. Carlos Eire, *A Very Brief History of Eternity* (Princeton: Princeton University Press, 2010), 21.
12. Ibid., 13–14.
13. Ibid., 16–17.
14. Ibid., 25.
15. Borges, *Selected Non-Fictions*, 123.
16. Ibid., 48.
17. Ibid., 50.
18. Ibid., 123.
19. Ibid., 126.
20. Arendt, "History and Immortality," *Partisan Review*, 13.
21. Ibid., 14.
22. Ibid., 19.
23. Ibid.
24. Ibid., 15.
25. Ibid., 21.
26. Borges, *Selected Non-Fictions*, 118.
27. Fassbinder, *The Anarchy of the Imagination*, 29.
28. Ibid.
29. Adorno, *Minima Moralia*, 184.
30. Ibid., 182.
31. Borges, *Selected Non-Fictions*, 485.
32. Balibar, *Politics and the Other Scene*, 27.
33. Roth, *The Breast*, 69.
34. Ibid., 70.
35. Bataille, *Visions of Excess*, 236.
36. Ibid., 237.
37. Ibid.
38. Elias Canetti, *Crowds and Power,* trans. Carol Stewart (New York: Continuum, 1973), 105.
39. Ibid.
40. Ibid., 106.
41. Ibid.
42. Rimbaud, *Oeuvres Complètes*, 184 [my translation].

43. Kafka, *The Basic Kafka*, 263.
44. Bataille, *Visions of Excess*, 237.

Chapter 3

1. Nietzsche, *The Will to Power, Volume II*, 191.
2. For a detailed account of this, see David Cay Johnston, *The Fine Print: How Big Companies Use "Plain English" to Rob You Blind* (New York: Portfolio, 2012).
3. Satyajit Chatterjee and Dean Corbae, "Monetary and Financial Forces in the Great Depression," *New Palgrave Dictionary of Economics*, June 2006, www.philadelphiafed.org.
4. Ibid.
5. Adorno, *Minima Moralia*, 182.
6. Nathanael West, *Miss Lonelyhearts & The Day of the Locust* (New York: New Directions, 1969), 9–10.
7. Ibid., 14.
8. Ibid., 24.
9. Ibid., 35–38.
10. Ibid., 1.
11. Balibar, *Politics and the Other Scene*, 27.
12. Ibid.
13. See the website deadpeasantsinsurance.com, accessed 12 December 2012.
14. Fassbinder, *The Anarchy of the Imagination*, 105.
15. Bataille, *Visions of Excess*, 235.
16. Nietzsche, *Beyond Good and Evil*, 153–54.
17. Ibid., 154.
18. Ibid., 146.
19. Werner Herzog, DVD commentary, *Even Dwarves Started Small* (Fantoma, 1999).
20. Ibid.
21. Ibid.

Chapter 4

1. Roth, *The Breast*, 49.
2. Ibid., 50–51.
3. Ibid., 55.
4. Ibid., 81.
5. Ibid., 82.
6. Ibid., 3.
7. Ibid., 5.
8. Ibid., 8.
9. Ibid., 7.
10. Ibid., 81.
11. Ibid., 10–11.
12. Ibid., 21.
13. Quoted in Lucy R. Lippard, *From the Center: Feminist Essays on Women's Art* (New York: Dutton, 1976), 105.
14. Lippard, *From the Center*, 88–89.
15. Roth, *The Breast*, 3.
16. Ibid., 8–9.
17. Ibid., 25.
18. Lawrence Kramer, *After the Lovedeath: Sexual Violence and the Making of Culture* (Berkeley: University of California Press, 1997), 117.
19. Ibid., 119.
20. Ibid.
21. Walt Whitman, *Leaves of Grass* (New York: Signet, 2000), 82.
22. Norman Mailer, *The Prisoner of Sex* (New York: Signet, 1971), 93–115.
23. Roth, *The Breast*, 41–42.
24. Ibid.
25. Lippard, *From the Center*, 106.
26. Ibid.
27. Ibid., 107–108.
28. Roth, *The Breast*, 26–27.
29. Ibid., 32.
30. In the BBC series *Absolutely Fabulous*, daughter Saffy (Julia Sawalha) tells her media-obsessed, self-centered mother Edina Monsoon (Jennifer Saunders): "There isn't a course in redemption…. Just start living your life and stop trying to find yourself fascinating!"
31. Lippard, *From the Center*, 125.
32. Ibid., 124.
33. Ibid.
34. Ibid., 89.
35. Ibid., 106.
36. Ibid.
37. Roth, *The Breast*, 3.

38. Ibid., 88.
39. Ibid., 77.
40. Ibid., 4.
41. Ibid., 24.
42. Ibid., 25.
43. Ibid., 31.
44. Ibid.
45. Ibid., 79–80.

Chapter 5

1. DeLillo perhaps alludes to the Rimbaud of "Après le Déluge" here. The novelist writes: "You know more surely who you are on a strong bright day after a storm when the smallest falling leaf is stabbed with self-awareness.... [T]he world comes into being, irreversibly, and the spider rides the wind-swayed web" (*The Body Artist*, 7). This echoes the beginning of Rimbaud's prose poem from *The Illuminations*: "Aussitôt que l'idée du Déluge se fut rassise, un lièvre s'arrêta dans les sainfoins et les clochettes mouvantes, et dit sa prière à l'arc-en-ciel à travers la toile de l'araignée." "The instant that the idea of the Flood receded, a rabbit paused among the sainfoins and the swaying lilies of the valley, and said its prayer to the rainbow through the gauze of a spider web" (*Oeuvres Complètes*, 176, my translation). Both poem and novel are renderings of a world, or several microcosmic overlapping worlds, reborn after a violent storm, and the concomitant revelation of nature's secrets (in Rimbaud's poem, precious gemstones and magic fires in the earth; in DeLillo's novel the secrets of the body, and of lives that are themselves like forces of nature) which are uncanny and transformative.
2. DeLillo, *The Body Artist*, 65.
3. Ibid.
4. Ibid., 12.
5. Ibid., 9.
6. Ibid., 33.
7. Lippard, *From the Center*, 82–83.
8. DeLillo, *The Body Artist*, 14.
9. Ibid., 20.
10. Ibid., 70. This off-kilter family snapshot again suggests, at least obliquely, the Rimbaud of *Illuminations*, especially in the way the adults have seemingly abandoned their children, as well as the way landscapes are rendered absurd or terrifying by the presence of the human figures: "C'est elle, la petite morte, derrière les rosiers.—La jeune maman trépassée descend le perron.—La calèche du cousin crie sur le sable.—Le petit frère—(il est aux Indes!) là, devant le couchant, sur le pré d'oeillets.—Les vieux qu'on a enterrés tout droits dans le rempart aux giroflées." "That is she, the dead little girl, behind the rose bushes.—The deceased young mother walks down the staircase.—The cousin's carriage cries upon the sand.—The kid brother—(he is in the Indies!) standing in front of the sunset on a field of carnations.—The old ones, buried standing up on the wallflower-covered hillside" (*Oeuvres Complètes*, 176–77, my translation).
11. Ibid., 57.
12. Ibid., 23.
13. Ibid., 85.
14. Ibid., 20.
15. Ibid., 16.
16. Ibid., 27.
17. This "thousand tales" comes from Jean-Luc Godard's *Histoire(s) du Cinéma* (Gaumont, 1988–97).
18. Jean-Luc Godard, *Godard on Godard,* trans. and ed. Tom Milne (New York: Da Capo Press, 1986), 66.
19. DeLillo, *The Body Artist*, 34.
20. Ibid., 10 and 23.
21. Ibid., 38.
22. Ibid., 38–39.
23. Ibid., 38.
24. Ibid., 109.
25. Ibid., 94.
26. Kafka, *The Basic Kafka*, 90.
27. DeLillo, *The Body Artist*, 15.
28. Rimbaud, *Oeuvres Complètes*, 220 [my translation].

29. DeLillo, *The Body Artist*, 124.
30. Ibid., 84.
31. Lippard, *From the Center*, 82–83.
32. Bataille, *Visions of Excess*, 7.

Chapter 6

1. Jorge Luis Borges, *The Book of Sand*, trans. Norman Thomas di Giovanni (New York: E. P. Dutton, 1977), 122.
2. Ibid., 121.
3. DeLillo, *The Body Artist*, 41.
4. Ibid.
5. Ibid., 65.
6. Ibid., 64.
7. Ibid., 45.
8. Borges, *The Book of Sand*, 121.
9. Nietzsche, *Beyond Good and Evil*, 222.
10. Let me counteract the perhaps overly cautionary tone here. I am attempting to describe cyberspace phenomenologically. There is much that is wonderful about the Internet, particularly its use as a public forum of opinion, and also as a kind of sprawling free festival where people commingle and make contact with each other. It marks a renewal of the "social contract," and in that sense I have great hopes for it.
11. Shaviro, *Connected*, 7.
12. John Edginton, *Robyn Hitchcock: Sex, Food, Death ... and Insects* (Sundance Channel, 2007).
13. DeLillo, *The Body Artist*, 48–49.
14. Ibid., 93.
15. Ibid., 46.
16. Borges, *The Book of Sand*, 117.
17. DeLillo, *The Body Artist*, 62.
18. Ibid., 15.
19. Shaviro, *Connected*, 167.
20. DeLillo, *The Body Artist*, 33.
21. Ibid., 44.
22. Bataille, *Visions of Excess*, 55.
23. Ibid.
24. Ibid.
25. Ibid., 51.
26. Adorno, *Minima Moralia*, 16.
27. Ibid., 72.
28. Ibid., 151.
29. Jameson, *Marxism and Form*, 268.
30. Ibid., 143.
31. Ibid., 143–44.
32. Bataille, *Visions of Excess*, 109.
33. Ibid., 107.
34. Jameson, *Marxism and Form*, 258.

Chapter 7

1. Stan Brakhage, Interviews, DVD extras, *By Brakhage: Anthology 2* (The Criterion Collection, 2010).
2. Ibid.
3. Ibid.
4. Ibid.
5. Ibid.
6. Ibid.
7. Borges, *Selected Non-Fictions*, 116.
8. Ibid., 126.
9. Brakhage, Interviews, DVD extras, ibid.
10. Godard, *Godard on Godard*, 43.

Chapter 8

1. Bataille, *Visions of Excess*, 121.
2. Ibid., 123.
3. Evan Schwartz, "Rapper Tyga Crashes Lamborghini," posted 17 December 2012, http://www.vibe.com/article/rapper-tyga-crashes-lamborghini. This article happened to be an Internet buzz item when I was writing this chapter. Tyga's crash was accidental and he was luckily unharmed; but the news stories all made mention of how expensive the Lamborghini had been. It reminded me, in formal terms, of a potlatch ceremony, the costly loss seen as a kind of tribute to Tyga's success.
4. Nietzsche, *Beyond Good and Evil*, 213–14.
5. Bataille, *Visions of Excess*, 121.
6. Ibid., 119.
7. Nietzsche, *Beyond Good and Evil*, 205.

8. Canetti, *Crowds and Power*, 46.
9. Shannon Winnubst, ed., *Reading Bataille Now* (Bloomington: Indiana University Press, 2007), 39.
10. Bataille, *Visions of Excess*, 111.
11. Adorno, *Minima Moralia*, 16.
12. Bataille, *Visions of Excess*, 6.
13. Adorno, *Minima Moralia*, 17.
14. Ernesto Laclau and Chantal Mouffe, *Hegemony and Socialist Strategy: Towards a Radical Democratic Politics* (London: Verso, 1985), 111.
15. Bataille, *Visions of Excess*, 113.
16. Quoted in Nealon, *Alterity Politics*, 167.
17. Nietzsche, *The Will to Power, Volume II*, 189.
18. Nealon, *Alterity Politics*, 170.
19. Ibid., 166.
20. Adorno, *Minima Moralia*, 55.
21. Arendt, "History and Immortality," *Partisan Review*, 25.

Chapter 9

1. The title of this chapter was inspired by Luce Irigaray's *This Sex Which Is Not One*.
2. Kafka, *The Basic Kafka*, 237.
3. DeLillo, *The Body Artist*, 57.
4. We must be somewhat wary of *The Will to Power*, a book that was published after Nietzsche's death after being edited together from his last notebooks. The thought in the book is coherent, and much of it is already familiar to readers of earlier texts by the philosopher; yet it has a bluntness at times, as well as an inflammatory quality in several passages mainly having to do with German and Jewish national identity, that make it a difficult, even cautionary book. Bataille emphatically states that any anti–Semitism in Nietzsche's writing was "taken up by Nietzsche in order to mock it" (*Visions of Excess*, 184). Nietzsche himself suggests, in a resonant passage from the earlier *Beyond Good and Evil*, that he viewed provocation as the future of philosophy, specifically for the most nimble future philosophers whom he christens "*attempters*" and whom he says will mainly be distinguished by their ability to speak in riddles (32). Whether we can accept all of Nietzsche's thought, or whether some of the passages were in fact forged, as Bataille suggests (*Visions of Excess*, 182–84), we might be able to attribute some excesses here and there to the cause of those philosophical riddles of the future. After all, Nietzsche subtitled *The Will to Power* "An *Attempted* Transvaluation of All Values." In this reading of *The Will to Power*, I wish to stress Nietzsche's concept of transvaluation as an important and intended function of the process of reading Nietzsche himself, perhaps nowhere as much as in this vitriolic but often exhilarating posthumous work. In a larger sense, we might also mention Nietzsche's literary ability to transfer his own moods to the reader: if something in Nietzsche makes us angry when we read it, it is probably because it made Nietzsche feel angry as well.
5. Nietzsche, *The Will to Power, Volume II*, 175.
6. Ibid., 129–30.
7. Ibid., 130.
8. Ibid., 211.
9. Nietzsche, *Beyond Good and Evil*, 185.
10. David Thomson, *The New Biographical Dictionary of Film, Updated and Expanded* (New York: Alfred A. Knopf, 2010), 501.
11. Borges, *Selected Non-Fictions*, 120.
12. Ibid., 119.
13. Nietzsche, *The Will to Power, Volume II*, 422–23.
14. Ibid., 427.
15. Ibid., 189.
16. Ibid., 135.

17. Ibid., 213–14.
18. Ibid., 214.
19. Ibid., 185.
20. Balibar, *Politics and the Other Scene*, 7.
21. Nietzsche, *The Will to Power, Volume II*, 175.
22. Ibid., 183.
23. Ibid., 216.
24. Ibid.
25. Ibid., 188.
26. Ibid., 130.
27. Ibid., 124.
28. Ibid., 217.
29. Ibid., 428.
30. Ibid., 424.
31. Ibid., 231.
32. Ibid., 227.
33. Ibid., 189.
34. Nietzsche, *Beyond Good and Evil*, 222–23n.

Chapter 10

1. Robert Nozick, *Anarchy, State, and Utopia* (New York: Basic Books, 1974), 255.
2. Ibid., 255–56.
3. Bataille, *Visions of Excess*, 122–23.
4. Nozick, *Anarchy, State, and Utopia*, 256.
5. Adorno, *Minima Moralia*, 190.
6. Ibid., 191.

(In)conclusion

1. This sentence is spoken in Godard's *Oh, Woe Is Me*.

Works Cited

Absolutely Fabulous: Absolutely Everything. BBC Video, 2008.

Adorno, Theodor W. *Minima Moralia: Reflections from Damaged Life.* Translated by E. F. N. Jephcott. London: Verso, 2002.

Alam, Julhas. "Bangladesh Factory Fire Leads to Protests As Workers Demand to Return to Work or Get Paid." www.huffingtonpost.com, 11/30/2012.

Arendt, Hannah. "History and Immortality." *Partisan Review* 1 (Winter 1957).

Balibar, Étienne. *Politics and the Other Scene.* Translated by Christine Jones, James Swenson, and Chris Turner. London: Verso, 2011.

Barthes, Roland. *Camera Lucida: Reflections on Photography.* Translated by Richard Howard. New York: Hill & Wang, 1983.

Bataille, Georges. *Visions of Excess: Selected Writings, 1927–1939.* Edited by Allan Stoeckl. Translated by Allan Stoeckl with Carl R. Lovitt and Donald M. Leslie, Jr. Minneapolis: University of Minnesota Press, 1985.

Borges, Jorge Luis. *The Book of Sand.* Translated by Norman Thomas di Giovanni. New York: E. P. Dutton, 1977.

_____. *Selected Non-Fictions.* Edited by Eliot Weinberger. New York: Penguin, 1999.

Bowie, David. *Diamond Dogs.* RCA Victor, 1974.

Brakhage, Stan. *Burial Path.* 1972.

_____. *Cat's Cradle.* 1959.

_____. *Crack Glass Eulogy.* 1995.

_____. Interviews, DVD extras, *By Brakhage: Anthology 2.* The Criterion Collection, 2010.

_____. *The Stars Are Beautiful.* 1974.

_____. *Window Baby Water Moving.* 1959.

Brecht, Bertolt. *Baal, A Man's a Man & The Elephant Calf.* Translated by Eric Bentley. New York: Grove Press, 1978.

Browning, Tod. *Freaks.* MGM, 1932.

Buñuel, Luis. *Le fantôme de la liberté* [*The Phantom of Liberty*]. Euro International Film, 1974.

Canetti, Elias. *Crowds and Power.* Translated by Carol Stewart. New York: Continuum, 1973.

Clooney, George. *Confessions of a Dangerous Mind.* Miramax, 2002.

Curtiz, Michael. *The Mystery of the Wax Museum.* Warner Brothers, 1933.

Deleuze, Gilles, and Félix Guattari. *Kafka: Toward a Minor Literature.* Translated by Dana Polan. Minneapolis: University of Minnesota Press, 1986.

Works Cited

DeLillo, Don. *The Body Artist*. New York: Scribner, 2001.

Edginton, John. *Robyn Hitchcock: Sex, Food, Death ... and Insects*. Sundance Channel, 2007.

Eire, Carlos. *A Very Brief History of Eternity*. Princeton: Princeton University Press, 2010.

Fassbinder, Rainer Werner. *The Anarchy of the Imagination: Interviews, Essays, Notes*. Translated by Krishna Winston. Edited by Michael Töteberg and Leo A. Lensing. Baltimore: Johns Hopkins University Press, 1992.

_____. *Plays*. Translated and edited by Denis Calandra. New York: PAJ Publications, 1985.

Fox, Richard Wightman, and T. J. Jackson Lears, eds. *The Culture of Consumption: Critical Essays in American History 1880–1980*. New York: Pantheon, 1983.

Frey, Hans-Jost. *Studies in Poetic Discourse: Mallarmé, Baudelaire, Rimbaud, Hölderlin*. Translated by William Whobrey. Stanford: Stanford University Press, 2006.

Godard, Jean-Luc. *Godard on Godard*. Translated and edited by Tom Milne. New York: Da Capo Press, 1986.

_____. *Hélas pour moi [Oh, Woe Is Me]*. Les Films Alain Sarde, 1993.

_____. *Histoire(s) du Cinéma*. Gaumont, 1988–97.

Gondry, Michel. *Eternal Sunshine of the Spotless Mind*. Focus Features, 2004.

_____. *Human Nature*. Fine Line Features, 2001.

Goodman, Paul. *Adam and His Works: Collected Stories*. New York: Vintage, 1968.

Hendrix, Jimi. *Axis: Bold as Love*. Reprise, 1968.

Herzog, Werner. DVD commentary, *Even Dwarves Started Small*. Fantoma, 1999.

Jameson, Fredric. *Marxism and Form*. Princeton: Princeton University Press, 1974.

Johnston, David Cay. *The Fine Print: How Big Companies Use "Plain English" to Rob You Blind*. New York: Portfolio, 2012.

Jonze, Spike. *Adaptation*. Beverly Detroit, 2002.

_____. *Being John Malkovich*. Gramercy Pictures, 1999.

Kafka, Franz. *The Basic Kafka*. New York: Simon & Schuster, 1979.

_____. *The Great Wall of China: Stories and Reflections*. Translated by Willa and Edwin Muir. New York: Schocken Books, 1970.

_____. *Letters to Milena*. Translated by Philip Boehm. New York: Schocken Books, 1990.

Kenton, Erle C. *Island of Lost Souls*. Paramount, 1933.

Kramer, Lawrence. *After the Lovedeath: Sexual Violence and the Making of Culture*. Berkeley: University of California Press, 1997.

Laclau, Ernesto, and Chantal Mouffe. *Hegemony and Socialist Strategy: Towards a Radical Democratic Politics*. London: Verso, 1985.

Lippard, Lucy R. *From the Center: Feminist Essays on Women's Art*. New York: Dutton, 1976.

Mailer, Norman. *The Prisoner of Sex*. New York: Signet, 1971.

Mankiewicz, Joseph L. *Suddenly, Last Summer*. Columbia, 1959.

Nealon, Jeffrey T. *Alterity Politics: Ethics and Performative Subjectiv-*

ity. Durham: Duke University Press, 1998.

Nietzsche, Friedrich. *Beyond Good and Evil: Prelude to a Philosophy of the Future*. Translated by Walter Kaufmann. New York: Vintage, 1966.

———. *The Will to Power: An Attempted Transvaluation of All Values, Volume II*. Translated by Anthony M. Ludovici. London: George Allen & Unwin, 1924.

Nozick, Robert. *Anarchy, State, and Utopia*. New York: Basic Books, 1974.

Oxford English Dictionary Online. www.oed.com.

Poe, Edgar Allan. *Stories*. New York: Platt & Munk, 1961.

Pred, Allan, and Michael John Watts. *Reworking Modernity: Capitalisms and Symbolic Discontent*. New Brunswick: Rutgers University Press, 1992.

The Ramones. *Leave Home*. Sire, 1977.

Rilke, Rainer Maria. *Selected Poetry*. Translated by Stephen Mitchell. New York: Vintage, 1989.

Rimbaud, Arthur. *Oeuvres Complètes*. Paris: Librairie Gallimard, 1954.

Ross, Herbert. *Play It Again, Sam*. Paramount, 1972.

Ross, Kristin. *The Emergence of Social Space: Rimbaud and the Paris Commune*. London: Verso, 2008.

Roth, Philip. *The Breast*. New York: Vintage, 1994.

Schwartz, Evan. "Rapper Tyga Crashes Lamborghini," posted 17 December 2012, http://www.vibe.com/article/rapper-tyga-crashes-lamborghini.

Scorsese, Martin. *Taxi Driver*. Columbia, 1976.

Sennett, Richard. *Authority*. New York: W. W. Norton, 1993.

Shaviro, Steven. *Connected, Or What It Means to Live in the Network Society*. Minneapolis: University of Minnesota Press, 2003.

Sprague, Mike. "Ex-Bumble Bee Employee Says Major Error Must Have Caused Fatal Accident." *Los Angeles Daily News* online, 15 October 2012, www.dailynews.com.

Thomson, David. *The New Biographical Dictionary of Film, Updated and Expanded*. New York: Alfred A. Knopf, 2010.

Ulmer, Edgar G. *The Black Cat*. Universal, 1934.

West, Nathanael. *Miss Lonelyhearts & The Day of the Locust*. New York: New Directions, 1969.

Whitman, Walt. *Leaves of Grass*. New York: Signet, 2000.

Winnubst, Shannon, ed. *Reading Bataille Now*. Bloomington: Indiana University Press, 2007.

Index

Absolutely Fabulous 196n30
Adaptation (Jonze) 143, 144, 145, 146, 152, 153, 154
Adorno, T.W. 13, 16, 50, 66, 71, 115, 123, 133, 135, 136, 139, 165, 174–175, 179, 193n43
Antin, Eleanor 86
Appel, Jacki 93, 105
Arendt, Hannah 11, 38, 47–48, 140
Arlen, Richard 64
Arquette, Patricia 149
Atwill, Lionel 70
Augustine, Saint 46, 47

Baal (Brecht) 27, 29
Bacon, Lloyd 79
Balibar, Étienne 15, 30, 39, 50, 69, 158
Barris, Chuck 143, 154
Barthes, Roland 192n13
Bataille, Georges 16, 17, 43, 44–45, 52–53, 56, 74, 115, 117, 130, 131–132, 133, 137, 156, 162, 164, 169–170, 173, 199n4
Baudelaire, Charles 26, 28
Bauman, Zygmunt 137
Bean, Orson 143
Being John Malkovich (Jonze) 142, 145, 146, 147–149, 161
Benjamin, Walter 26, 72
Bitter Victory (N. Ray) 102
The Black Cat (Ulmer) 70, 75–76
The Body Artist (DeLillo) 23, 97–106, 110–111, 112–113, 114
"The Book of Sand" (Borges) 107–108, 111, 123, 155
Borges, Jorge Luis 10, 16, 35, 39, 46–47, 49, 50, 107, 122, 123, 155
Brakhage, Stan 119–128, 154
The Breast (Roth) 41, 51, 83–96, 106
Brecht, Bertolt 26, 27
Bremen Freedom (Fassbinder) 38
"The Bridge" (Kafka) 32–39

Brown, W. Earl 148
Browning, Tod 66, 79
Buñuel, Luis 152–153
Burial Path (Brakhage) 119–120, 121, 127
Burke, Kathleen 63

Cage, Nicolas 143, 154
Call, Annie Payson 20
Calvin, John 18, 38, 130, 171, 173, 186
Canetti, Elias 53–55, 130
Carrey, Jim 142
Carroll, Kevin 147
The Castle (Kafka) 35, 147
Cat's Cradle (Brakhage) 124–125, 126
Céline, Louis-Ferdinand 58
Confessions of a Dangerous Mind (Clooney) 143, 145, 154
Cooper, Chris 152
Crack Glass Eulogy (Brakhage) 121
Curtiz, Michael 70, 72, 74
Cusack, John 142

Darwin, Charles 159
Deleuze, Gilles 36–37, 194n54
DeLillo, Don 23, 97–106, 110, 141, 197n1
Deren, Maya 120
Descartes, René 30
Diaz, Cameron 147
Dostoevsky, Fyodor 68
Down by Law (Jarmusch) 118
"The Drunken Boat" (Rimbaud) 26–32
Dunst, Kirsten 147

Earles, Harry 76
Eberle, Bo 191n3
Eire, Carlos 46
Empire (Warhol) 124
Engels, Friedrich 18, 26, 133
Eternal Sunshine of the Spotless Mind (Gondry) 142, 144, 145, 147, 150, 155

205

Index

Even Dwarves Started Small (Herzog) 80–81

Falling Man (DeLillo) 98
Farrell, Glenda 70
Fassbinder, Rainer Werner 8, 16, 38, 44–45, 49, 74
42nd Street (Bacon) 79
Freaks (Browning) 66–67, 69, 76–82

Godard, Jean-Luc 102, 120, 179
Gogol, Nikolai 84
Gondry, Michel 46
Goodman, Paul 40–42
Guattari, Félix 36–37, 194n54

Hayek, Friedrich 167
Hegel, Georg 12, 37–38, 57, 61, 115, 138, 139, 177
Heidegger, Martin 164
Hendrix, Jimi 45, 49, 116
Herzog, Werner 80–81
Hitchcock, Robyn 112
Homer 48
Horkheimer, Max 136, 193n43
Human Nature (Gondry) 46, 144–145, 149, 150, 152, 154, 157, 159, 177
"A Hunger Artist" (Kafka) 104–105

If I Had a Million 81–82
Ifans, Rhys 144
The Illuminations (Rimbaud) 30, 197n1, 197n10
Island of Lost Souls (Kenton) 60, 62–69, 152

James, Henry 13
Jameson, Fredric 7, 10, 116
Jarmusch, Jim 118

Kafka, Franz 26, 34–39, 56, 84, 104, 141, 193n9, 194n52, 194n54
Karloff, Boris 75
Kaufman, Charlie 141–166, 177
Kaufmann, Walter 163
Keener, Catherine 147
Kenton, Erle C. 60
Kramer, Lawrence 88–89

Laughton, Charles 62
Lawrence, D.H. 90
Lears, T.J. Jackson 19
Libra (DeLillo) 98

Lippard, Lucy R. 86, 91, 92–93, 99
Livingston, Ron 144
Lugosi, Bela 75

MacLuhan, Marshall 58
Mailer, Norman 90
Malkovich, John 143, 161
Manners, David 76
Marcuse, Herbert 112, 135
Marx, Karl 8, 18, 26, 37, 38, 57, 61, 137, 140, 158, 165, 166, 167, 168, 172, 177, 181, 182–184
Maxwell, Edwin 70
McHugh, Frank 71
Melena, José 2–4
Melville, Herman 13, 144
Mencken, Marie 120
Miss Lonelyhearts (West) 67–69
Morrissey 131
The Mystery of the Wax Museum (Curtiz) 70–75

Nealon, Jeffrey T. 138
Nietzsche, Friedrich 8, 12–13, 36–37, 45, 47, 52, 57, 76–78, 111, 131, 132, 136, 137, 139–140, 141–142, 146, 149–150, 151, 153–154, 155–166, 169–170, 172, 177, 181, 188, 199n4
Nirvana 185
Nozick, Robert 167–174

Oh, Woe Is Me! (Godard) 179, 200n1
Otto, Miranda 149

Pericles 48, 181
The Phantom of Liberty (Buñuel) 152
Piper, Adrian 91
Place, Mary Kay 146, 152
Plato 46–47, 181, 194n54
Poe, Edgar Allan 21–26, 30, 177
Pollock, Jackson 73
Potser, Mary 152
Proust, Marcel 26

Ramones 69
Ray, Nicholas 102
Rilke, Rainer Maria 44, 92, 94, 103, 106, 114, 128, 145–146, 188
Rimbaud, Arthur 10, 13, 19, 26–32, 39, 55, 105, 110, 128, 161, 188, 197n1, 197n10
Robbins, Tim 144
Rockwell, Sam 143
Ross, Kristin 26–27, 32

206

Index

Roth, Philip 41, 51, 83–96, 106, 113, 115
Ruffalo, Mark 147

Sartre, Jean-Paul 164
Saunders, Jennifer 196*n*30
Sawalha, Julia 196*n*30
Shaviro, Steven 18, 24, 112, 114, 158
Smith, Patti 91
Socrates 10, 30, 50
Spinoza, Baruch 165
The Stars Are Beautiful (Brakhage) 125, 128
Stein, Gertrude 122
Streep, Meryl 143
Suddenly, Last Summer (Williams) 123
Swift, Jonathan 20, 84, 193*n*9

Talking Heads 186
Teacher, Kelly 154
The Tempest (Shakespeare) 106
"Terry Fleming—Or, Are You Planning a Universe?" (Goodman) 40–42
Thomson, David 154, 155
Tyga 198*n*3

Ulmer, Edgar G. 70

Van Gogh, Vincent 73
The Velvet Underground 188
Verlaine, Paul 32

Warhol, Andy 124
Watts, Michael 18
Wells, H.G. 63
West, Nathanael 67–68
Whitman, Walt 88
Wilkinson, Tom 142
"William Wilson" (Poe) 21–26, 28, 30, 33, 177
Williams, Tennessee 123
Wilson, Martha 92, 93, 105
Window Baby Water Moving (Brakhage) 120–121, 126, 127, 128, 154
Wood, Elijah 147
Wray, Fay 70
Wright, Richard 19

Zeno 35, 39

www.ingramcontent.com/pod-product-compliance
Ingram Content Group UK Ltd.
Pitfield, Milton Keynes, MK11 3LW, UK
UKHW042004140426
5217IPUK00015B/973